WINDOWS VISTA FOR XP PROFESSIONALS

Raymond P.L. Comvalius

After climbing a great hill, one only finds
that there are many more hills to climb.
Nelson Mandela

Thomas,

Enjoy reading!

Ray

Production Editor Irene Venditti, *i-write*

Cover designer Marco Muis

Publishing Rob Bastiaansen - Books4Brains

Acknowledgements

Thanks to my wife and family for supporting me to get this book completed. I know that I had to hide sometimes to get the job done.

Jeroen Starrenburg from HP deserves thanks for triggering me to start the research that led to the realization of the book. Rob Bastiaansen deserves credit for inspiring me to start authoring my first book and helping me to get it published.

Irene Venditti deserves credit for taking care of the editorial review. She really saved the project after so many people failed to keep their word.

WEKA publishers in Amsterdam deserve thanks for picking up the concept of this book and having it translated into the Dutch version that came out before I finished the original.

A number of people read parts of the book and provided valuable feed-back to refine the approach, test coding examples and generally provide input.

Finally, I would like to thank Marcel Vonk, Harry Westerman, Didier van Eetvelt, Constant Werkhoven, Toon Wortelboer and the rest of the team that I worked with to realize what has become one of the first Windows Vista enterprise deployments in the financial world.

About the Author

Raymond Comvalius, an independent consultant and Microsoft Certified Trainer in the Netherlands. He has more than ten years of experience implementing network infrastructures based on Microsoft products and technologies. Raymond his specialties contain topics like Security, Active Directory, Network services, PKI, Windows Terminal Services and Windows Server and Client operating systems. Raymond produced several articles and columns about his expertise and is an occasional blogger on bink.nu and his own website at www.xpworld.com.

Raymond is a frequent visitor of Microsoft's Tech Ed and IT Forum events and has worked with the Windows Vista product team at the conference in Boston in 2006. Raymond is co-author of the Dutch Windows Security Handbook by WEKA in The Netherlands and is also known as a speaker.

Book license

Published by Books4Brains, September, 2008
P.O. Box 345
3830 AJ Leusden
The Netherlands

ISBN 978-90-72389-01-5

Disclaimer
The author and publisher of this book have made every effort to make this book as complete and accurate as possible. The author and publisher make no representations or warranties of any kind as to the accuracy or the contents of this book and accept no liability whatsoever with respect to any loss or damages that may arise from the information contained in this book or from the use of any programs described in this book.

The author and publisher do not guarantee that the information in this book will continue to work with future versions of Windows.

Trademarks
The names of actual companies and products mentioned herein may be the trademarks of their respective owners.

Contents

1 Introduction

A nice thing about Windows Vista is that the product feels familiar from the start. The familiarity makes it feel like Vista is actually nothing more than a mere upgrade to Windows XP. Well, this is the same logic that made a lot of technological novices think they mastered previous versions of Windows when they were magically able to run through a wizard and complete their jobs. The fact that Windows Vista almost feels like Windows XP is probably one of Microsoft's biggest mistakes, if I may call it a mistake. I can't tell how many people I met say: "Vista is not so new, I could even install it at home!" .

The truth is that when you start digging deeper into the product you find so many new elements, that my current opinion about Vista is that one of Microsoft's biggest accomplishments with Windows Vista probably is the fact that it often still feels and looks a lot like Windows XP, but certainly is a very different product.

This book is intended to aid the IT specialist, who is responsible for Desktop management, in dealing with the most important changes in Windows Vista. The subjects are based on my years of experience in upgrading Windows based network infrastructures and giving of courses for IT professionals on all levels.

The five parts of this book cover the following topics:

- What's new in Windows Vista (and not discussed in this book)
- Deploying Windows Vista
- Managing Windows Vista
- Securing Windows Vista
- Windows Vista mobility features
- Migrating to Windows Vista

Each topic will explain the most important changes in Windows Vista for that topic. Most topics will span multiple paragraphs that briefly explain what has changed and how you can use the changes on your new Vista based clients.

2 What's new in Windows Vista and not discussed in this book

When you start gathering information about Windows Vista on the Microsoft website or when you just browse through a bookstore, you will discover that most of the material you find about Windows Vista is geared towards end user features and the "wow" factor of the product. I tried to restrict the "wow" remarks in this book to a few geeky comments. So I won't try to "wow" you with descriptions about the cool 3D user interface or gorgeous pictures in Media Center. I will try to "wow" you with stuff like the feature set of the Windows Recovery Environment and the new ways you can configure Windows Vista's built-in firewall.

To do that, I had to go through the painful process of selecting features that will not be discussed in this book. Of course you can read a lot about these features in other sources. A good place to start would be the Windows Vista Product Guide, which can be downloaded from the Microsoft website.

2.1 A summary of some new features not discussed in this book

Ok, the complete list of new features in Windows Vista is almost endless. That's why I cannot pretend that my list of skipped features contains every non-discussed feature. It is my single attempt to list the most obvious ones that I could come up with while selecting the topics for this book.

Here is the list of items that will not be treated in this book, with a short description.

- **User Interface**
Numerous items were moved in the Windows Vista user interface (UI). Be prepared for more clicks.

- **Instant Search**
Almost anywhere, when you start typing in Windows Explorer, Vista will start searching for you. This is especially useful in the Start Menu and Control Panel.

- **Windows Flip**
Press Alt-Tab and Windows Vista will show you a current view of all current windows. This makes it easier to select the right program.

- **Flip 3D**
Probably the biggest "wow" in Windows Vista. Press ⊞-Tab to find out why.

- **Windows Sidebar and Gadgets**
The new bar that contains items like clocks, calendars, the weather and other gadgets that you can download from the Internet.

- **XPS (XML Paper Specification)**
Microsoft's "PDF killer" format is natively supported in Windows Vista.

- **Automatic Disk Defrag**
Vista does automatic disk defragmentation once a week out of the box.

- **Windows Experience Index**
A performance index that reports the overall speed of your computer.

- **Sleep**

Vista by default uses hybrid sleep. In hybrid sleep a computer first enters sleep modus and then later turns to Hibernation to save battery lifetime. Windows Vista allows you to configure Power Management and Sleep with Group Policy.

- **Presentation settings**

Presentation settings allow you to temporarily change the settings for display, desktop and screensaver when a presentation device is connected to your system.

- **Network Projection**

Vista natively supports projection over Wi-Fi and wired networks.

- **Windows SideShow**

A rarely used technology for displaying information, such as a calendar or inbox, on a separate screen on the outside of a device.

- **Disk partitioning**

Vista supports GUID (GPT) partitioning to support partitions larger then 2TB and the upcoming EFI standard that will replace the current BIOS.

- **Built –in diagnostics**

Vista keeps an eye on running applications and will try to solve issues when applications unexpectedly stop functioning.

- **Recovery from application crashes**

Vista keeps track of how an application closes. When Vista is under the impression that the application did not end in an appropriate way, it will notify the user, try to restart the application and look for a solution for the problem.

- **Fast user switching on domain joined workstations**

Vista now supports fast user switching when the system is joined to a domain. This feature in Windows XP was only available for computers that were not joined to a domain.

I am sure I could come up with some more interesting new features, but this is what you get from me now. Now prepare for the rest in the upcoming chapters.

2.2 Windows Vista Versions

The following table shows the global feature sets of Windows Vista's five main editions. I'm excluding the N-versions (that nobody buys anyway) and the very stripped down Starter Edition that is only sold in developing countries.

	Home Basic	Home Premium	Business	Enterprise	Ultimate
Aero		✓	✓	✓	✓
Multiple CPU			✓	✓	✓
Domain Member			✓	✓	✓
Media Center		✓			✓
Data Backup & Restore	✓	✓	✓	✓	✓
Movie Maker		✓			✓
DVD Maker		✓			✓
Parental Controls		✓			✓
Tablet PC Support		✓	✓	✓	✓
Complete PC Backup			✓	✓	✓
Windows Fax & Scan			✓	✓	✓
Network and Sharing Center			✓	✓	✓
Wireless Network provisioning			✓	✓	✓
Encrypted File System			✓	✓	✓
Policy Based QoS			✓	✓	✓
NAP Client			✓	✓	✓
BitLocker Driver Encryption				✓	✓
Multiple UI Languages				✓	✓
Subsystem for					✓

	Home Basic	Home Premium	Business	Enterprise	Ultimate
Unix					
Remote Desktop			✓	✓	✓
Windows Meeting Space		✓	✓	✓	✓
Offline Files and Folders			✓	✓	✓

Bottom line: You can see that Windows Home Premium certainly lacks a few features that you would really want to use in a business environment such as domain membership and Remote Desktop. At the same time there is the strange omission of BitLocker Drive Encryption in Vista Business Edition, which is sold with most retail business laptops nowadays.

If you want it all, you should choose Windows Vista Ultimate Edition. This version contains every available feature of the product; however, it comes with a big "but...". Vista Ultimate Edition is not suitable for the purposes of an enterprise because there is no Volume Licensing available and is only sold with a retail license. You can read more about Volume Licensing in paragraph 3.1.4.

2.3 Using Multiple Languages or changing the System Language

Windows Vista is language neutral. This means that Windows Vista has no basic language and that any language can be added to the language neutral basis. It also means that Service Packs for Windows Vista will no longer be related to a single language. Despite this fact, only Windows Vista Enterprise and Ultimate editions allow running multiple UI languages on a single system. Other versions of Windows Vista only allow a single UI language to be installed on the computer.

It is possible to change the UI language on a Windows Vista system not running the Enterprise or Ultimate editions. You can do this by installing the language pack as an lp.cab file for a different language. This file can be downloaded from the Microsoft Web site, although the links are not actively promoted by Microsoft (see www.xpworld.com for a list). However, after installing the extra language, you must make sure that you define the newly installed system language as the system default language within 24 hours after installation. This is necessary, because the Windows Vista editions that do not support multiple languages will remove all "non default" languages after 24 hours.

Even though Service Packs are language neutral in Windows Vista, be aware that the Language Packs have to be updated with each change in the UI. This is why there are still Service Pack downloads for different languages available. Those are actually the same Service Pack with different language pack updates in each download.

Use **lpksetup.exe** to install a UI Language Pack on Windows Vista.

2.4 SuperFetch and ReadyBoost

Microsoft's claims for the better performance of Windows Vista are largely based on two really cool named features in Windows Vista: SuperFetch and ReadyBoost. This chapter explains how each feature works and how it improves Vista's performance.

2.4.1 SuperFetch

SuperFetch' main purpose is to improve Vista's user experience right after the user has started the system. SuperFetch monitors user behavior and tries to predict which programs will be started by the user after logon. Windows Vista searches for the most frequently, as well as for the most regularly used programs. It then pre-caches the bits for these programs in otherwise unused random access memory (RAM). When a program that is already loaded in RAM is used, the time required to start the program is significantly shortened. Hard drives are rather slow in comparison to RAM (60-90 MB/s disk transfer rate vs. 5-7 GB/s RAM throughput). SuperFetch provides faster application launch times. Typically, 512MB RAM is not enough memory for SuperFetch to offer a significant increase in performance. A minimum of 1 GB is suggested if you want to experience the benefits of SuperFetch.

2.4.2 ReadyBoost

ReadyBoost is another performance enhancing technology that is closely related to SuperFetch. ReadyBoost is especially handy when there is a limited amount of RAM available in the computer. For example, when Windows Vista is running on a system with 512 MB of RAM, most of that memory will be in use and SuperFetch will not have much RAM available to pre-cache programs in memory. ReadyBoost uses static memory instead of RAM to eliminate disk seek times on the hard disk and immediately have the data available that SuperFetch would otherwise have cached in RAM. Although no static memory device offers the throughput of a fast hard drive (20-25 MB/s max for USB 2.0 Flash devices vs. 60-90 MB/s for hard drives), the lack of seek time on a Flash storage device makes it a faster alternative than the hard disk that requires a relative long time to move the heads to the right position before retrieving the data.

In order for static memory to be available for ReadyBoost, the following pre-requisites apply:

- The static memory device can be a USB stick or an SD card.
- If the device has a USB interface, it must be at least USB 2.0.

- The device must be able to deliver 3.5 MB/s for 4 KB random reads uniformly across the entire device and 2.5 MB/s for 512 KB random writes uniformly across the device.
- The device must have at least 64 MB of free space.
- ReadyBoost is not supported on external USB card readers or USB hard drives.

In order to prevent misuse of data on a storage device used for ReadyBoost, Windows uses AES-128 encryption.

Various performance tests show that ReadyBoost especially improves performance on systems with less than 1 GB RAM available. As the amount of available RAM increases, the benefit of ReadyBoost declines.

Using ReadyBoost

After plugging in a USB 2.0 Flash memory stick into an unused USB 2.0 port, Windows Vista recognizes the new mass storage device and wants to know what to do with it. One option is to select it to improve system performance. Vista will then test the device for its capacity to be used for ReadyBoost. If the test result is positive, you may limit the size of the ReadyBoost cache, or use its full capacity to a maximum of 4 GB. After successful installation, Windows Vista will use the additional storage capacity to speed up application startup through SuperFetch by populating the Flash drive with frequently used applications.

2.5 32- or 64-bit Windows Vista

Windows Vista is available in 32- and 64-bit versions. The 64 bits versions are theoretically able to address 2^64 or 16 Exabytes of RAM. This is over 4 billion times the 4 GB limit which applies to 32-bit versions of Windows. Be aware that the 4 GB limit on 32-bit systems includes memory for display and BIOS. Probably even Microsoft thought 16 Exabytes was a bit too much. The practical limit of 64-bit Windows Vista currently is “only” a mere 16TB. Read the following KB article to find out why you will never see the full 4 GB of RAM on a 32-bit Windows Vista system: *http://support.microsoft.com/kb/929605/en-us*.

If RAM availability was the only motive for choosing a system, the choice would have been easy. Microsoft included a few differences between 32- and 64-bits versions of Windows Vista that will make the choice more difficult than it seems at first sight.

The following paragraphs provide an overview of the most important differences between 32- and 64-bit Windows Vista.

64-bit Vista requires 64-bit drivers.
The fact that 32-bit drivers don't work on 64-bit Windows, limits the amount of hardware available on 64-bit systems.

64-bit Vista only accepts signed kernel mode drivers.
The 64-bit versions of Windows Vista and Windows Server 2008 require that all kernel mode device drivers be signed with a Software Publishing Certificate issued by a certification authority. If you use a 64-bit version of Windows Vista, then you need a driver package that is already signed, or you should have access to a Software Publishing Certificate with which you can sign the driver package. If you sign a 64-bit kernel mode device driver incorrectly, it will not load or run successfully. If the device driver is required to start the computer, your computer might fail to start.

16-bit applications will not run on 64-bit Vista.
While this sounds like a non-issue, one has to be aware that quite a lot of known 32-bit applications use 16-bit installers.

Windows on Windows 64 or WoW64 enables compatibility for 32-bit applications.
WoW64 lets 32-bit applications run like they are on a 32-bit system. This works for a lot of applications as long as they don’t contain Shell Extensions (like WinZip).

More memory may even boost performance for 32-bit applications.
More memory is always better. This also goes for 64-bit systems. When your memory grows (beyond 4 GB), it allows more processes to actively reside in physical memory simultaneously. This may eliminate or reduce the time spent loading and switching between processes.

Patchguard or Kernel Patch protection.
Kernel Patch Protection was first introduced on x64 (AMD64 and Intel EMT64T) CPU architecture versions of Windows including Windows Server 2003 SP1 and Windows XP Professional x64 Edition. Patch protection is currently not supported on x86 or ia64 architectures. It provides protection against “Kernel Patching” or “Kernel Hooking”, which is the practice of using unsupported mechanisms to modify or replace kernel code. Kernel patching can result in unpredictable behavior, system instability and performance problems. Kernel patching has been used by the good as well as the bad guys in the industry. Anti-malware vendors, for example, use it to intercept system calls to prevent applications from doing harm to your systems. Malware authors, on the other hand, use kernel patching to attack the same system. Rootkits are well known for kernel patching in order to hide their presence.

Kernel Patch Protection monitors if key resources used by the kernel or kernel code itself have been modified. When the operating system detects an unauthorized patch of certain data structures or code, it will initiate a shutdown of the system.

So what version do you chose?
If performance is your main reason for running 64-bit Windows Vista, your gain depends on the availability of RAM. When using less than 4 GB of RAM, the overall performance of 64-bit Vista is more or less the same as 32-bit Vista. Otherwise you just have to make sure that you can live with the restrictions of running 64-bit Windows Vista.

3 Deploying Windows Vista

Windows Vista exhibits great differences in deployment, compared to Windows XP. Windows Vista introduces a shipload of new technologies and tools to Windows deployment that will significantly increase flexibility. It is about time to forget everything you know about Windows XP deployment and start all over, to learn how to deploy Windows Vista.

Here is a short list of changes to the Windows deployment process:

- Windows deployment is now image based.
- Get used to deployment images of 2GB+.
- When deploying keep security in mind: BitLocker requires a different partitioning scheme.
- Windows installation is component based.
- Patches, Service Packs and Languages are also components.
- Drivers can be injected as components at install time.
- Boot.ini does not exist anymore.
- (Almost) all ini-files are now XML based.
- Images are HAL independent.
- Installation starts with Windows PE (Windows Pre-installation Environment). DOS is definitively a thing of the past.
- Setup.exe replaces winnt32.exe to start Windows installation.
- Vista is language neutral. No more language-specific patches or service packs.
- If you must deploy now and don't have time to learn all new tools at present, Microsoft Deployment Toolkit can save you a lot of time and probably provides you with much better results then you expected.

3.1 Vista Product Activation

Windows Product Activation was introduced in Windows XP, as a counter measure for software piracy. Product Activation forces the software to get uniquely activated during the grace period, in order to stay fully functional. In Windows XP, product activation was required in all versions except the Volume Licensing (VL) and OEM versions of the product. Due to those exceptions, the VL version of Windows XP turned out to be the most pirated piece of software on the planet. While this was bad for Microsoft's cash flow, it also had some more serious side effects. As Microsoft decided to decline software updates for Windows installations with known pirated VL product codes, loads of Windows based clients were no longer updated for security vulnerabilities. This and the fact that a lot of so called "specialists" who install pirated versions of Windows still recommend that you don't really need those updates, created numerous willing systems on the Internet, ready to be hacked and used in some kind of botnet or other criminal activity.

Windows Vista extends product activation to the VL versions of the product. This creates three kinds of activation for Windows Vista:

- Retail Activation
- OEM Activation
- Volume Activation

Before diving into the differences between these activation schemes, let's first explore what activation states exist on a Windows Vista client and what this means for its functionality.

3.1.1 License states

The Windows Vista license state defines the need to activate a client. Windows Vista uses five license states:

- Licensed
  A Windows Vista client enters the licensed state when it is properly activated. Activation can be executed online, via telephone or by using a KMS Server.
- Initial Grace
  The Initial Grace period for a Windows Vista client starts right after installation. This state is also called the OOB (Out-of-Box) Grace. Every Windows Vista client installed with or without a product key will enter the OOB Grace period after install and will be fully functional in this state. The

OOB Grace can be restarted three times using *sysprep /generalize* or *slmgr.vbs –rearm*.

- Non-Genuine Grace
  Windows Vista clients attain the non-Genuine Grace state when the Windows Genuine Advantage (WGA) ActiveX control fails genuine validation. If this happens, non-Genuine Grace provides 30 days to re-activate the client and perform a valid genuine validation using the WGA ActiveX control. When a Windows Vista system enters non-Genuine Grace, Windows Aero and ReadyBoost features are disabled, and Windows Defender and Windows Update will have limited capabilities (optional updates will not be available through Windows Update, and Windows Defender will only remove critical and severe threats).
- Out-of-Tolerance Grace
  Out-of-Tolerance (OOT) Grace begins when significant hardware changes push an already activated system beyond a tolerance level, or when the client did not contact a KMS for longer than 180 days (see Volume Activation). OOT Grace provides 30 days to re-activate. When using a KMS, there is no limit for the number of times a system can enter OOT Grace.
- Unlicensed
  A Windows Vista client becomes unlicensed when any grace period expires. When this happens, the system operates in Reduced Functionality Mode (RFM). In RFM the system can no longer be used for normal operation and can only return to full functionality after activation. In Windows Vista with Service Pack 1, RFM has undergone some changes. Due to those changes RFM no longer removes functionality from Windows Vista, but turns the background black and present regular warnings for the fact that the product does not meet the license policy.

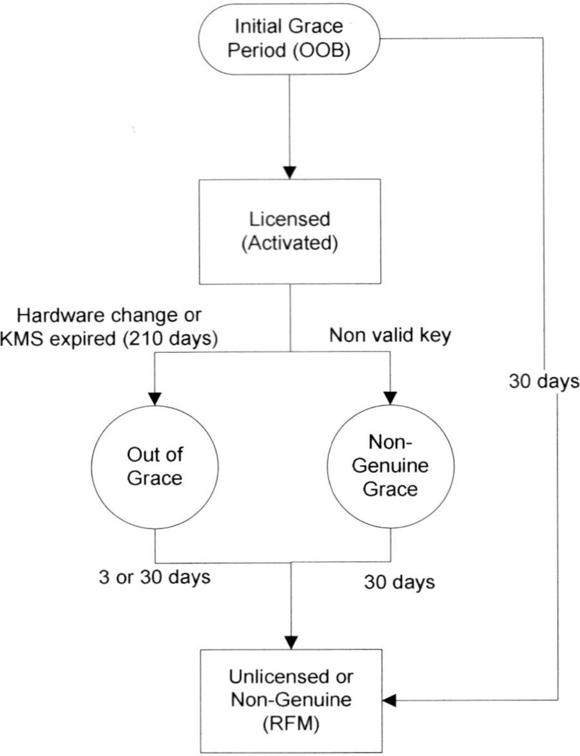

Figure 3-1 Windows Vista license states

3.1.2 Retail Activation

Retail Activation applies to all retail versions of Windows Vista. Retail versions of Windows Vista have a unique product key for each installed instance. Installations using retail keys can be activated once on the Internet. When Internet activation fails or is not possible, activation can usually be requested by telephone.

3.1.3 OEM Activation

OEM Activation is the only non-activating installation left of Windows Vista. In order to use OEM Activation, one must use an especially crafted version of the Windows Vista media that looks for specific system characteristics defining the OEM. In combination with the correct product key, the installation will not request activation and run out of the box.

Due to its non-activating nature, OEM activation has become the latest target for people trying to run unlicensed copies of Windows Vista. Currently, the only known well working hack for Windows Vista was created using OEM Activation. This may change overtime.

3.1.4 Volume Activation 2.0

With Volume Activation 2.0, even enterprise customers using Windows Vista must now activate their software. In order to create some flexibility when adhering to this new requirement, Microsoft introduced two new kinds of product keys and three methods of Activation:

- Multiple Activation Key (MAK)
    - MAK Proxy Activation
    - MAK Independent Activation
- Key Management Server (KMS) Key
    - KMS Activation

Enterprise customers are free to use one or more of these keys or activation methods.

3.1.5 Multiple Activation Key

Systems installed with a MAK use the same activation on the Internet as in the retail versions of Windows Vista. The only difference is, that this key is the same for each client under the specific contract. This may look like the old VL concept we know from Windows XP, but there is one major difference: systems installed with this key do activate and a counter is keeping track of the number of activations that have taken place.

Depending on the type of activation, MAK clients will contact an activation server from Microsoft on the Internet or on the local network. When the MAK client directly contacts a Microsoft activation server on the Internet, this is called MAK Independent Activation. In cases where the MAK client cannot directly connect to the Internet, an intermediate server can be assigned to proxy the activation request to the Internet. This is called MAK Proxy Activation.

MAK Proxy activation is a manual procedure, executed on a system that is able to connect to the internet and has RPC-based access to the clients that need to be activated. In order to perform MAK Proxy Activation, an administrator installs the Volume Activation Management Tool (VAMT) on the MAK Proxy system. From there the admin can trigger client discovery using the "Add Machine" function and use Active Directory or workgroups on the network to select the systems that must be activated. After discovering the computers, the admin can perform MAK-independent or MAK Proxy Activation for those systems.

MAK Activation is executed only once for each system after installation, during OOB Grace period or in the OOT Grace period.

A MAK can be supplied to a system in the following ways:

- With an unattend file in the "specialize" pass.
- With the reference image.
- After installation, using:
    - The "Change Product Key" option in the Control Panel.
    - From the command line using:

      ```
      slmgr.vbs -ipk <MAK> & slmgr.vbs-ato
      ```

      NB <MAK> stands for the Manual Activation Key.
    - Volume Activation Management Tool (VAMT).

Note: The MAK <u>cannot</u> be supplied during setup.

3.1.6 Key Management Server (KMS)

A Key Management Server (KMS) host enables an organization to take product activation completely offline by installing its own activation server. The KMS is an extra service that can be enabled on any system running Windows Vista, Windows Server 2008 or Windows Server 2003 with SP1 or higher. The service has low impact on system performance and uses very few resources. A single KMS server is theoretically capable of handling up to 100.000 clients. Typically an organization will install two Key Management Servers in its network. A primary and backup KMS will do the job.

A KMS host must be activated using a KMS key. This can be done online or over the telephone. After activation, the KMS will no longer need to contact Microsoft, except when a significant hardware change has taken place. By default an organization with a VL enterprise agreement will get one KMS Activation key that can be used to activate up to 6 Key Management Servers which are allowed to reactivate up to 10 times.

Use the following commands to install KMS Server:

- Install the license key:

```
SLMGR -ipk <Volume License Key>
```

- Activate
    - online:

    ```
    SLMGR -ato
    ```

    - via telephone:

    ```
    SLUI.EXE 4
    ```

Note: Be careful while selecting the installation key for Windows Vista! It turns out that the Volume License Key which is supposed to activate the KMS, can also be used as a MAK for plain simple Vista client activation. After entering the key on six systems, your VL key will no longer work and you will have to contact Microsoft in order to get it fixed.

A KMS host will register a special SRV record in DNS, in order to be located by clients. Therefore the DNS must be running on Windows 2000 or higher, or BIND version 9 or higher. By default the KMS host uses TCP Port 1688 for client activation.

The KMS can be easily located in DNS. Type the following command in the command prompt and press Enter:

```
nslookup -type=srv _vlmcs._tcp.
```

The reply will include the following information for each KMS SRV resource record in DNS:

```
vlmcs._tcp.contoso.com SRV service location:
          priority = 0
          weight   = 0
          port     = 1688
          svr hostname    = KMS1.contoso.com
```

Clients will only activate when the KMS is servicing a minimum of 25 clients. The clients are keeping track of this. The number of clients activated by the KMS is also called the n-count. The n-count increases with every client activating with the KMS Server. When a client does not contact the KMS for 30 days, the n-count decreases by one. While activating, the clients send a Client Machine ID (CMID) to identify themselves to the KMS. The KMS only keeps track of the last 50 clients it activated. In order to get a report of all activated clients one must query the event log of the KMS host.

KMS Client

Clients utilizing a KMS have the following characteristics:

- The clients are installed from VL media.
- The clients locate the KMS via DNS.
- The clients are installed without providing a product key.

After installation, KMS clients enter the 30 day OOB Grace Period and try to contact the KMS every two hours until Activation has taken place. This two hour interval is configurable. When activated, the activation is valid for 180 days. During this time the client will try to contact the KMS once every seven days. This interval is also configurable. The KMS activation stays valid for 180 after the last connection. When the 180 day activation period expires without a connection to the KMS, the client starts the 30 day OOT Grace period after which it reverts to RFM.

Virtual Machine clients can activate using a KMS, but they will not increase the n-count.

3.1.7 Licensing overview

Media	Activation	Refresh	Out of Tolerance (OOT)
Retail	Retail Key + online activation	Never	Hardware change
OEM	OEM Key + BIOS check		
VL	No key + KMS	Try every 7 days < 180 days	> 180 days no KMS contact n-count < 25 Hardware change WGA check failed
	MAK + online activation	Never	Hardware change WGA check failed
	No key + MAK proxy activation		

3.2 Windows Image Management

Windows Vista is deployed from a file based image; the Windows Image (WIM) file format is the new basis for Windows installations. The file format is said to be derived from the LHARC format that has also been used to create well-known formats like ZIP. The WIM file on the Windows Vista DVD contains all versions of Windows Vista for that DVD in a single file. The Windows Vista version that will be installed depends on the key entered at install time. WIM files use a single instance mechanism that ensures that every file it contains is stored only once. This mechanism uses a sound compression algorithm, so that all versions of Vista will fit in a WIM file of roughly 2.5 GB.

When the term 'image' is used, many people think of Ghost imaging. Ghost uses a sector based imaging technology that is basically different from the WIM file format, which is file based. Because of its file based background it is a lot easier to manipulate WIM files than it will ever be to change the contents of a Ghost file.

Sector-based images in Windows XP imposed a number of limitations that created a lot of work for the systems administrator. A number of known issues for images based on Windows XP are:

- The destination computer has to use the same Hardware Abstraction Layer (HAL) as the master or source computer.
- The destination computer is required to boot from the same mass-storage controller as the master computer.
- The existing contents of the destination computer's hard drive are destroyed, thus complicating Windows deployment scenarios.
- The hard drive is exactly duplicated; therefore, the image can be deployed only on partitions of the same type as the master computer, and will be at least the same size as the partition on the master computer.
- Direct modification of imaged files is not enabled.
- The purchase of third-party applications and services might be required to use images for deployment.

The Windows Vista WIM files can be easily manipulated to create a customized installation. Using tools like ImageX and the Windows System Image Manager, it is rather easy to add files, device drivers, languages, service packs or other options to an existing WIM-image.

3.2.1 ImageX

ImageX is a command-line tool that enables the SysAdmin to capture, modify and apply file-based images for the deployment of Vista, Windows PE or Windows Server 2008. ImageX provides the opportunity to mount an image and then treat the contents as any ordinary folder structure. You can add, copy, paste and delete files with any file management tool, like Windows Explorer.

A common scenario for using ImageX, is to customize the default Windows Vista WIM image on the DVD in order to add, remove, edit or copy files to the image by using the Windows Imaging File System Filter (WIM FS Filter). The WIM FS Filter allows an Administrator to mount an image in a WIM file and then access it as if it is part of the existing file system.

ImageX main features are:

- Capture and apply Windows Vista images for deployment.
  ImageX is perfectly capable of capturing or applying an image for rapid deployment. This scenario requires booting into Windows PE, capturing an image to a network location and then applying the image to destination computers.
- Capture and apply Windows XP SP2 and Windows Server 2003 SP1 images.
  ImageX can also be used to capture and apply images for these other operating systems. Only, those images cannot be mounted for offline manipulation.
- Mount Windows Vista based WIM files.
  ImageX can only mount image files with Windows Vista installations. Images from other operating systems cannot be mounted. To mount an image for reading and writing, the image file must be based on an NTFS volume. Image files stored on FAT , ISO or UDF formatted media can only be mounted for reading.

Accessing a WIM-file

A WIM-file can contain one or multiple images. Each image consists of a folder structure that can represent an random set of files. On the retail version of the Windows Vista DVD, Install.wim contains 7 Windows Vista images; one for each edition of Windows Vista.

ImageX can report the contents of a WIM-file. Using the INFO argument one can tell which images are in the WIM-file and what their global parameters are. When querying Install.wim on the retail version of the Windows Vista DVD, part of the output will look like this:

```
Administrator: Windows PE Tools Command Prompt
E:\sources>imagex /info install.wim

ImageX Tool for Windows
Copyright (C) Microsoft Corp. 1981-2005. All rights reserved.

WIM Information:
----------------
GUID:          {03071445-5d93-4792-ba6d-5e5ccca3b18d}
Image Count: 7
Compression: LZX
Part Number: 1/1
Attributes:  0xc
             Integrity info
             Relative path junction

Available Image Choices:
------------------------
<WIM>
  <TOTALBYTES>2412491164</TOTALBYTES>
  <IMAGE INDEX="1">
    <NAME>Windows Vista BUSINESS</NAME>
    <DESCRIPTION>Windows Vista Business</DESCRIPTION>
    <FLAGS>BUSINESS</FLAGS>
    <WINDOWS>
      <ARCH>0</ARCH>
      <PRODUCTNAME>Microsoft« Windows« Operating System</PRODUCTNAME>
      <HAL>acpiapic</HAL>
      <PRODUCTTYPE>WinNT</PRODUCTTYPE>
      <PRODUCTSUITE>Terminal Server</PRODUCTSUITE>
      <LANGUAGES>
        <LANGUAGE>en-US</LANGUAGE>
        <DEFAULT>en-US</DEFAULT>
      </LANGUAGES>
      <VERSION>
        <MAJOR>6</MAJOR>
```

Figure 3-2 View image information in a WIM image

The "WIM information" section provides general information about the WIM file, the number of images contained in the file and the type of compression that was used.

The "Available Image Choices" section provides more detailed information about each image contained in the WIM, in XML format. Each XML record starts with <IMAGE INDEX="n">. This provides an easy way to identify each image in the WIM, because you must refer to the image index number "n" when accessing information contained in a specific image.

It is very easy to get more information about the files contained in each image. If you only want to get a file listing, you can simply use the IMAGEX /DIR command and view a list of files contained in an image. You must refer to the image index number when using this command. You will usually not use this command to search a Windows Vista image in a WIM file, because it will return the complete list of more than 35.000 files.

Use the following command to view the full list of files contained in the first image contained in E:\Sources\Install.WIM:

```
IMAGEX /DIR E:\Sources\Install.WIM 1
```

Mounting an image

Another way of accessing the information contained in an image in a WIM file is by mounting the image. By mounting an image you connect the contents of the image to an empty "mount folder" on the local file system. After the image is mounted, its contents are accessible as files and subfolders of the mount folder.

Use IMAGEX /MOUNT to get read-only access to the contents of an image. Use IMAGEX /UNMOUNT to unmount a folder when you want to dismount the image from the folder.

The following screenshot shows what happens when the first image in E:\Sources\Install.WIM is mounted to C:\Mount.

```
Administrator: Windows PE Tools Command Prompt
C:\>md Mount

C:\>imagex /mount e:\sources\install.wim 1 c:\Mount

ImageX Tool for Windows
Copyright (C) Microsoft Corp. 1981-2005. All rights reserved.

Mounting: [e:\sources\install.wim, 1] ->
          [c:\Mount]

Successfully mounted image.

C:\>dir Mount
 Volume in drive C has no label.
 Volume Serial Number is 2A86-AA99

 Directory of C:\Mount

21-01-2008  04:32    <DIR>          PerfLogs
02-11-2006  15:01    <DIR>          Program Files
21-01-2008  03:41    <DIR>          Users
21-01-2008  04:55    <DIR>          Windows
18-09-2006  23:43                24 autoexec.bat
18-09-2006  23:43                10 config.sys
               2 File(s)             34 bytes
               4 Dir(s)  483.364.294.656 bytes free

C:\>imagex /unmount c:\Mount

ImageX Tool for Windows
Copyright (C) Microsoft Corp. 1981-2005. All rights reserved.

Unmounting: [c:\Mount]...

Successfully unmounted image.
```

Figure 3-3 Mounting a WIM image

Using ImageX to create a WIM file

As you can tell from previous examples, Microsoft distributes Windows Vista as a series of images in a WIM file. You can also create your own WIM file with your own files or customized Windows installation. Make sure you store the new WIM file on another volume than the one you are capturing, when creating a WIM file from a custom Windows Installation.

When you like to exclude specific files or folders from the captured WIM, you can define which files should not be captured and which files should not be compressed.

IMAGEX /CAPTURE by default excludes the following files:

```
[ExclusionList]
\$ntfs.log
\hiberfil.sys
\pagefile.sys
"\System Volume Information"
\RECYCLER
\Windows\CSC

[CompressionExclusionList]
*.mp3
*.zip
*.cab
\WINDOWS\inf\*.pnf
```

Create a file called WIMSCRIPT.INI in the directory where imagex.exe is located to extend or override the default exclusion list. Create a section [ExclusionException] to override default exclusions for IMAGEX /CAPTURE.

Use the following command to create Z:\CUSTOM_IMAGE.WIM with the contents of C: in an image called "Drive C":

```
IMAGEX /CAPTURE C: Z:\CUSTOM_IMAGE.WIM "Drive C"
```

Adding and removing images from a WIM file

A WIM file can contain multiple images. ImageX is used from the command-line to add or remove images from a WIM file. There is no GUI available in Windows Vista to perform these operations.

Adding images to a WIM file

Use the IMAGEX /APPEND command to append an image to an existing WIM file. Multiple images in a WIM file can save a lot of disk space, because the single instance functionality built in the WIM file may significantly reduce the disk space needed by the extra image.

Use the following command to add the contents of D: to Z:\CUSTOM_IMAGE.WIM in a new image:

```
IMAGEX /APPEND D: Z:\CUSTOM_IMAGE.WIM "Drive D" /verify
```

Deleting images from a WIM file
Use IMAGEX /DELETE to delete an image from an existing WIM file.

The following command will remove the first image from Z:\CUSTOM_IMAGE .WIM:

```
IMAGEX /DELETE Z:\CUSTOM_IMAGE.WIM 1
```

Extract an image for a new WIM file
With IMAGEX /EXPORT you can create a new WIM file that contains an image from an existing WIM file. This method is used in chapter 4.8 to create a WIM file with Windows RE.

Use the following command to extract the second image as a bootable image from BOOT.WIM to WINRE.WIM:

```
IMAGEX /EXPORT /BOOT BOOT.WIM 2 C:\WINRE.WIM "Windows
Recovery Environment"
```

Customizing a WIM file with ImageX

By mounting an image in Read/Write mode, the contents of a WIM file can be edited within the file. You can add, remove and edit files in the mounted folder structure. Changes will not be written to the image until they have been explicitly committed using the IMAGEX /COMMIT command.

The following example shows how IMAGEX.EXE is added to WINPE.WIM and the results are committed to the WIM file.

```
Administrator: Windows PE Tools Command Prompt
C:\>md Mount

C:\>imagex /mountrw d:\winpe.wim 1 Mount

ImageX Tool for Windows
Copyright (C) Microsoft Corp. 1981-2005. All rights reserved.

Mounting (RW): [d:\winpe.wim, 1] ->
               [C:\Mount]

Successfully mounted image (RW).

C:\>copy "c:\Program Files\Windows AIK\Tools\x86\imagex.exe" c:\Mount
        1 file(s) copied.

C:\>imagex /unmount /commit Mount

ImageX Tool for Windows
Copyright (C) Microsoft Corp. 1981-2005. All rights reserved.

Unmounting: [C:\Mount]...

Successfully unmounted image.
```

Figure 3-4 Customizing a WIM image

Splitting a WIM file

When the WIM file becomes too big for the storage medium, the file can be split into multiple files. The result will be a number of SWM files. Each SWM file is capped at the maximum size defined in the IMAGEX /SPLIT command. A split WIM file can be applied with ImageX, but cannot be edited or loaded in Windows Deployment Services.

Use the following command to split INSTALL.WIM into 650 MB SWM files:

```
IMAGEX /SPLIT Z:\CUSTOM_IMAGE.WIM 650
```

Using a WIM file for deployment

Use IMAGEX /APPLY to apply an image in a WIM file to an existing volume. This is one of the ways one can apply a custom image from a sysprep-ed reference system to a new system for deployment.

Use the following command to apply the first image in *CUSTOM_IMAGE.WIM* to the C:-volume of the local system:

```
IMAGEX /APPLY Z:\CUSTOM_IMAGE.WIM 1 C:\
```

3.3 Automating Windows Setup

Installing a single system using the installation wizard is a blast with Windows Vista. Just like Windows XP, Vista allows you to automate the installation so that you can skip parts of the installation wizard and create an unattended installation. Only thing is that Vista has so many more options to define and so much more flexibility to provide that creating an unattended installation becomes a whole other story. The following paragraphs discuss how Windows Vista installation can be automated and how this is different from Windows XP.

3.3.1 Windows Vista answer files

Windows Vista uses an XML based answer file that will often be referred to as Unattend.XML. This answer file replaces all of the answer files that were used in previous versions of Windows (Unattend.txt, Winbom.ini, Oobeinfo.ini, and Sysprep.inf). For example, an answer file can be used to partition and format a disk before installing Windows, then change the default setting for the Internet Explorer home page. An answer file can also be used to install third-party applications, device drivers, language packs, and other updates.

3.3.2 Catalog Files

A catalog file is required when you open or create an answer file in Windows System Image Manager (WSIM). If there is no catalog file, WSIM recreates the catalog based on the contents of the Windows image that you select. When a catalog is created, it queries the Windows image for a listing of all the settings in that image. Because the contents of a Windows image can change over time, it is important that you recreate the catalog file whenever you update a Windows image.

A "catalog" is a binary file that lists all the components in a Windows image (.wim) file. Catalogs are smaller and more portable than Windows image files. For example, catalogs are typically less than 5 MB, while Windows image files can be 1.5 GB or more. Due to their smaller size, catalogs can be easily copied to removable media, shared to a network folder, or sent as e-mail attachments. Catalog files can also be opened by users who are not administrators. More than one user can open a catalog at the same time.

The Windows Vista retail DVD includes pre-generated catalog files for each Windows image inside install.wim. These catalog files are in the Sources directory of the retail DVD and can be used to create an answer file for a Windows image in the default install.wim file. However, if you intend to create a catalog for a custom

Windows image, you should use Image Manager to recreate the catalog for that custom Windows image.

The catalog contains the following information:

- A list of component settings and current values.
- Windows features and package states.

3.3.3 Windows System Image Manager

Windows System Image Manager (WSIM) is kind of the successor to the unattended installation Wizard in Windows XP. Because of the XML based nature of the new answer files, it is unlikely that WSIM will often be replaced by Notepad. WSIM is delivered as part of the Windows Automated Installation Kit (WAIK).

WSIM is much more powerful and much more complex than any wizard for unattended installation we had in previous versions of Windows. Starting WSIM immediately proves the point. The UI of WSIM does not look like the unattended installation wizard.

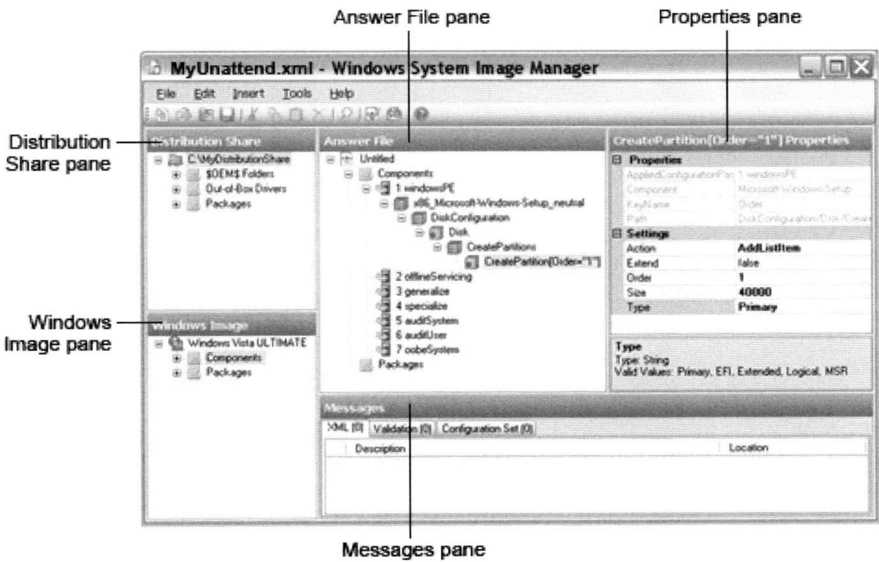

Figure 3-5 Windows System Image Manager UI

After starting WSIM you first have to load an image or a catalog file. This is because WSIM will present components and packages that are available in the image you are loading. A catalog only stores information about the components and packages without the ballast of a complete image.

The WSIM GUI

The WSIM GUI consists of five panes:

- Distribution Share Pane
  The Distribution Share pane displays the currently open distribution share folder in tree view. You can select, create, explore, and close distribution share folders by selecting the top node and then right-clicking in the pane. You can add items in an open distribution share folder to an answer file by right-clicking the item.
- Answer File Pane
  The Answer File pane displays the Windows Setup configuration passes, the settings to apply in each pass, and the packages to install. You can open and edit an existing answer file, validate the settings in an answer file against a Windows image, or create a new answer file.
- Windows Image Pane
  The Windows Image pane displays the currently open Windows image in tree view. When the tree is expanded, all the components and packages for the image are visible and available to add to an answer file in the Answer File pane.
- Properties Pane
  The Properties pane displays the properties and settings of a selected component or package. The Properties pane enables you to edit the settings, and, in the case of packages, Windows feature selections. At the bottom of the Properties pane, WSIM displays the name of the setting and the associated .NET type.
- Messages Pane
  The Messages pane consists of three tabs. The tabs displayed are XML, Validation, and Configuration Set. Clicking a tab in the Messages pane displays the type of message, a description, and the location of the issue. The types of messages that the Messages pane displays are informatory. Messages only appear in the Configuration Set messages tab if a configuration set has been created.

Creating an answer file

To create an answer file, you must first load or create a catalog file. Left Click **Select a windows image or catalog file** in the Windows Image pane and click

Select Windows image... This enables you to select a catalog or WIM file. After the catalog is selected or created, the Components and Packages nodes are populated.

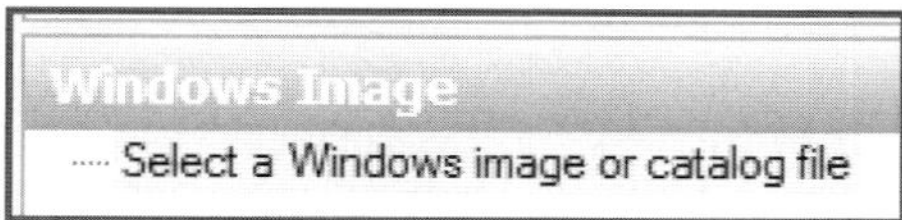

Figure 3-6 Selecting an image in WSIM

Then left click **Create or open an answer file** in the Answer file pane and select "**New Answer file**".

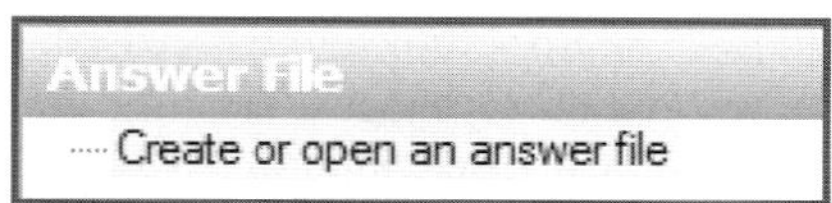

Figure 3-7 Creating an Answer File in WSIM

This creates another Components and a Packages folder in the answer file section. Under Components there is a view of the answer file, broken down in 7 sections. Each section stands for a "Windows Setup Configuration Pass". The sections are:

1. **WindowsPE**
   The WindowsPE section contains all modifications applied during the pre-boot phase of an installation. Settings included in the WindowsPE pass are:
   a. Partition and format a hard disk.
   b. Select a specific Windows image to install, the path of that image, and any credentials required to access that image.
   c. Select a partition on the destination computer where you install Windows.
   d. Apply a product key and administrator password.
   e. Run specific commands during Windows Setup.
2. **OfflineServicing**
   OfflineServicing contains unattended setup settings applied to offline images of Windows Vista. Here you can inject drivers, add language packs, QFE updates, or change default settings in an offline image.
3. **Generalize**
   The Generalize section contains settings that would be defined in winbom.ini in Windows XP. The section contains information about what a sysprep should

do when preparing a windows reference image. The generalize pass runs during sysprep.

4. **Specialize**
   The specialize pass contains settings that define the configuration at the system level during an automated installation.
5. **auditSystem**
   The auditSystem pass processes unattended Setup settings in system context in audit mode (using sysprep /audit, or sysprep /generalize /audit). Audit mode enables OEMs and corporations to install additional device drivers, applications, and other updates without running through the OOBE. This enables customizations of an image without running through the specialization routine after each customization. When Windows boots to audit mode, the auditSystem and auditUser unattended Windows Setup settings are processed.
   By using audit mode, you can maintain fewer Windows images, because you can create a reference image with a minimal set of drivers. The image can be updated with additional drivers during audit mode. You can then test and resolve any issues related to malfunctioning or incorrectly installed devices on the Windows image.
6. **auditUser**
   See auditSystem.
7. **oobeSystem**
   The oobeSystem pass configures settings that are applied during the first-boot experience for end users, also called Windows Welcome. oobeSystem settings are processed before a user first logs into Windows. Out-of-Box-Experience (OOBE) runs the first time the user starts a new computer. OOBE runs before the Windows shell or any additional software runs, and performs a small set of tasks necessary to configure and run Windows.

Editing an answer file

In order to actually insert information into the answer file, you have to add components and/or packages. Expanding the Components section in the Windows Image pane reveals the available components. When you select a component, this immediately shows its properties and settings in the Properties pane on the right.

When you right click a component the UI will show to which Windows configuration pass the component can be added. Select the pass and click on the component in the Answer file pane to actually change its properties.

The same procedure works for adding packages to the unattended install file. The only difference is, that packages will be added to the Packages section in the Answer file pane.

When all desired components and packages are added to the answer file, you can save it. Before actually saving the file, WSIM will check the contents for validity. All messages will be presented in the Messages pane on the bottom of the WSIM UI. You can also manually initiate the validation without saving the file. Just click **Validate Answer file** on the Tools menu.

Boot-critical device drivers
WSIM allows you to add boot-critical device drivers required for installation. They must be added during the windowsPE configuration pass. These device drivers are added by using the Microsoft-Windows-PnpCustomizationsWindows PE component.

Hiding passwords in an answer file

1. Start **Windows System Image Manager**.
2. Open a Windows image.
3. Open or create an answer file.
4. Add one of the following password settings to your answer file:
   - **Microsoft-Windows-Shell-Setup | AutoLogon | Password**
   - **Microsoft-Windows-Shell-Setup | UserAccounts | AdministratorPassword**
   - **Microsoft-Windows-Shell-Setup | UserAccounts | LocalAccounts | LocalAccount | Password**
5. Add a value to one or more of the password settings.
6. On the Tools menu, check **Hide Sensitive Data**. This ensures that when the answer file is saved, the password information will be hidden.
7. Save the answer file and close **Windows System Image Manager**.

3.3.4 Common WSIM scenarios

The following sections describe common WSIM scenarios.

Create a New Answer File for a Windows Image

WSIM enables you to create an answer file that can be used during Windows Setup. You can view all of the components available in a Windows image, add component settings to your answer file, and choose when to apply a component setting by adding it to a particular configuration pass.

After component settings are added to an unattended answer file, you can view and customize the available settings for each component.

Edit an Existing Answer File

WSIM enables you to add new components, packages, or other updates to an existing answer file. You can also validate an existing answer file against a Windows image to ensure that the settings in that answer file can be applied to a specific Windows image. An answer file is typically associated with a specific Windows image. By using WSIM, you can open the Windows image, open an existing answer file, and then make changes to the answer file.

WSIM validates the component settings in the answer file against the settings available in the Windows image.

Add Additional Device Drivers to an Answer File

While automating Windows Setup, two type of drivers are being used:

- In-box drivers
  "In box" means that you will find this products' driver on the Microsoft Vista Installation DVD. In-box drivers are handled in the same way as packages.

- Out-of-box drivers
  Out-of-box drivers are automatically installed during install, but are not part of the installation DVD.

Out-of-box device drivers can be added during Windows Setup using an answer file. In this answer file, you can specify the paths to device drivers on a network share (or a local path), and the configuration passes in which you intend to install them. Device drivers can be installed in the windowsPE, offlineServicing, or auditSystem configuration passes.

By adding device driver paths to the windowsPE or offlineServicing configuration passes, you can add out-of-box device drivers to a Windows image before the system starts. This enables you to add boot-critical device drivers to a Windows image.

Adding drivers to auditSystem enables you to add additional out-of-box drivers during audit mode. This enables you to maintain a simple Windows image, and then add only the drivers that are required for a specific hardware configuration.

Extending an automated install with a distribution share or data image

You can add additional applications or drivers to be installed during Windows Setup with WSIM by using an optional set of folders called a distribution share. A distribution share is used to store all applications, device drivers, scripts, or other resources that you make available during Windows Setup.

You can also add additional applications, scripts, and other binaries by using a data image. A data image is packaged similarly to a Windows image. By using ImageX, you can capture a folder structure that contains the resources that you must add to Windows (or another partition on the system) during Windows Setup. You can specify where the data image is applied by using the DataImage setting in the Microsoft-Windows-Setup component.

You can also use OEM folder structures to place binary files and other applications in specific locations during Windows Setup. Applications are added from distribution shares through subfolders, called OEM folders. The RunSynchronous setting from the Microsoft-Windows-Setup component must be added to the answer file to launch the .msi file or .exe files that install the applications.

RunSynchronous and RunAsynchronous settings

Microsoft-Windows-Setup | RunSynchronous and RunAsynchronous settings specify one or more commands to run on the system during the windowsPE configuration pass. RunSynchronous commands are executed in the order specified in the section; each command must finish before the next command runs. Asynchronous commands are executed in the order specified in the section, but the system does not wait for the previous command to finish before it runs. Running a service would be an example of an asynchronous command.

RunSynchronous commands are always executed before RunAsynchronous commands in the same pass.

All RunSynchronous and RunAsynchronous commands run in the system context.

Add Updates to an offline Windows Image

WSIM enables the addition of offline updates to a Windows image, including software updates, device drivers, language packs, and other packages. Packages are provided by Microsoft.

Package Manager is the tool that is used to apply packages to Windows. You can use an answer file with Package Manager to apply packages to a Windows image. Any package installation, removal, or modifications in the answer file are applied to the Windows image.

Packages that exist in the offlineServicing pass are applied to the offline Windows image.

Configuration Set

A configuration set is a subset of files available in a distribution share that is explicitly called in an answer file. When you choose to create a configuration set, any files in a distribution share that are referenced in the answer file are saved to a specific local folder. Paths to these files are updated in the answer file to point to the specific folder.

Configuration sets are merely smaller, more portable versions of a distribution share. A configuration set is ideal for installations that cannot access a distribution share.

A typical configuration set may look like the following:

```
C:\MyDistributionShare\$OEM$ Folders

C:\MyDistributionShare\Packages

C:\MyDistributionShare\Out-of-Box Drivers
```

Import Packages to a Distribution Share

WSIM imports packages that are not part of a Windows image (.wim) file to an optional set of folders called a distribution share. The packages can then be added to an answer file from the distribution share. To import a package into a distribution share, you must use the WSIM tool or the CPI APIs.

You can also import a package directly into an answer file. The answer file includes a pointer to the path of the package.

3.3.5 Using the unattend file

When developing a large scale rollout of Windows, Unattended installation is the way to go. You start by creating an answer file using WSIM, and then use that file to instruct Windows Setup what to do during installation.

There are two ways in which an answer file can be applied to Windows Setup:

- Explicitly using setup.exe /unattend:*filename,* where *filename* is the path for the answer file. Because reboots are required, the answer file is cached on the system to %windir%\panther.
- Implicitly by creating an answer file with a specific name on a pre-defined location.

Every time a configuration pass starts, Windows Setup implicitly searches for an answer file on several different locations. There is an order of precedence when Windows Setup searches for an answer file. If an answer file is found in one of the valid locations, it must include a valid configuration pass. If an answer file is found and it includes no settings for the given configuration pass that is running, that answer file will be ignored.

Usually answer files will be named Unattend.xml. However, because some answer files contain destructive actions like disk partitioning, Unattend.xml must be renamed to AutoUnattend.xml when used in the WindowsPE and offlineServicing configuration passes. You typically use AutoUnattend.xml when running setup from the Windows Setup DVD, and supply an answer file on USB flash drive (UFD) or floppy disk.

The following table shows the implicit answer file search order:

Order	Location	Description
1	Registry HKLM\System\Setup!UnattendFile	Specifies a pointer in the registry to an answer file. The answer file is not required to be named Unattend.xml.
2	%WINDIR%\panther\unattend	The name of the answer file must be Unattend.xml or Autounattend.xml.

3	%WINDIR%\panther	Windows Setup caches answer files to this location. **Important**: Do not overwrite the answer files in these directories.
4	Removable read/write media in order of drive letter, at the root of the drive.	Removable read/write media in order of drive letter, at the root of the drive. The name of the answer file must be Unattend.xml or Autounattend.xml, and the answer file must be located at the root of the drive.
5	Removable read-only media in order of drive letter, at the root of the drive.	Removable read-only media in order of drive letter, at the root of the drive. The name of the answer file must be Unattend.xml or Autounattend.xml, and the file must be located at the root of the drive.
6	WindowsPE and offlineServicing passes: \sources directory in a Windows distribution. All other passes: %WINDIR%\system32\sysprep	In the windowsPE and offlineServicing passes, the name of the answer file must be Autounattend.xml. For all other configuration passes, the file name must be Unattend.xml.
7	%SYSTEMDRIVE%	The answer file name must be Unattend.xml or Autounattend.xml

3.3.6 Unattended setup

Windows Vista Setup requires a number of components to be defined in the answer file to completely automate the installation.

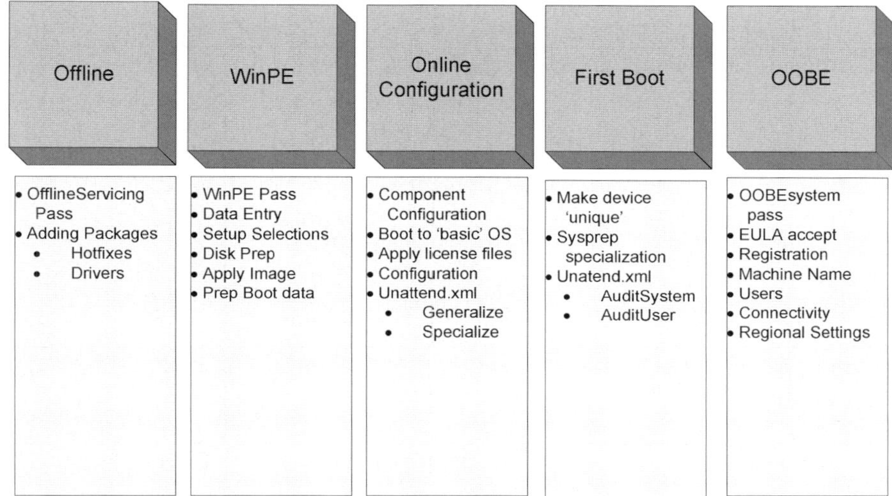

Figure 3-8 Image Based Setup Passes

The following table shows all components that must be entered into an answer file to provide a fully unattended installation.

Component[1]	Setting	Value
1 WindowsPE		
Setup_neutral\UserData	AcceptEula Full Name Organization	True <FullName> <Organization>
Setup_neutral\UserData\Product	Key	<Key>[2]

[1] All component names start with "x86_Microsoft-Windows-".

[2] The product key is not needed when installing a VL version of Windows Vista.

Component[1]	Setting	Value
Key	WillShowUI	False
4 Specialize		
International-Core_neutral	InputLocale SystemLocale UILanguage UILanguageFallback UserLocale	en-US en-US en-US en-US
Security-Licensing-SLC-UX_neutral	SkipAutoActivation	True
Shell-Setup_neutral	ComputerName RegisteredOrganization RegisteredOwner TimeZone	Client1 XPWorld XPWorld W. Europe Standard Time
UnattendedJoin_neutral\Identification	DebugJoin JoinDomain MachineObjectOU UnsecureJoin	False Contoso OU=VistaClients,DC=contoso,DC=com False

Component[1]	Setting	Value
7 oobeSystem		
International-Core_neutral	InputLocale SystemLocale UILanguage UILanguageFallback UserLocale	en-US en-US en-US en-US
Shell-Setup_neutral\OOBE	HideEULAPage NetworkLocation ProtectYourPC SkipUserOOBE	True Other 1 True
Shell-Setup_neutral\Themes	CustomDefaultTheme File DefaultThemesOff	C:\Windows\Reso urces\Themes\aer o.theme False
Shell-Setup_neutral\UserAccounts\LocalAccounts \LocalAccount	Action Description DisplayName Group Name	AddListItem Local Admin VistaAdmin Administrators VistaAdmin

3.3.7 Sensitive Data in Answer Files

Setup removes sensitive data in the cached answer file at the end of the current configuration pass.

However, if an answer file is embedded in a location with a higher precedence than the cached answer file, then the cached answer may be overwritten at the beginning of each subsequent configuration pass, if the embedded answer file matches the implicit search criteria. For example, if an answer file is embedded at %WINDIR%\panther\unattend\unattend.xml, the embedded answer file will replace the cached answer file at the beginning of each configuration pass. A second example: if the embedded answer file specifies both the specialize and oobeSystem passes, then the embedded answer file is discovered for the specialize pass, cached, processed, and sensitive data is cleared. The embedded answer file is discovered again during the oobeSystem pass and cached again. As a result, the sensitive data for the specialize pass is no longer cleared. Sensitive data for previously processed passes will not be cleared again. Unless the cached answer file must be overridden, it is recommended that answer files be embedded at a lower precedence location.

It is best practice to delete all the answer files on a Windows installation before delivering the computer to the end user. This includes any embedded answer files, as well as the cached answer file. However, if you have unprocessed settings in the oobeSystem configuration pass that you intend to run when an end user starts the computer, do not delete the cached answer file.

Setupcomplete.cmd

You can add a command to the *Setupcomplete.cmd* command script that deletes any cached or embedded answer files on the computer. At the end of the setup process, but before the logon screen appears, Windows Setup searches for the SetupComplete.cmd file in the *%WINDIR%\Setup\Scripts* folder. Windows executes the commands in SetupComplete.cmd in the LOCAL SYSTEM context.

Setup does not verify any exit codes or error levels in the script after executing SetupComplete.cmd.

The function of *Setupcomplete.cmd* differs from the RunSynchronous and RunAsynchronous commands, to the extent that *Setupcomplete.cmd* runs after Windows Setup completes, while the RunSynchronous and RunAsynchronous commands run during Windows Setup.

3.3.8 Troubleshooting Unattended Setup

Windows Vista setup logs its setup information in the *%windir%\Panther* folder. In this folder, Windows Setup caches the latest unattend.xml used during setup. As stated in the previous paragraph, unattend.xml is overwritten during each setup pass.

Some interesting information can be found in *%windir%\Panther\UnattendGC*. This folder contains the logfiles created during setup. When troubleshooting unattended setup, this folder contains two files that are of interest:

- Setupact.log
  Setupact.log contains information about each pass during setup. Here you will find information about the unattend file that was used, and about which settings have been applied during each pass.
- Setuperr.log
  Setuperr.log only contains error information. It is empty when no errors occurred during setup.

Both files are protected in such a way that they are only accessible by members of the Administrators group. Due to UAC you are not able to just double-click those files to open them with Notepad. Use one of the following ways to open the logfiles and view their contents:

- Open a command prompt with administrative privileges (Run as Administrator) and use Notepad to open the files.
- Browse to *%windir%\Panther\UnattendGC* and copy the files. You can then open them with Notepad by just double-clicking each file.

A special situation occurs when setup did not complete due to an error. In this case, setup will stop indicating that an error has occurred during setup. In this situation you can open a Command Prompt by pressing **Shift-F10**. From the Command Prompt you can use Notepad to view the logfiles and start troubleshooting.

Tip: Disable the command prompt during the Windows Vista installation process

In some cases, you may want to use the command prompt to troubleshoot the Windows Vista installation process. By default, the command prompt is enabled during Windows Vista Installs.

To start a command prompt during the Windows Vista installation process, press **SHIFT+F10**.

During all phases of the Windows Vista Enterprise installation process, Windows Setup and the related setup files examine the Windows Vista Enterprise setup directory for a file that is named *DisableCMDRequest.tag*. When Windows Setup and the related setup files find the file *DisableCMDRequest.tag*, Windows Setup disables the command prompt for the duration of the Windows Vista Enterprise installation process.

Windows Pre-installation Environment (Windows PE) runs when you start Windows Setup for the first time. To disable the command prompt during the Windows Vista installation process, follow these steps:

1. Verify that the computer has Windows Automated Installation Kit (Windows AIK) or Windows OEM Preinstall Kit (Windows OPK) installed.
2. Click **Start**, click **All Programs**, click **Windows AIK** or **Windows OPK**, and then click **Windows PE Tools Command Prompt**.
   Note: If you follow these steps on a Windows Vista Enterprise-based computer, right-click the **Command Prompt** icon, and then click **Run as Administrator**.
3. Use the ImageX tool to mount the Boot.wim file to a folder. To do this, run the following command:

```
md \mount
imagex /mountrw WimFileFolderName\boot.wim 2 \mount
```

   Note: In this command, **WimFileFolderName** is a placeholder for the name of the folder that contains the *Boot.wim* file.
4. In the Windows Vista setup directory, create the *DisableCMDRequest.tag* file. To do this, run the following command:

```
md \mount\windows\setup\scripts
cd \mount\windows\setup\scripts
echo . > DisableCMDRequest.TAG
```

5. Apply the changes to the Boot.wim file. To do this, run the following command:

```
Imagex /unmount /commit \mount
```

6. Deploy the image. To do this, use the methods that are specified in the documentation for Windows AIK, for Windows OPK, or for Windows Deployment Services.

Note: After having executed these steps, you cannot run audit mode by pressing **CTRL+SHIFT+F3**.

3.4 Offline Servicing of Windows

Windows Vista offers the possibility to change component statuses and manage drivers even when the Operating System is not running. This kind of management is called Offline Servicing. Offline Servicing of Windows Vista can be done in a WIM file, or by starting the system with Windows PE. One of the most important tools for Offline Servicing is the Package Manager. This chapter describes how the Package Manager can be used for Offline Servicing.

3.4.1 Package Manager

Package Manager (*Pkgmgr.exe*) is a command-line tool that you can use offline to install, remove, or update Windows packages. You can add packages, provided as .cab files, to an offline Windows image. Package Manager can also enable or disable Windows features, either offline or on a running Windows installation. Package Manager can also use an unattended installation answer file to perform offline servicing of WIM files in order to do stuff like:

- Install language packs.
- Add out-of-box drivers to the driver store.
- Enable or disable Windows features.
- Accept an answer file as input.
- Add packages to an offline Windows image.

Limitations of Package Manager

Package Manager has a very limited user interface. It must be invoked with the start /w pkgmgr command. Otherwise it will simulate console behavior.

Package Manager is only supported to service WIM files on the local system. Package Manager can pick up packages on a network share, but it will copy them to a temporary local, writable directory called a sandbox directory.

Package Manager can only install packages from .CAB files. Packages from MSI files must be installed using OCSetup.

If you specify an answer file with Package Manager, only the settings specified in the offlineServicing configuration pass are applied. All other settings in the answer file are ignored.

Which pkgmgr.exe to use?

When investigating Windows Vista, there appear to be two available instances of *pkgmgr.exe*. One in the Windows\System32 directory and one installed with WAIK in the *\Tools\Servicing* directory. Both instances are identical. But when performing offline servicing, the version from the servicing directory must be used, as this folder contains the servicing stack.

How Package Manager works

Package Manager is a lightweight client of the Windows Module Installer (*TrustedInstaller.exe*). TrustedInstaller.exe is the online interface to the servicing stack. The installer is native to the operating system, but Package Manager and the servicing stack are also distributed in the Windows OEM Preinstallation Kit (Windows OPK) and the Windows Automation Installation Kit (WAIK).

You can specify which packages to install or remove at a command prompt or in an answer file.

Package Manager can be used to service offline applied images in Windows PE, but ImageX mount operations are not supported.

Package Manager detects whether the files to be serviced are in use, and restarts the computer if necessary. Package Manager can prompt the user to restart the computer immediately, or it can operate in non-interactive (quiet) mode.

Package Manager can also enable or disable Windows features, even if the files are in use, and can change the state of multiple packages within one transaction.

You can use Package Manager to install out-of-box drivers to an offline Windows image. Use an answer file to specify a device driver location in the Microsoft-Windows-PnpCustomizationsNonWindows PE component. All drivers are imported into the driver store. Boot-critical drivers are reflected so that the image can boot. Other drivers are installed by Plug-and-Play once the system is online. The best match is determined by driver ranking.

Detailed error information is available in *%WINDIR%\logs\cbs\Cbs.log* or the user-specified logfile.

3.4.2 Enabling or disabling Windows Features

Enabling or Disabling Windows Features
Use the following steps to enable or disable Windows features: 1. Create an unattend file using WSIM. 2. In the Windows Image pane, browse to **Packages	Foundation**.

3. Right-click **x86_Microsoft_Windows_Foundation_Package_...** and click **Add to Answer File.**
4. Enable or Disable the Windows Features in the Windows Foundation Properties pane.
5. Save the answer file as *C:\COMPCONF.XML.*
6. Mount the Windows image with ImageX.

```
IMAGEX /MOUNTRW C:\Dist\CUSTOM_IMAGE.WIM 1 C:\Mount
```

7. Use Package Manager to apply the changed feature selections.

```
PKGMGR /o:"c:\Mount;c:\Mount\windows"
/n:"c:\COMPCONF.xml" /l:c:\COMCONF.log
```

8. Commit the changes and unmount the WIM file:

```
IMAGEX /unmount /commit C:\Mount
```

3.4.3 Adding a language pack to an offline image

Adding a Language Pack to an Offline Windows Image

Use the following steps to install a language pack to an offline Windows image:

1. Create an unattend file using WSIM.
2. In the Answer File pane, right click **Packages** and click **Insert Package(s)….**
3. Select the Language Pack file and click **Open.**
4. Save the unattend file as *ADDLANG.XML.*
5. Open the "Windows PE Tools Command Prompt" with administrative privileges.
6. Mount the Windows image with ImageX.

```
IMAGEX /MOUNTRW C:\Dist\CUSTOM_IMAGE.WIM 1 C:\Mount
```

7. Use Package Manager to apply the language pack to the offline Windows image:

```
START /w pkgmgr /o:"C:\Mount;C:\Mount\Windows"
/n:"C:\ADDLANG.xml" /L:C:\Language.log
```

8. Check *c:\Language.log* for errors.
9. When the WIM file is located in the sources folder, recreate sources\lang.ini:

```
INTLCFG -genlangini -dist:C:\Dist -image:C:\Mount -
defaultlang:nl-NL -all:nl-NL
```

10. Verify that INTLCFG has added the new language.

```
INTLCFG -report -dist:C:\Dist -image:C:\Mount
```

11. Commit the changes and unmount the WIM file:

```
IMAGEX /unmount /commit C:\Mount
```

3.4.4 Offline Driver Injection

With Offline Driver Injection, you can add drivers to the local driver store of a system. When a driver is in this store, a user without administrative privileges is able to add a device and install the driver in the Operating System.

Adding an Out-of-Box Driver to an Offline Windows Image

1. Locate the device driver .inf files that you intend to install on your Windows image.
2. Use Windows System Image Manager (Windows SIM) to create an answer file that contains the paths to the device drivers that you intend to install.
3. Add the **Microsoft-Windows-PnpCustomizationsNonWindows PE** component to your answer file in the offlineServicing pass.
4. Expand the **Microsoft-Windows-PnpCustomizationsNonWindows PE** node in the answer file. Right-click **DevicePaths**, and then select **Insert New PathAndCredentials**. A new **PathAndCredentials** list item appears.
5. For each location that you intend to access, add a separate **PathAndCredentials** list item.
6. In the **Microsoft-Windows-PnpCustomizationsNonWindows PE** component, specify the path to the device driver and the credentials used to access the file if the file is on a network share.
7. Save the answer file and exit Windows SIM.
8. Mount the Windows image to which you intend to install the drivers by using

ImageX. For example:

```
imagex /mountrw
C:\windows_distribution\sources\install.wim 1
C:\wim_mount
```

9. Enable logging of specific device driver injection actions in a separate logfile. Edit the following registry key on the computer on which you are running Package Manager:
   Path: HKLM\Software\Microsoft\Windows\CurrentVersion\Device Installer.
   - Key: DebugPkgMgr
   - Type: REG_DWORD
   - Value: 0x01

   This will create a Drivers.log file during the driver package injection. This logfile will log all actions of the driver injection process.
10. Use Package Manager to apply the unattended installation answer file to the mounted Windows image. Specify a location for the creation of the logfile. For example:

```
pkgmgr /o:"C:\wim_mount\;C:\wim_mount\Windows"
/n:"C:\unattend.xml" /l:"C:\pkgmgrlogs\logfile.txt"
```

3.5 Windows Pre-boot Environment

As mentioned before, Vista will not use DOS anymore in the install process. Instead of DOS, Vista will immediately boot a minimal version of Windows based on the Vista kernel from the DVD or USB stick in the preface of setting up a new Windows installation.

Before the release of Windows PE 2.0 with Windows Vista, Windows PE existed in a number of versions based on Windows XP. These versions were only available to Enterprise customers and provided limited functionality compared to the full version of Windows XP. Its limited availability led to a number of initiatives to create a non-Microsoft provided version of Windows PE from Windows XP. Most famous of these is BartPE, which is a very flexible and extensible Windows XP based Pre-boot Environment that can easily be booted from CD-ROM or USB stick.

3.5.1 What does Windows PE do and what not

Windows PE is not designed to be the primary operating system on a computer. It is supposed to be used as a standalone pre-installation environment and as an integral component of other setup and recovery technologies, such as Setup for Windows Vista, Windows Deployment Services (Windows DS), the Systems Management Server (SMS) Operating System (OS) Deployment Feature Pack, and the Windows Recovery Environment (Windows RE).

Windows PE as a pre-boot environment offers some really interesting possibilities compared to DOS before. Its architecture is designed in such a way that you can choose extra components to be in Windows PE and extend some of its functionality. Just keep in mind that Microsoft does not want Windows PE to be a primary OS and will not likely extend its functionality in such a way that it will replace a thin client OS for example.

Windows PE does	Windows PE does not
Completely support NTFS	Support RDP as a client or server
Support native network	Act as a file server
Support 32-bit (or 64-bit) Windows device drivers	Support the Windows .Net framework or the Common Language Runtime (CLR)
Support WMI	Support Dfs domain roots
Have Windows Script host support (VBScript and Jscript)	Support MSI packaged applications
Have HTA support	Support the WIM File System Filter

Windows PE does	Windows PE does not
Boot from CD, DVD, USB stick (UFD) or Windows Deployment Service (WDS)	Run for longer than 72 hours
	Boot from floppy ;-)

3.5.2 Windows PE architecture and system requirements

Windows PE 2.0 is a minimal Win32 subsystem with limited services, based on the windows Vista kernel running in protected mode.

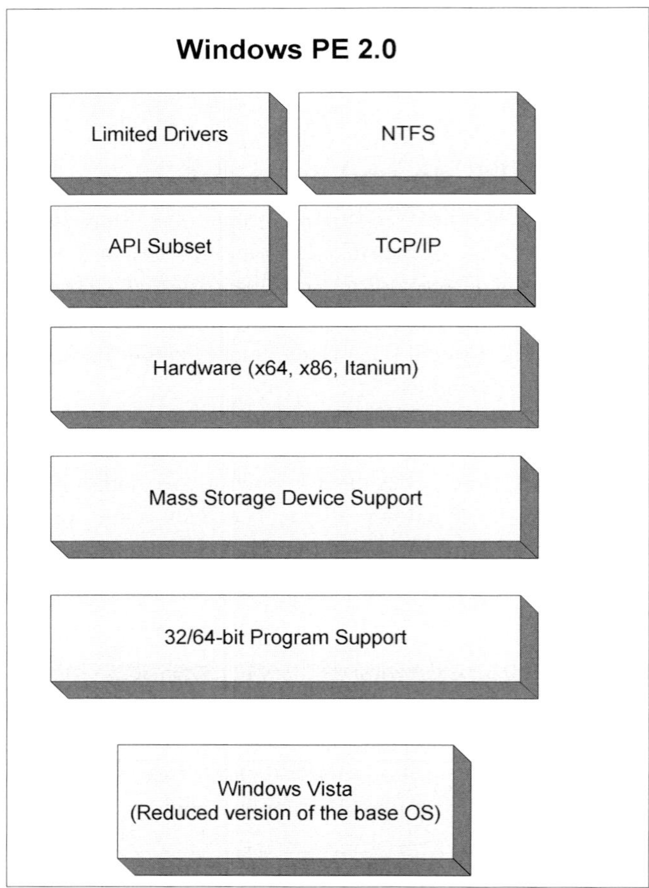

Figure 3-9 Windows PE 2.0 Architecture

In order to run Windows PE smoothly, the environment should have the following characteristics:

- Sufficient RAM for RAM disk boot (>= 512 MB recommended).
- An appropriate network adapter.
- Mass storage drivers.
- When using a USB boot device, it must meet requirements for booting Windows PE.
- When using WDS, all client computers must have PXE enabled.

3.5.3 Windows PE boot process

The boot process of Windows PE is as follows:

1. The boot sector on the particular media is loaded. Control is passed to Bootmgr. Bootmgr extracts basic boot information from the Boot Configuration Data (BCD) and passes control to winload.exe that is contained in Boot.wim. Winload.exe then loads the appropriate Hardware Abstraction Layer (HAL), and loads the System registry hive and necessary boot drivers. After it finishes loading, it prepares the environment to execute the kernel, Ntoskrnl.exe.

   Note: If you start Windows PE from read-only media such as a CD, Windows PE stores the registry hives in memory so applications can write to the registry. Any changes made to the registry by the applications do not persist across different Windows PE sessions.
2. Ntoskrnl.exe is executed and finishes the environment setup. Control is passed to the Session Manager (SMSS).
3. SMSS loads the rest of the registry, configures the environment to run the Win32 subsystem (Win32k.sys) and its various processes. SMSS loads the Winlogon process to create the user session, and then starts the services and the rest of the non-essential device drivers and the security subsystem (LSASS).
4. Winlogon.exe runs setup based on the registry value HKLM\SYSTEM\Setup\CmdLine. Windows PEshl.exe will launch *%SYSTEMDRIVE%\sources\setup.exe* if it exists, otherwise it looks for an application specified in *%SYSTEMROOT%\system32\Windows PEshl.ini*. If no application is specified, Windows PEshl.exe will execute cmd /k *%SYSTEMROOT%\system32\startnet.cmd*. By default, Windows PE contains a Startnet.cmd file which will launch *Wpeinit.exe*. *Wpeinit.exe* loads network resources and coordinates with networking components like DHCP.
5. When Wpeinit.exe completes, the Command Prompt window is displayed. The boot process of Windows PE is complete.

3.5.4 Building a Windows PE image

The first step in creating a custom Windows PE 2.0 image is to modify the base Windows PE image (Windows PE.wim) by using ImageX and PEImg tools. ImageX is required to extract the files to a local directory. PEImg enables you to add and to remove packages, and to add out-of-box drivers and language packs. ImageX then enables you to recapture changes back into a .wim file.

The Windows AIK contains a full Windows PE image to start from and build your own image.

1. To start the process, you first copy the sample file to your custom location using *copype.cmd.*

```
copype.cmd x86 c:\custom_pe
```

2. Then use ImageX to mount Windows PE.wim.

```
imagex /mountrw c:\custom_pe\Windows PE.wim 1
c:\custom_pe\mount
```

3. Using PEImg you can now disable or enable packages in the Windows PE image. The following packages are available in Win PE:

Package Name	Description
Windows PE-HTA-Package	HTML application support
Windows PE-MDAC-Package	Microsoft Data Access Component support
Windows PE-Scripting-Package	Windows Script Host support
Windows PE-SRT-Package	Windows Recovery Environment component
Windows PE-XML-Package	Microsoft XML (MSXML) parser support

4. Use the following command to list all available packages and their status:

```
peimg c:\custom_pe\mount\windows /list
```

5. Use PEImg to enable (install) a package (HTA Package) in Windows PE.

```
peimg c:\custom_pe\mount\windows /install=*HTA*
```

6. Use PEImg to Add drivers to the image. Drivers can also be loaded at runtime using *drvload.exe.*

```
peimg /inf=c:\drivers\driver.inf
c:\custom_pe\mount\windows
```

7. Use PEImg to remove all unused packages from the images (/prep).

```
peimg c:\custom_pe\mount\windows /prep
```

8. You can now also add extra software to the image or change its startup behavior. Change startup behavior with one of the following commands:
    a. *Unattend.xml* with Microsoft-Windows-Setup. I RunSynchronous or RunAsynchronous added to the Windows PE pass.
    b. By creating Winpeshl.ini as described in paragraph 4.8.
9. When finished customizing the image, commit the changes using Imagex.

```
imagex /unmount c:\custom_pe\mount /commit
```

The following diagram illustrates how a custom Windows PE image is built.

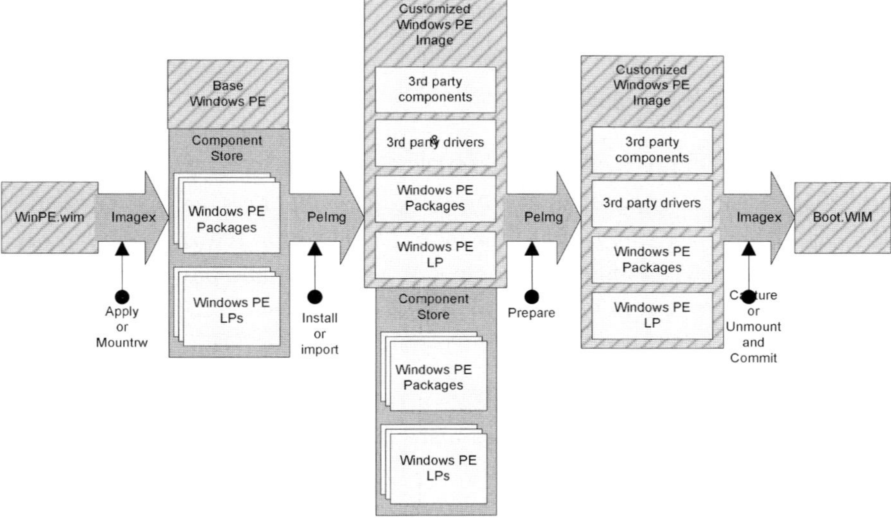

Figure 3-10 Building a custom Windows PE image

3.5.5 Adding a network driver to a running Windows PE instance

Once in a while you will find yourself in a situation where you boot a system to Windows PE, and find out that Windows PE does not contain the required driver for the network adapter. When you have the driver on a USB stick, there is an easy way to get the network running without creating a new Windows PE image that contains the required drivers. The procedure is as follows:

1. Boot the system with Windows PE.
2. Check network connectivity using **ipconfig** from the command prompt. When IPConfig shows no network adapters, the required drivers are not loaded.
3. Locate the storage containing the driver. For instance a USB stick on drive D:
4. Load the driver in Windows PE using **DrvLoad**:

```
DrvLoad D:\Folder\Driver.inf
```

5. Initialize the network using **WPEUtil**:

```
wpeutil InitializeNetwork
```

6. Verifiy the network using **ipconfig**.

More information on this procedure can be found in KB article 92834 at *http://support.microsoft.com/kb/923834*.

3.5.6 Booting Windows PE from a USB stick or CD ROM

After creating a custom Windows PE in a wim file like the one created in paragraph 4.8, it is a very simple process to take the wim file and use it to boot from a USB stick. The following procedure describes a simple way to create a USB stick that boots the custom Windows PE image. Please make sure that disk 1 really is the USB stick, otherwise you may be whipping the wrong disk:

1. Connect the USB stick to a Windows Vista system.
2. At the command prompt, type **diskpart**, and then press **ENTER**.
3. Now type the following commands in the Diskpart console:

```
DISKPART
SELECT DISK 1
CLEAN
CREATE PARTITION PRIMARY
ACTIVE
FORMAT FS=FAT32
EXIT
```

4. Copy the custom WIM file and overwrite *c:\custom_pe\iso\sources\boot.wim*.

```
xcopy /Y c:\custom_pe\Windows PE.wim
c:\custom_pe\sources\boot.wim
```

5. Copy the entire contents of *c:\custom_pe\iso* and its subfolders to the root of the USB stick.

```
xcopy /s /e /f C:\custompe\iso D:
```

6. The USB stick is now ready to boot from.

When you need a CD ROM to boot Windows PE from, you must first create an ISO that you can burn to CD or mount in a Virtual Machine. Use the following procedure to create a bootable CD ROM that boots your customized Windows PE:

1. Copy the custom WIM file and overwrite *c:\custom_pe\iso\sources\boot.wim*.

```
xcopy /Y c:\custom_pe\Windows PE.wim
c:\custom_pe\ISO\sources\boot.wim
```

2. Create *C:\custom_pe\custom_pe.iso* using *oscdimg.exe*.

```
oscdimg -n -bc:\custom_pe\etfsboot.com c:\custom_pe\ISO
c:\custom_pe\custom_pe.iso
```

3. Burn *C:\custom_pe\custom_pe.iso* to CD ROM.

3.5.7 Booting a locally stored WIM file

The Windows PE WIM file that you just created can also be used to boot from when it is stored on the local hard drive. Enabling this feature just requires a couple of modifications of the BCD and the addition of a boot file. In this example we create an extra boot entry to boot the system from our custom Windows PE WIM file C:\custom_pe\custom_pe.wim. We assume C: is also the system volume.

1. Copy *boot.sdi* from *%PROGRAMFILES%\Windows AIK\Tools\PETools\x86\boot* to the hidden system folder C:\Boot.
2. Use the following set of commands to create a **ramdiskoptions** object in the BCD store. The string "{ramdiskoptions}" is the well-known name for the object's GUID:

```
bcdedit /create {ramdiskoptions} /d "Ramdisk options"
bcdedit /set {ramdiskoptions} ramdisksdidevice
partition=c:
```

```
bcdedit /set {ramdiskoptions} ramdisksdipath
\boot\boot.sdi
```

3. Create a new boot entry:

```
bcdedit -create /d "Custom Windows PE" /application
OSLOADER
```

4. Step 3 returns the GUID that is associated with the newly created boot entry. It is referred to as NewGUID in the remaining examples. Run the following set of commands to configure the new boot entry:

```
bcdedit /set {NewGUID} device
ramdisk=[c:]\custom_pe\custom_pe.wim,{ramdiskoptions}
bcdedit /set {NewGUID} path
\windows\system32\boot\winload.exe
bcdedit /set {NewGUID} osdevice
ramdisk=[c:]\custom_pe\custom_pe.wim,{ramdiskoptions}
bcdedit /set {NewGUID} systemroot \windows
bcdedit /set {NewGUID} winpe yes
bcdedit /set {NewGUID} detecthal yes
bcdedit /displayorder {NewGUID} /addlast
```

Now when you boot the system, an extra boot option "**Custom Windows PE**" is presented and can be used to boot from *c:\custom_pe\custom_pe.wim.*

3.6 Components in a running Windows Image

It is obvious that you can also manage components on a running Windows Vista system. Contrary to Offline Servicing, Online Servicing is not done with a single main tool for everything. Driver management for instance, uses other tools than the management of Operating System components.

3.6.1 Driver management

In previous chapters we've seen a number of tools being used to manage device drivers in online and offline instances of Windows Vista and Windows PE. In the end every situation requires a different tool. In order not to get lost in this myriad of device driver management tools, this table should help you to find out which tool is needed in which situation to manage the drivers.

	Online (running)	Offline
Windows PE	Drvload	PEImg
Windows Vista	PnpUtil	PkgMgr

PnpUtil is used to perform online management of drivers in Windows Vista. PnpUtil is used to manage drivers in the local driver store. Drivers in the local driver store are automatically loaded when a plug-and-play device is connected to the system and the supported driver is available in the store. Drivers from the local driver store are installed without the need of administrative rights from the user.

Pnputil can only be used from an elevated Command Prompt. If the driver is not digitally signed or has an invalid signature, Pnputil will pop up a warning in the GUI.

Use the following command to add the driver with *DEVICE.INF* to the local driver store:

```
pnputil.exe -a device.inf
```

3.6.2 Using a share as a source for device drivers

Windows Vista and Windows Server 2008 can be configured to use a shared folder on the network to search for a driver when a matching driver was not found in the local driver store. When the matching driver is found on the network, a user must have administrative rights in order to actually load the drivers on the system. Use the following value in the registry to define the location where Windows must look for drivers when not available in the local driver store:

Location:
HKEY_LOCAL_MACHINE\SOFTWARE\Microsoft\Windows\CurrentVersion

Value (REG_EXPAND_SZ): DevicePath

3.6.3 OCSetup

OCSetup is a command-line utility that allows you to add or remove optional components in an installed instance of Windows Vista. The option is also available from the Control Panel as "Turn Windows features on or off". OCSetup is the functional successor of SYSOCMGR in Windows XP. OCSetup can only run from an elevated command prompt.

Because OCSetup does not wait until finished before returning the command prompt, always use start /w when running *OCSetup.exe* to monitor that it actually finished.

Look for a page called "Windows Vista Packages" on the Microsoft Technet site for the complete list of packages that can be installed using the ocsetup command.

Here are some of the most common optional components:

Windows Feature	Command
Desktop Experience	`Start /w ocsetup Desktop Experience`
Internet Information Services	`Start /w ocsetup IIS-WebServerRole`
Telnet Client	`Start /w ocsetup TelnetClient`
ActiveX Installer Service	`Start /w ocsetup AxInstallService`
Tablet PC components	`Start /w ocsetup TabletPCOC`

3.7 Windows Deployment Services

Microsoft Windows Deployment Services (WDS) is the updated and redesigned version of Remote Installation Services (RIS). Windows Deployment Services is part of the Windows Server 2008. It is also distributed with the Windows Automated Installation Kit (WAIK) as an update for Windows Server 2003 with SP1. Using Windows Deployment Services, you can deploy Windows operating systems over a network, without having to be physically present at the destination computer, and without using installation media.

3.7.1 What´s new in Windows Deployment Services

The main differences between RIS and WDS are:

- WDS supports Windows PE to boot over the network with PXE.
- WDS has integrated tools for capturing and deploying Windows Vista.
- WDS has a complete new UI based on MMC 3.0 to easily manage deployments.
- When running in mixed mode WDS also supports old-style DOS boot to install Windows XP, for example.
- When running on Windows Server 2008, WDS enables Windows deployment using multicast.

3.7.2 Prerequisites for running WDS

The prerequisites for WDS are the same as they have always been for RIS:

- Active Directory must be available and running.
- DHCP.
- DNS.
- Installation media.
- A partition not containing the operating system to store the installation sources.

3.7.3 Installing Windows Deployment Services

Depending on the Service Pack version running on Windows Server 2003, use one of the following methods to install Windows Deployment Services:

Windows Server 2003 with SP1	Windows Server 2003 with SP2
1. Install RIS. 2. Download and install Windows AIK. 3. Open the Command prompt and type the following command: `windows-deployment-services-update-XXX.exe /quiet /forcerestart` Replace XXX with x86 or amd64 depending on the CPU architecture.	Windows Server 2003 with SP2 has replaced RIS with WDS. There are two options here: • If RIS was already installed, it is upgraded with the installation of SP2 for Windows Server 2003. • Install Windows Deployment Services as a Windows Component from Add/Remove Components in the Control Panel.

3.7.4 WDS Modes

When running on Windows Server 2003 with SP1, WDS has three modes of operation:

1. Legacy Mode
   A system running Windows Server 2003 with RIS enabled, is running in Legacy mode when upgraded with SP2. In Legacy Mode, WDS behaves like RIS and can only be managed like RIS (using the RIS toolset). In Legacy mode WDS uses the DOS based OSChooser as the boot environment and supports RISETUP and RIPREP for OS deployment.
2. Mixed Mode
   Once an Administrator starts the Windows Deployment Services management console for the first time on a system with RIS images installed, WDS starts running in Mixed Mode. Now WDS supports both the RIS based boot environment and images and the new Windows PE and WIM images. Both the WDS management console and the RIS toolset can be used to manage the service.
3. Native Mode
   WDS runs in native mode when the WDS management console is started after installation without RIS images installed. WDS in native mode only supports Windows PE and WIM images and can only be managed by the WDS management console. A system running mixed mode can be updated to native mode using the following Command:

```
WDSUTIL /forceNative
```

3.7.5 WDS image types

Windows Deployment Services works with WIM files that can be uploaded from various sources. The following image types are typically used by WDS:

- Boot Images
  Boot images are Windows PE images that enable a system to boot over the network using PXE. Administrators can upload custom PE files or just the boot.wim from the Windows Vista or Windows Server 2008 product DVD.
- Install Images
  Install images are images containing full Operating Systems. These can be Windows Vista, Windows Server 2008, Windows XP or Windows Server 2003 systems. Uploaded Install images are available through the WDS share (Reminst$) or by using multicast on Windows Server 2008 WDS Servers.
- Discovery Images
  A discovery image is the boot.wim from the Vista product DVD, customized by WDS to enable easy deployment of Install images.
- Capture Images
  A capture image is the boot.wim from the Vista product DVD, customized to capture and upload a (sysprep-ed) image to the WDS Server.

3.7.6 Configuring Windows Deployment Server

Windows Deployment Server has two configuration tools:

- The Windows Deployment Services MMC 3.0 snap-in
- WDSUTIL command-line utility

Actually there is not very much to configure about WDS. After installation, configuration involves the following actions:

- Creating and assigning a shared folder that contains the boot files for PXE, Windows PE and OS Installations.
- Uploading Windows PE boot images in WIM format.
- Uploading OS Install images of Windows Vista, Windows Server 2008, Windows XP or Windows Server 2003 in WIM format.
- Configuring the PXE listener to define if and how the server will service PXE boot requests.

Known issues when configuring WDS

There are a few things to keep in mind when configuring Windows Deployment Services. Knowing these issues will probably save you a lot of time when you setup WDS for the first time:

- Spanned WIM files cannot be uploaded to WDS. You must create a single WIM image before uploading.
- PXE clients should send their architecture to the WDS server using DHCP option 93. Unfortunately, not every PXE implementation acts this way. In that case you will not see 64-bits (x64) boot images on x64 capable systems. In order to fix this situation you can enable architecture discovery in the PXE boot program. This runs an architecture discovery program (NBP) on the client before PXE boot. Run the following command to enable architecture discovery in the boot programs[3]:

```
WDSUTIL /set-server /architecturediscovery:yes
```

- Keep in mind that the PXE listener is nothing else than a slightly modified DHCP Server. That's the reason why the system needs special configuration when DHCP is running on the same server. In that case, configure WDS not to listen on port 67 and configure Option 60 to 'PXE Client'.
- When the DHCP server is running in another subnet, make sure all DHCP requests are also forwarded to the WDS server and add DHCP options 66 and 67 on the DHCP Server.
- When a firewall is located between the clients and the WDS server, enable traffic from the clients to UDP port 4011.

Initializing WDS

During initialization the administrator defines the distribution share location for WDS. There are two options to start WDS initialization:

1. Using the Windows Deployment Services MMC console (WdsMgt.msc):
   a. If the server is not in the servers list, right-click the **Servers** node to add a server.
   b. In the **Add Server** dialog box, click **Another computer**, and then browse to select the computer to manage.
   c. In the **Add Server Warning** dialog box, click **Yes** to add the server.

---

[3] The NBP is extracted from the Boot image with the same architecture. Booting a x64 capable system will fail when there is no x64 boot image available on the server. Add a x64 boot image or tell the server to extract the NBP from the x86 boot image by changing the default boot program in the WDS boot properties for x64 architecture to a x86 boot image (for instance *boot\x86\pxeboot.com*).

d. Right-click the server that you want to manage, and click **Configure Server** to start the Windows Deployment Services Configuration Wizard.
e. At the **Welcome** page, click **Next**.
f. At the **Remote Installation Folder Location** page, click **Next** to accept the default location (D:\RemoteInstall).
g. If the Microsoft DHCP service is on the server that is being configured as a Windows Deployment Services server:
   i. Set **DHCP Option 60** to **PXEClient**
   ii. Set **Windows Deployment Services** to **Do not listen on Port 67**.
h. On the **PXE Server Initial Settings** page, click **Respond to all (known and unknown) client computers**.

2. Using WDSUTIL with the following command:

```
WDSUTIL /initialize-server
/reminst:"<driveletter>\<foldername>"
```

Uploading boot images to WDS

The boot.wim file from the sources folder on the Windows Vista product DVD is an easy target to start and try adding boot images to WDS. You can also try adding one of your own custom PE files from chapter 3.5.4.

Adding a boot image to Windows Deployment Services from the UI

Use the following steps to add a boot image to Windows Deployment Services:

1. In the left pane of the Windows Deployment Services MMC snap-in, expand the server list, and locate the server for which you want to add the boot image.
2. Right-click the **Boot Image** node, and then click **Add Boot Image**.
3. Browse to select the boot image, and then click **Open**.
4. On the **Image File** page, click **Next**.
5. On the **Image Description** page, click **Next** to select the default name and description.
6. On the **Summary** page, click **Next**.
7. Click **Finish**.

Adding a boot image to Windows Deployment Services from command-line

Use the following command to add a boot image to Windows Deployment Services:

```
WDSUTIL /add-image
/imagefile:\\server\share\sources\boot.wim
/imagetype:boot
```

Creating a discover image

A discover image is a customized boot image enabled to start a Windows installation from WDS over the network, using the REMINST$ share. The discover image is created from the original boot.wim from the Windows Vista or Windows Server 2008 product DVD. Use the following procedure to create a discover image in WDS:

Creating a discover image in Windows Deployment Server

Use the following steps to create a discover image with Windows Deployment Services:

1. In the left pane of the Windows Deployment Services MMC snap-in, expand the server list, and locate the server where the setup boot image is located.
2. Right-click the Setup boot Image, and then click **Create Discover Boot Image**.
3. Type the name of the new boot image at "**Location and filename:**".
4. Type the fqdn of the WDS Server at "**Windows Deployment Server to Respond:** "
5. Click **Next**.
6. Wait for the discover image to be created, and click **Finish**.

Creating a capture image

A capture image is a customized boot image enabled to capture an install image from a sysprep-ed Windows system. The image boots Windows PE and starts a wizard that captures the contents of the local hard disk to the REMINST$ share on the WDS Server. The captured image is extracted from any bootable Windows PE WIM image. Use the following procedure to create a capture image in WDS:

Creating a capture image in Windows Deployment Server

Use the following steps to create a capture image with Windows Deployment Services:

1. In the left pane of the Windows Deployment Services MMC snap-in, expand the server list, and locate the server where the Windows PE boot image is located.
2. Right-click the Setup boot Image, and then click **Create Capture Boot Image**.
3. Type the name of the new boot image at "**Location and filename:**".
4. Click **Next**.
5. Wait for the capture image to be created, and click **Finish**.

Uploading install images to WDS

Install images are installation images captured from sysprep-ed systems or taken from the product DVD. Add an install image to install Windows Vista with a discover image created by WDS.

Adding an install image to Windows Deployment Services from the UI

Use the following steps to add an install image to Windows Deployment Services:

1. In the left pane of the **Windows Deployment Services** MMC snap-in, expand the server list, and locate the server for which you want to add the install image.
2. Right-click the **install Image** node, and then click **Add Install Image**.
3. Browse to select the install image, and then click **Open**.
4. On the **Image File** page, click **Next**.
5. In the list of available images, select the required image(s), click **Next**.
6. On the **Image Description** page, click **Next** to select the default name and description.
7. On the **Summary** page, click **Next**.
8. Click **Finish**.

Booting a system using Windows Deployment Services

When the boot and install images are loaded in Windows Deployment Services, you can start installing the operating system, using the created discover image and an uploaded install image. The following procedure will do the job:

Starting a PXE booted installation of Windows Vista using WDS
1. Configure the client BIOS to Enable PXE boot, and set the boot order so that "Boot from network" is first. 2. When prompted, press **F12** to initiate the PXE boot process. 3. Select the appropriate Windows PE boot image from the boot menu. 4. On the Install Windows page, select your locale and keyboard layout, and then click **Next**. 5. When prompted, enter a user name and password with sufficient credentials to read images from the Windows Deployment Services server. 6. Select an available operating system, and then click **Next**. 7. On the **Where do you want to install Windows?** page, select the disk and partition for your Windows installation. You may optionally load a mass storage driver, if required, by pressing **F6**, or choose **Advanced options** to format or partition the disk. 8. Click **Next** to begin the image copy phase of installation. 9. If there is an existing copy of Windows on the selected partition, you will be presented with a warning dialog. Click **OK** to rename the previous installation to *windows.old*. 10. When the image installation is complete, the computer will reboot and Windows Setup will continue.

3.8 Boot Configuration Data (BCD)

Compared to previous versions of Windows, Vista has a completely new mechanism to boot the system. System Boot options will no longer be available from boot.ini, but stored in a datastore called the Boot Configuration Data (BCD) store. The Boot Configuration Data (BCD) store contains boot configuration parameters and controls how the operating system is started in Windows Vista and Windows Server 2008.

You can use the Bcdedit.exe command-line tool for adding, deleting, editing, and appending entries in the BCD store. Bcdedit.exe is located in the *%WINDIR%\System32* directory.

BCD was created to provide an improved mechanism for describing boot configuration data. With the development of new firmware models (for example, the Extensible Firmware Interface (EFI)), an extensible and interoperable interface was required to abstract the underlying firmware. This new design provides the foundation for a variety of new features in Windows Vista (for example, the Startup Repair tool, and Multi-User Install shortcuts).

Depending on the type of system, the BCD can be located in two places on the system:

- On BIOS-based operating systems, the BCD registry file is located in the *\Boot\Bcd* directory of the active partition.
- On EFI–based operating systems, the BCD registry file is located on the EFI system partition.

3.8.1 How to modify BCD

Depending on what you want to change, you can use the following tools to modify BCD:

- **Startup and recovery.**
  The **Startup and recovery** dialog box enables you to select the default operating system for starting the system, if you have multiple operating systems installed on your computer. You can also change the time-out value. These settings are located on the **Advanced** tab in the System Properties dialog box.
- **System Configuration utility (Msconfig.exe)**.
  Msconfig.exe is a more advanced tool to manage the startup configuration of Windows Vista. It includes possibilities to define which applications and services should start at Windows startup. It also includes advanced Windows

startup options like: **/debug, /safeboot, /bootlog, /noguiboot, /basevideo,** and **/numproc**.

- **BCD WMI provider.**
  The BCD Windows Management Instrumentation (WMI) provider is a management interface that you can use to script utilities that modify BCD. This is the only programmatic interface available for BCD.
- **BCDEdit.exe.**
  BCDEdit.exe is a command-line utility that replaces Bootcfg.exe in Windows Vista. BCDEdit became known as the most user-unfriendly utility during the beta of Windows Vista. Compared to editing *boot.ini*, it is hard to use, and has a number of hard-to-guess parameters available when manipulating the BCD.

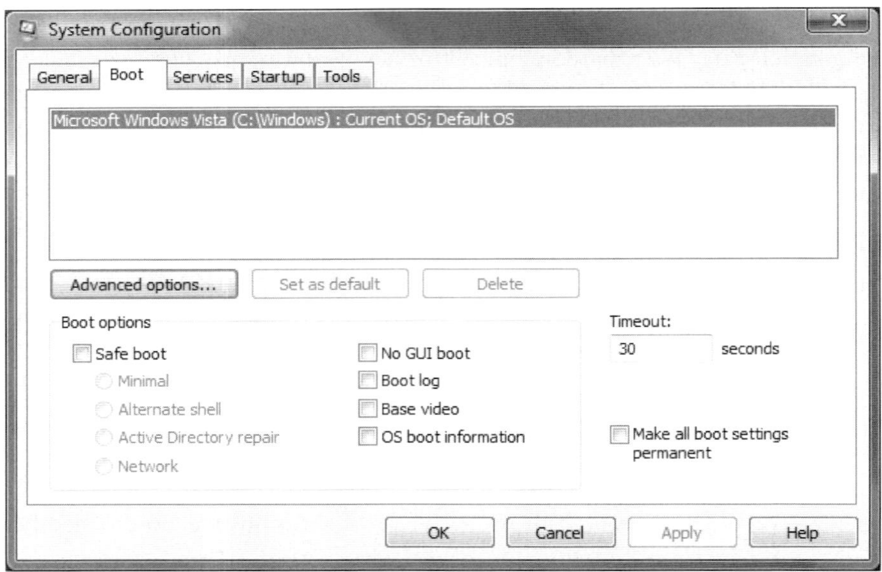

Figure 3-11 Using msconfig.exe to configure the BCD

3.8.2 Using BCDEDIT

Even though it's not the most intuitive utility in Windows Vista, BCDEDIT provides some useful functionality when it comes to managing the startup options of your system.

First it is good to have some basic understanding of the Boot Configuration Database (BCD). The BCD exists on the active partition of the system and contains records for each startup entry. This is the same as it used to be in boot.ini in previous versions of Windows, except for the fact that the BCD is a binary blob and cannot be edited with Notepad.

Let's have a look at a common BCD scenario. To display the contents of the BCD, type BCDEDIT. The output of the command may look like this:

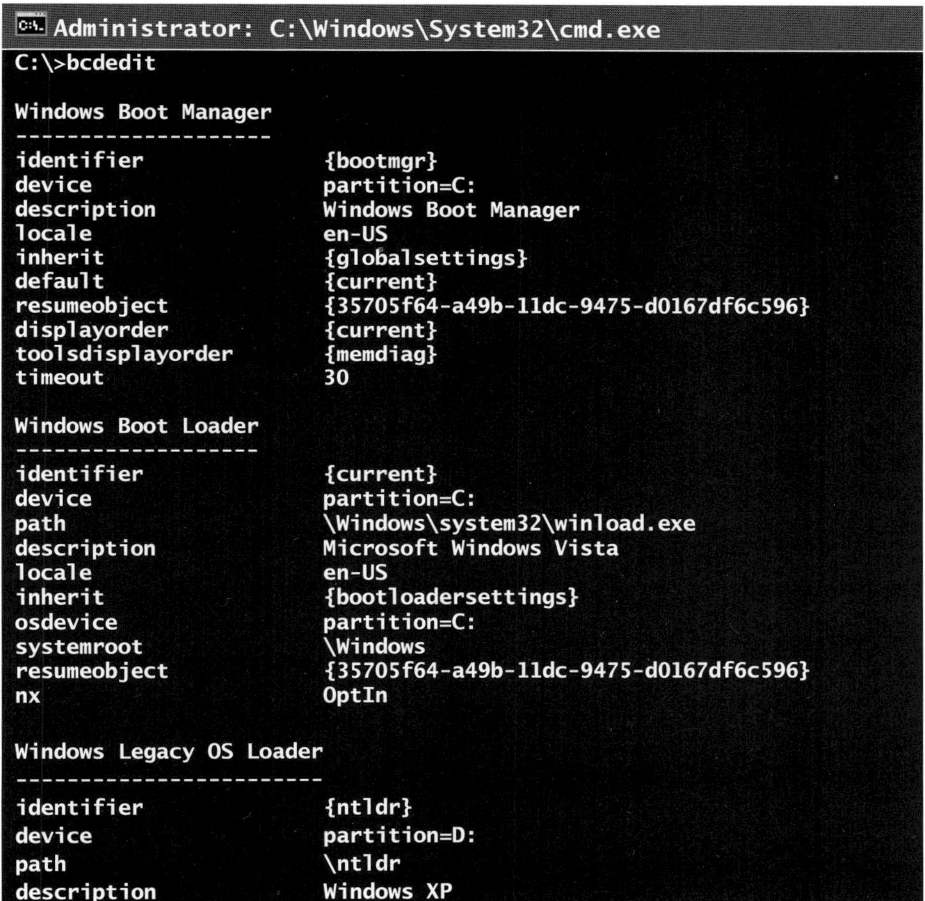

Figure 3-12 Display of the contents of the Boot Configuration Database

Notice the three sections in the report:

- Windows Boot Manager
  This section is about the boot manager configuration. It involves parameters like the location of the BCD, the default OS to boot and the time out of the boot menu.

- Windows Boot Loader
  Each instance of Windows Vista gets a boot loader record, just like in the [boot loader] section of boot.ini. The section defines specifics like the location of the OS and boot parameters to use when loading the OS.
- Windows Legacy OS Loader
  The Legacy OS Loader section is for backwards compatibility with previous versions of Windows.

Each section is identified by a GUID between {}. The real GUID is a 28-byte number like: {3ce90b6e-b226-11db-9a1d-9a97c185ef25}. The report above doesn't show any values like this, but shows identifiers like:

- {default}
  This is de default OS entry in the Boot Manager.
- {current}
  This is the currently booted OS entry.
- {bootmgr}
  This is the Boot Manager entry.
- {ntldr}
  This is the NTLDR based entry for previous Windows versions.
- {memdiag}
  This is the entry for the memory diagnostics utility.

These are all virtual identifiers that represent a GUID in a well readable format. Type "BCDEDIT /v" to display the list with full GUIDs.

Changing the Boot Manager Timeout

Use the following command to change the Boot Manager time out (to 15 seconds):

```
BCDEDIT /timeout 15
```

Adding a Boot Manager entry

The easiest and probably most common way to add a boot entry to the BCD, is by copying and then modifying an existing entry in the BCD. For instance, let's create a boot entry for the current OS without Data Execution Prevention (DEP).

In order to do this in boot.ini, we would do the following:

1. Copy and paste an existing line.
2. Change the description.
3. Add "/NoExecute=AlwaysOff" to the line.

In the BCD it will look like this:

1. Copy an existing record in the BCD to an entry with the new name.
2. Change the nx entry option to disable DEP.

In the BCD example above, we would act as follows:

1. First we copy the current default entry to an entry we call "Windows Vista without DEP".

```
BCDEDIT /copy {default} /d "Windows Vista without DEP"
```

The response to this command is:

```
The entry was successfully copied to {803cc364-777b-
11dc-acaa-005056c00008}
```

2. We need the GUID of the new OS entry to change the nx option to AlwaysOff. The following command will do this:

```
bcdedit /set {803cc364-777b-11dc-acaa-005056c00008} nx
AlwaysOff
```

3. Now we can see what it looks like by typing BCDEDIT at the command-line:

```
Windows Boot Loader
-------------------
identifier              {803cc364-777b-11dc-acaa-
005056c00008}
device                  partition=C:
path                    \Windows\system32\winload.exe
description             Windows Vista without DEP
locale                  en-US
inherit                 {bootloadersettings}
osdevice                partition=C:
systemroot              \Windows
resumeobject            {3ce90b6f-b226-11db-9a1d-
9a97c185ef25}
nx                      AlwaysOff
```

When we reboot the system we get an extra boot entry to choose from.

Changing the default Boot Manager entry

When we decide that our new entry must be the new default entry in the Boot Manager, the following command will change this for us:

```
BCDEDIT /default {803cc364-777b-11dc-acaa-005056c00008}
```

Deleting a BCD OS entry

Okay, this was just a demo. So now we revert the original entry to the default settings and delete the new entry using BCDEDIT:

```
BCDEDIT /delete {803cc364-777b-11dc-acaa-005056c00008}
```

3.9 Microsoft Deployment Toolkit

Microsoft Deployment Toolkit provides the ideal framework to develop an automated desktop deployment framework that can be easily expanded. Microsoft Deployment Toolkit is the successor of Business Desktop Deployment 2007 (BDD2007). The main difference between the two is that the Microsoft Deployment Toolkit also support deployment of servers, while BDD was only supporting desktop systems.

Microsoft Deployment Toolkit uses all best practices and tools of Windows Vista to provide a solution that contains various deployment scenarios:

- Scripted installation of the OS, applications and hotfixes.
- Automated installation through Windows Vista built-in imaging technologies.
- Installation customization based on a central database.

One of the easiest and most efficient ways to use Microsoft Deployment Toolkit in the Windows Vista client development process, is to build a scripted installation of Windows Vista first, containing all required OS components, applications and settings. When this procedure passes initial tests, Microsoft Deployment Toolkit can be used to create an ImageX based WIM image containing the complete installation. This WIM image can then be used for rapid deployment.

3.9.1 Building a Microsoft Deployment Toolkit development lab

The Microsoft Deployment Toolkit development lab can be built on Windows Server 2003 with at least SP1 and preferably SP2. The development network should at least contain the following infrastructure components:

- Active Directory
- DNS
- DHCP

The components needed for Microsoft Deployment Toolkit are:

- Windows Deployment Server (see paragraph 0)
- Windows Automated Installation Kit (Windows AIK)
- Microsoft Deployment Toolkit

3.9.2 Installing Microsoft Deployment Toolkit

Installation of Microsoft Deployment Toolkit is relatively simple. Make sure you install Windows AIK first. Windows AIK installs with two components required for Microsoft Deployment Toolkit:

- Microsoft .NET Framework 2.0
- Microsoft XML 6.0

Besides these two components, Microsoft Deployment Toolkit also requires MMC 3.0. MMC3.0 can be downloaded from *http://support.microsoft.com/kb/907265*.

During installation, Microsoft Deployment Toolkit sets the following options:

- Microsoft Deployment Toolkit program files location
  The Microsoft Deployment Toolkit program files folder contains the binary files for Microsoft Deployment Toolkit, a few configuration files and a lot of documentation.
- Microsoft Deployment Toolkit distribution share location
  Microsoft Deployment Toolkit will use the distribution share to store all its resources. This will include operating system source files, applications, drivers, patches and language packs. Additionally there may be a number of captured builds and boot images. As this will cause a shipload of Gigabytes for storage, it is recommended to allocate at least 30 GB of disk space for the Microsoft Deployment Toolkit distribution share. Microsoft Deployment Toolkit will automatically choose the disk with the most disk space as the default location for the distribution share. It is recommended not to use the OS disk for this purpose. Also be careful when you have WDS running on the same system. WDS will enable the Single Instance Store Groveler service on the volume with the WDS share.

3.9.3 Using Microsoft Deployment Toolkit

After installing Microsoft Deployment Toolkit, the Microsoft Deployment Toolkit Deployment Workbench is the program where it all happens. The Deployment Workbench is a MMC 3.0 snap-in that is supposed to help you walk through your first automated Windows Vista Deployment. On the left side of the console you find the three as shown in Figure 3-13.

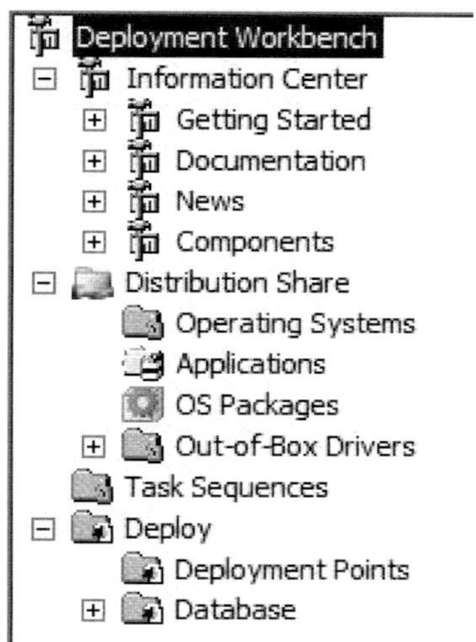

Figure 3-13 Deployment Workbench UI tree

By following this tree starting at 'Distribution Share', you're building an automated installation that is complete by the time you enter 'Deployment Points'.

Information Center

The Information Center in the Deployment Workbench is the primary point to find documentation in Microsoft Deployment Toolkit. Actually, all previous versions of Microsoft Deployment Toolkit (Business Desktop Deployment or BDD) laid a strong emphasis on documentation. Microsoft Deployment Toolkit is the first edition that actually contains a lot of tooling as well, to provide guidance in developing automated deployment for Windows Vista.

The Components node is the only node under Information Center that has something to do with the operation of the toolset. The Components node lists all additional software that can or must be loaded to successfully use Microsoft Deployment Toolkit. It also provides options to immediately download and install the software so that you don’t have to go out and hunt all of it down with Google (or Live Search).

Microsoft Deployment Toolkit has only one required component:

- Windows Automated Installation Kit (AIK)
  This kit contains all tools needed to automate Windows Vista installation.

Optional software for Microsoft Deployment Toolkit is:

- User State Migration Tool 3.01
- Application Compatibility Toolkit 5.0
- Key Management Server
- Volume Activation Management Tool
- Office Migration Planning Manager
- Windows Vista Hardware Assessment

Distribution Share

The Distribution Share node is where you collect all the software needed to build an automated installation. Each Node quite clearly describes which software is supposed to be available:

- Operating Systems
  Here you can load each operating system image to be installed. These can be images straight from the product CD, or images captured from a sysprep-ed installation of an OS. It is required that at least one of the imported images is a complete Windows Vista installation from the product DVD. This is because Microsoft Deployment Toolkit uses some components of the DVD to build a new deployment.
- Applications
  Each application to be deployed with the image must be loaded here with the command-line needed to do an unattended install. Keep in mind that you don't want the image to grow too big. That is why you usually only install some base applications, like management clients for SMS or Altiris with the image, and let them take care of the rest of the applications. The UI of the workbench has no option to define the order in which the applications must be installed. To work around this omission you can disable each application and then create one application that has the other applications as a dependency. Now you can change the order of the dependencies. This creates a way to control the installation order.
- OS Packages
  OS Packages consist of Language Packs, Hotfixes and Service Packs. Each of these can be loaded here and will be recognized as such.
- Out-of-Box Drivers
  This is where all the desired drivers are loaded into the local driver store of your newly installed systems. Be aware that the network and storage drivers will be loaded both in Windows PE and in Windows Vista. You might not want to load too many drivers here. Make sure that at least the Network and Storage drivers are

present in the local driver store. All other drivers can then be copied to a share that you point to from unattend.xml. Those drivers will be loaded over the network during installation, when needed. This will also reduce the time needed to maintain the image built with Microsoft Deployment Toolkit. Drivers can be put together in user-defined groups. This allows drivers to be associated with specific builds, reducing the risk of possible conflicts.

Note: Make sure you let at least one application take care of rebooting the system. This ensures completion of all component installations, including hotfixes and language packs. The OS images do not trigger a reboot of the system during the build process, which may lead to unexpected results.

Task Sequences

A Task Sequence associates source files in the Distribution Share with:

- The Operating System source
- A Driver Group
- Unattended Settings and an Unattend.xml
- A Task Sequence

When creating a Task Sequence, the following options must be defined:

- Task Sequence ID
- Task Sequence Number
- Task Sequence Version
- Operating System images to be used
- Product Key (or specify not to use one)
- Full Name
- Organization
- Internet Explorer Home Page
- Local Administrator password

After the Task Sequence has been generated, you can customize the unattend.xml associated with the Task Sequence by right clicking the Task Sequence and then clicking Properties. On the 'OS Info' tab you can click 'Edit Unattend.xml' to open the file.

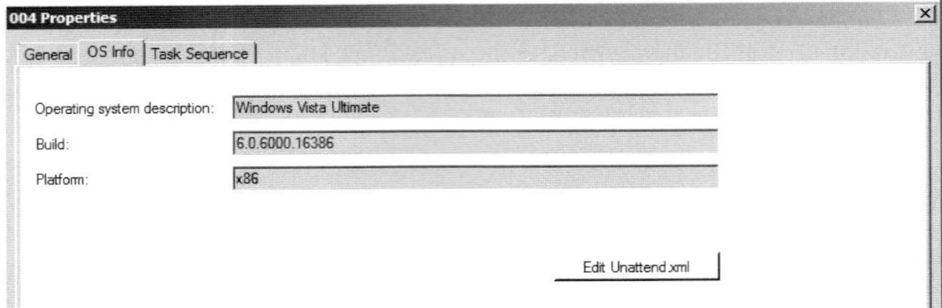

Figure 3-14 OS Info tab in Deployment Properties

Be aware that some of the settings in unattend.xml (for instance TimeZone) will be changed by the wizards in Microsoft Deployment Toolkit, and changing them here may not cause the required results. Edit Distribution\Control\CustomSettings.ini in order to configure those settings.

Deploy

The final part of preparation, when using the Microsoft Deployment Toolkit workbench, involves configuring a Deployment Point. From the four deployment point types available in Microsoft Deployment Toolkit I will describe and use two types:

- Lab or Single server deployment
  This creates a single distribution share on the Microsoft Deployment Toolkit server for deploying configured Task Sequences. This is most appropriate for a lab environment.
- Removable Media
  This allows the Microsoft Deployment Toolkit installation to be deployed from removable media such as a DVD or a USB flash device on disconnected workstations.

When creating a Deployment Point, the following options must be supplied:

- The deployment point type
  Choose from Lab or Single server, Removable Media, Separate Deployment Share or SMS 2003 OSD.
- The deployment point name
  Define a name for the deployment point.
- Allow users to select additional applications on upgrade
  Define whether or not to show this option when using the wizard.

- Ask if an image should be captured
  Define whether the wizard will show the option to capture a WIM file from the installed system after installation. Microsoft Deployment Toolkit will start capturing immediately after completing the installation.
- Ask user to set the Local Administrator password
  Define whether or not to show this when using the wizard.
- Ask user for a product key
  Define whether or not to show this when using the wizard.
- Server name, Share name and Path for share
  All these options should be automatically filled and don't need to be changed.
- Specify user data defaults
  Choose whether or not to provide options to run USMT to save the user state in an upgrade.

After the Deployment Point has been generated, a number of advanced options can be defined by right clicking the Deployment Point and then clicking Properties. The Deployment point properties window consists of three tabs: General, Rules and Windows PE.

- **General**
  The General tab provides the option to determine which platforms must be supported by Microsoft Deployment Toolkit.
- **Rules**
  The Rules tab is a representation of the CustomSettings.ini file. Customizing this file defines which parts of the wizard must be shown during installation, and allows for the definition of options that are skipped in the wizard. Use "Configuration Reference.doc" from the Microsoft Deployment Toolkit Documentation folder to look up the options that can be defined in CustomSettings.ini.
- **Windows PE**
  The Windows PE tab defines which Windows PE boot images should be generated by Microsoft Deployment Toolkit. This is also the tab where you can define which drivers must be injected in Windows PE. A WIM file is needed when you will boot your systems from a Windows Deployment Server. The ISO should be booted from a DVD.

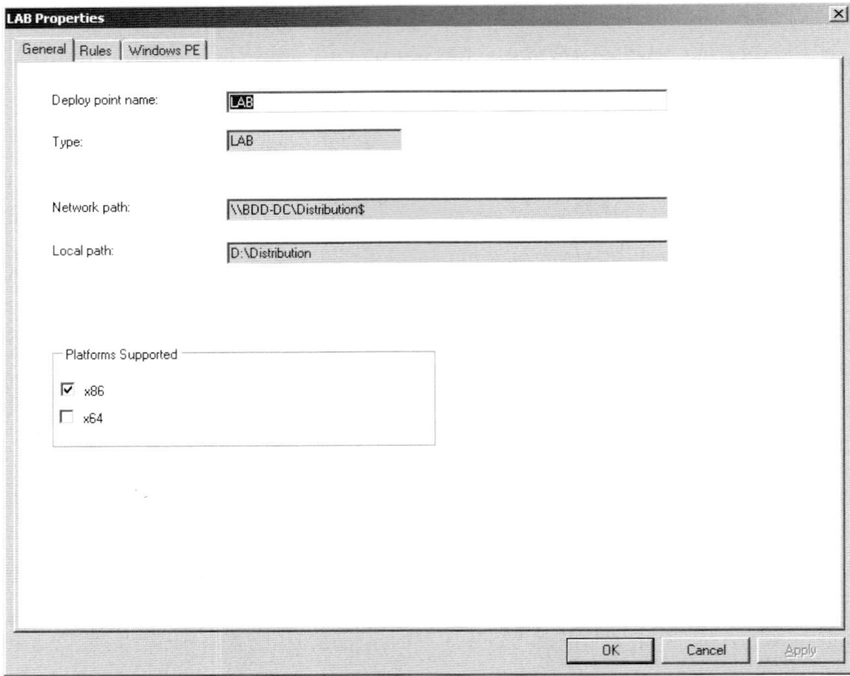

Figure 3-15 Configuring a deployment point

Right click the deployment point and click Update to generate the Windows PE boot image and copy all required files to the distribution share.

Once this process has been completed for a LAB or single server deployment, the Widows PE boot image can be found on the Microsoft Deployment Toolkit Distribution share, under Boot folder, as *LiteTouchPE_x86.wim*. This file will be imported into WDS. When a client boots from this WIM, it will startup the wizard for installing Microsoft Deployment Toolkit from the distribution share on the Microsoft Deployment server.

When the process is completed for Removable Media, an ISO file can be found as *LiteTouchPE_x86.ISO* in the Media folder.

4 Managing Windows Vista

4.1 WinRM

WinRM or Windows Remote Management is Microsoft's implementation of Web Services for System Management (WS-Management). WS-Management provides a universal language that is used to obtain data concerning the the systems, to improve manageability. The WS-Management specification describes a general SOAP-based protocol for managing any type of device on a network.

WinRM provides the possibility to securely obtain management information on a Windows Vista system. It communicates over http or https and sends its data in XML packets. This feature enables easy communication across firewalls, and is user-friendly to program and store in a database.

Out of the box, WinRM exposes WMI information and Windows Remote Shell capabilities. This enables new ways of getting information from remote systems and using that information in scripts. Actually, Windows Vista Event Forwarding in chapter 4.2.4 plugs into WinRM, to forward eventlog information to a central system on the network.

WinRM is running as a web service on the host and has a lot in common with IIS in terms of protocol support (http and https) and authentication options (Kerberos, basic and digest). By default the WinRM client only supports Kerberos authentication.

4.1.1 Configuring WinRM

WinRM is disabled by default on Windows Vista. Enabling WinRM is a single command. This enables the WSMan Service and opens the firewall for incoming traffic on port 80 (http). Make sure you know the security risks when enabling WinRM.

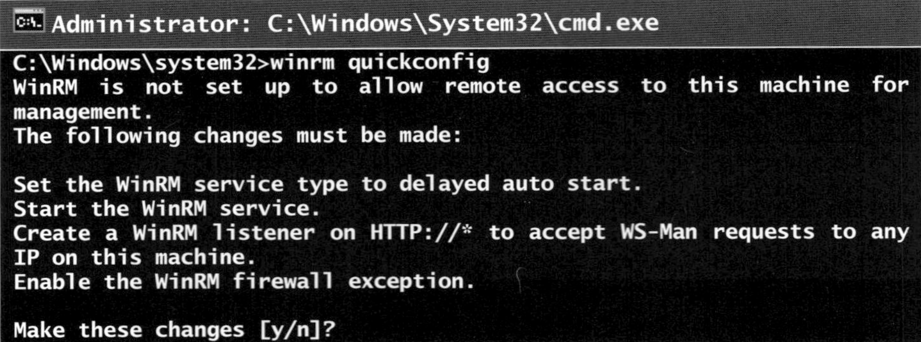

Figure 4-1 Initializing WinRM from the Command-line

By default the listener accepts connections from any network. This may not be exactly what you want when the system is running in a DMZ, for instance.

WinRM configuration commands	
`Winrm Quickconfig`	Enable WinRM and configure its default configuration
`Winrm get winrm/config`	Display WinRM configuration
`winrm delete winrm/config/ listener?Address=* +Transport=HTTP`	Disable WinRM (delete the listener)
`Winrm id -auth:none - remote:<remote system>`	Ping WSMan on a remote system
`Winrm id -remote:<remote system>`	Test WinRM access to a remote system
`Winrm get winrm/Config [- r:<remote system>]`	Get a [remote] machine's WSMan configuration

4.1.2 Using WinRM for remote console

WinRM can be used as a remote command-line console to administer Windows Vista and Windows Server 2008 systems over the network. It looks like an alternative to telnet or SSH. In fact it is, when you take into account that WinRM supports both http and https with various authentication options.

WINRS is the command-line program to get remote access with WinRM. Here is an example:

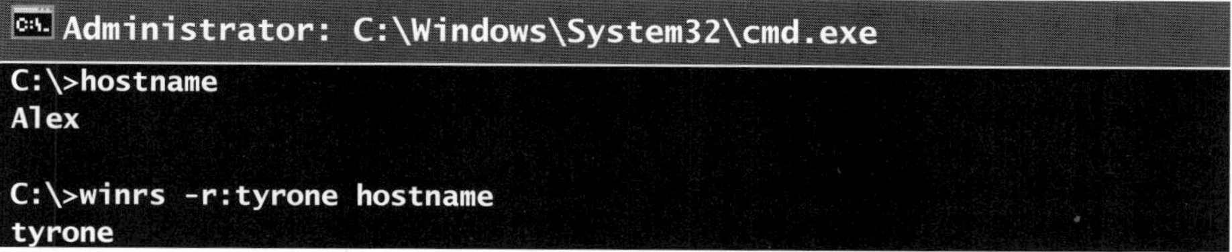

Figure 4-2 Example of WinRM in a remote console session

When you are skilful in using the command-line (think Windows Server Core), you now have a remote system at hand to use tools like netsh, netdom, powershell etc., to do almost anything you can imagine.

4.1.3 Using WinRM for systems management

WinRM provides some interesting built-in possibilities to collect information from remote systems over the network and perform basic configuration.

WinRM uses the following commands for systems:

- Get
  The WinRM get-command is used to retrieve management information from a specific object.
- Set
  WinRM set is used to modify management information.
- Enumerate
  WinRM enumerate is used to list all instances of a management resource.
- Invoke
  WinRM invoke, executes a method on a management resource.

Here are a few examples:

Systems management with WinRM	
Display OS properties	`Winrm get wmicimv2/Win32_OperatingSystem`
Display basic hardware info and output in XML	`Winrm get wmicimv2/Win32_ComputerSystem /format:pretty`

Display the status of the spooler service	Winrm get wmicimv2/Win32_Service?Name=spooler
Display disk configuration	Winrm enumerate wmicimv2/* - filter:"select * from win32_DiskDrive"
Display network interfaces of a remote system	Winrm enumerate wmicimv2/* -filter: "select * from win32_NetworkAdapterConfiguration where IPEnabled=True" -r:<remote system>
Start a service on a remote system	Winrm invoke startservice wmicimv2/win32_Service?name=w32time - r:<remote system>
Reboot a system	Winrm invoke reboot wmicimv2/win32_OperatingSystem - r:<remote system>

4.2 Event Viewer

Windows Vista provides a new centralized event logging system and Event Viewer based on Microsoft Management Console (MMC) version 3. Features such as cross-log querying, scheduled task integration, and page support in filtered views make the Event Viewer the ideal tool to monitor the health of the computer. The new Event Log is now XML-based and offers some nice new features:

- It can collect events from many systems to one system's log, allowing centralization of event logs.
- It provides an easy way to configure actions based on the occurrence of an event, like telling it to send you an e-mail, run a program or do something else.
- It allows the creation of custom queries to show only the events you want to see.
- By default it creates a consolidated view of all event logs to let one identify the latest events of a specific severity.

The Event Viewer can still be executed through the "Control Panel\Administrative Tools", by accessing "Computer Management", or by entering the command "**EVENTVWR**" into a Command Prompt or the "**Run**" dialog box.

If you want to view the Vista Event Log from a remote Windows XP machine, make sure the Remote Registry Service is running on the system being monitored. This service is set to Manual by default and thus may not be running.

4.2.1 The new event viewer UI

When you start the new event viewer in Windows Vista, you may not see too many differences at first site. Of course it now is a MMC 3.0 snap-in with the Actions pane on the right. The default logs on the left side of the UI enumerating the System, Security and Application logs are still there. But besides those, there is a massive group of new logs. At first you will see two of those alongside the ones you already knew from previous Windows versions. The **Setup** and "**ForwardedEvents**" logs are containers that will respectively collect application installations and events forwarded from other systems. I'll tell you more about that later on.

Then there are two news folders that constitute the biggest change in the Event Viewer:

- Custom Views
  Custom Views allow for the creation of customized views of the Event Log's contents. This offers great possibilities to collect targeted information for troubleshooting specific components, not restricted to the source of the events.

- Applications and Services Logs
  These logs store events from a single application or component, rather than events that might have system-wide impact. This category of logs includes four subtypes or channels:
    - Admin
      Events in Admin logs are of particular interest to IT Professionals and support personal use of the Event Viewer to troubleshoot problems. These events should provide guidance about how to respond to them.
    - Operational
      Events in the Operational log are also useful for IT Professionals, but they are likely to be less descriptive and require more knowledge for correct interpretation. They can be used to trigger tools or tasks based on the problem or occurrence.
    - Analytic
      The Analytic logs are disabled by default. They store events that trace an issue and, often, a high volume of events is logged.
    - Debug logs
      Debug logs are meant to provide information for developers when debugging applications and are also disabled by default.

All events in the event entries have three views:

- General
  This looks like it used to be in previous Windows versions.
- Details
    - XML View
      As all entries in the event log are stored as XML, you can also view them as XML. This is not always interesting for humans, but might be useful when you keep in mind that very often, more information is presented in XML than in the general view. XML is also easier to process in automation schemes.
    - Friendly View
      Friendly Views shows an easy-to-read view of the XML data contained in the event entry.

4.2.2 Custom Views

Probably one of the most useful new features of the Windows Vista Event Viewer is the possibility to create custom views. With Custom Views, you can create queries that span multiple logs, to collect and display simply the information you need to troubleshoot your component of choice. After creating the correct query, it can be stored and copied to other systems when required.

The query for a custom view can consist of just about every piece of information that can be found in the event logs. The easiest way to create a query is the Create View wizard. This wizard has the following options to create a query:

- Time Period
  To filter events based upon their time of occurrence.
- Event level
  Select from:
  - Critical
  - Error
  - Warning
  - Information
  - Verbose
- Event log
  To filter events from specific event logs.
- Event source
  To filter the component(s) that generated the events.
- Event IDs
  To filter event IDs.
- Task category
  To filter task categories.
- Keywords
  To filter keywords that must be included in the events.
- User
  To filter users. Multiple users can be entered, separated by a comma.
- Computer(s)
  To filter by computers. Multiple computers can be entered, separated by a comma.

Blank fields are considered as "select all". If the GUI does not provide enough flexibility, a query can be created in XML using XPath expressions.

When you created a really complex query, it comes in handy that you can export and import custom views for the Event Viewer. This creates an XML file that you can edit in Notepad for instance and import on another system when appropriate.

4.2.3 Using events to trigger actions

Windows Vista allows for the definition of various actions based on the occurrence of a certain event. Event triggers can be based on any event, with the exception of events in an analytic or debug log.

Every action based on an event is stored as a task in the Windows Task Scheduler. The creation of the task is automated using a wizard in the event viewer. When you right click an event, the option "Attach Task based on this event..." is shown. This opens the Task Wizard. The Task Wizard provides the following actions based on the occurrence of an event:

- Start a program
- Send an e-mail
  Allows for the definition of a message to be sent to a specified mail address and SMTP server. Make sure your mail server will accept mail from the client sending the mail.
- Display a message
  Sometimes you just wished that Windows popped up a message for a certain event (for example when your disk is causing errors). This is the option to define your own criteria for popping up messages.

4.2.4 Event forwarding

Event forwarding is a long awaited feature in Windows that has been promised by Microsoft for a long time. Those who followed the story might recall a product once announced for Windows Server 2003 SP1, called MACS (Microsoft Audit Collection System). MACS was supposed to become a free optional component that collects events from multiple systems in a network in a single database. In the end, Microsoft decided to build this functionality in Microsoft Operations Manager.

Event forwarding in Windows Vista is certainly a feature that is primarily built for Windows Server 2008. Finally, there is a way to detect strange occurrences on, let's say, 500 systems at about the same time. The mechanism for event forwarding is based on web services. It is based on the following principles:

- A subscription
  A subscription is the designation of a Windows Vista system to collect events from one or more other computers.
- The collector
  The collector is the system where the events are collected.
- Source computers
  Source computers are the computers where the collector gets the events.

Event forwarding is based on a polling mechanism. The collector will poll the source computers every 15 minutes for new events. By default these events will be collected in the "ForwardedEvents" container. But this is configurable.

The underlying technology for event forwarding is WS-Management. On the source computer you can see this, because the configuration of event forwarding enables the WinRM listener that listens on port 80 for http requests. Even though this might look like a web server running on the system, it is not a fully functional web server and it is not possible to use it for anything else than WS-Management.

How to set up event forwarding

This scenario implies that all systems involved are running in the same Active Directory domain.

Setting up event forwarding involves the following steps:

1. Set up the sources
    a. Configure the WinRM listener service.
    b. Add the collector to the local "Event Log Readers" group.
2. Set up the Collector
    a. Configure the "Windows Event Collector" Service.
    b. Create the subscriptions.

Set up an event forwarding source computer

1. Open a command prompt running as Administrator.
2. Type: **winrm quickconfig**
   The Windows Remote Management Tool will respond, telling WinRM is not set up to allow remote access and will require a number of changes.
3. Respond typing: **y [enter]**
   The Windows Remote Management Tool responds that it set up an http listener for WinRM and has made changes to the Windows Firewall.
4. Add the computer account of the collector to the local group "Event Log Readers", using the following command:
   ```
   net localgroup "Event Log Readers"
   Computername$@DNSdomainname /add
   ```
   Where Computername$ stands for the computer name of the collector computer, followed by a "$" character, and DNSdomainname stands for the fully qualified domain name of the domain the systems are running in.

Check connectivity to the source computer

WinRM provides an easy way to check if a source computer is properly accessible. It is good practice to use this check from the collector computer to see if everything will work properly after configuration of the subscriptions.

The command "winrm id –remote:*sourcecomputerfqdn*" is essentially a "ping" to the WinRM service on the source computer. The command is used to test WinRM connectivity when setting up or troubleshooting Event subscriptions.

Set up an event collector computer

1. Start the event viewer.
2. Right click **Subscriptions.**
3. Click **Create Subscription.**
4. When this is the first subscription, the system will request if it should configure the Windows Event Collector Service.
   Click **Yes**
   Alternatively you could have typed **wecutil qc** from an elevated command prompt before starting the wizard.
5. In the Subscription Properties dialog box fill in the following:
   a. Subscription Name
   b. Description
   c. Destination Log
   d. Source Computers
6. Click **Select Events…** to define an event query like in Custom Views.
7. Leave the User Account as default (Machine Account).
8. Click **Ok**

Event collection interval

After configuring the collector computer it will take up to 15 minutes before the system actually starts collecting events for the subscription. This interval is configurable using wecutil. The interval is defined in milliseconds.

Change the event collection interval to 10 seconds

1. Start an elevated Command Prompt on the collector computer.
2. Type:

```
wecutil ss <SourceComputer> /cm:custom
```

   (this command returns no response).
3. Type:

```
wecutil ss <SourceComputer> /hi:10000
```

4.3 Task Scheduler

Windows Vista contains a completely revamped version of the Task Scheduler. The Task Scheduler that once started as AT.exe in Windows NT is nothing like the old tool anymore. It seems that Microsoft, for once, thought they should create a tool good enough to use it themselves for OS maintenance purposes. When you open the Task Scheduler UI in a clean installed instance of Windows Vista, you will find 16 active scheduled tasks out-of-the-box taking care of business.

4.3.1 What's new in the Task Scheduler

The Task Scheduler is about scheduling tasks. But what is a Task?

In Windows, a task is the construct that defines a unit of operation, consisting of launching conditions, including *triggers*, *conditions*, *settings* and one or more execution operations known as *actions*.

Hint: Running as System

In previous versions of Windows, the Task Scheduler provided an excellent option to open an interactive command prompt running as System. This proved to be very successful for both hacking and troubleshooting. Because of numerous security enhancements in Windows Vista, it is no longer possible to start an interactive program as System. As far as I know there currently is no new workaround available for this functionality.

4.3.2 Pulling the trigger

In previous versions of Windows the Task Schedulers' only trigger (almost), was the time. Windows XP added a few triggers like system startup, logon and idle time. Most of these did not turn out to be very useful. The approach for Windows Vista appears to me to be much more flexible. First of all there is the possibility to create multiple triggers for a task. This allows you to create single tasks to run based on more than one trigger. Then there is this master of new triggers we've seen in the previous chapter: the event trigger. This trigger will certainly be used for a lot of scenarios to add self healing capabilities to possible error conditions. Other new triggers include:

- At task creation/modification
  This trigger adds the possibility to run a task when a new task is created or an existing task is modified.

- On disconnect from user session
  This trigger causes a task to run when a local user disconnects a session by using the "switch user" feature. Remote users activate this trigger by disconnecting a Remote Desktop session.
- On workstation lock
  This trigger will initiate a task when the system is locked. The trigger allows differentiating between the user or user group of the user that locks the system.
- On workstation unlock
  Like the previous trigger this one will initiate the task when a user unlocks the system.

Triggers contain a number of Advanced settings to fine-tune the task. Some of these like "Repeat task every", "Enabled" and "Stop any task that runs longer than" have remained the same as in previous versions of Windows. New advanced settings are:

- Delay task for or Delay task for up to (random delay)
- This setting allows you to specify an amount of time to delay the task from running, after the task is triggered. If you are using a time-based trigger (On a schedule), then the delay time will be a random time between the time the task is triggered and the time specified in this setting.
- Stop the task if it runs longer than .
- This setting allows you to set the maximum time that a task may run.
- Expire
- This setting allows you to set a date and time for the trigger to expire. When a trigger is expired, it cannot cause the task to run.

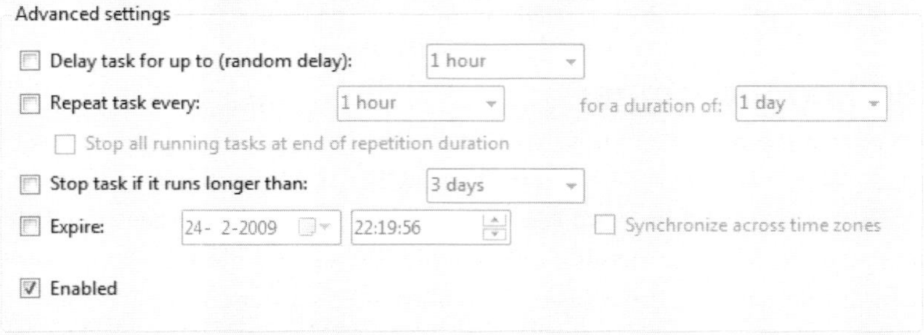

Advanced settings
Delay task for up to (random delay): 1 hour
Repeat task every: 1 hour for a duration of: 1 day
Stop all running tasks at end of repetition duration
Stop task if it runs longer than: 3 days
Expire: 24- 2-2009 22:19:56 Synchronize across time zones
Enabled

Figure 4-3 Advanced settings for a task trigger

Trigger times

When defining the advanced settings Activate and Expire, there is a new Universal ('Synchronize across time zones' in SP1) check box available. By default all times defined in the Task Scheduler are relative to the time zone that is set on the computer that runs the task. Enabling the Universal check box will make the time relative to UTC time instead of the time zone on the local system. Use this check box to coordinate tasks that have to run at the same moment in different time zones.

4.3.3 Redefining the action

The new actions are very similar to the actions defined for events for the Event Viewer. By default you can choose from:

- Start a program
- Send an e-mail
- Display a message

What's new in Windows Vista is the fact that you can define multiple actions for a single task. This enables easy synchronization of multiple actions, which was almost impossible in earlier versions of Windows.

Conditions

Conditions specify extra pre-requisites for a trigger to hit. The idle and power conditions are not new for Windows Vista. The configurable conditions are:

- **Idle**
  The Task Scheduler service will check if the computer is in an idle state every 15 minutes. A computer is considered to be in an idle state when a screen saver is running. If a screen saver is not running, then the computer is considered to be in an idle state if there is 0% CPU usage and 0% disk input or output for 90% of the past fifteen minutes and if there is no keyboard or mouse input during this period of time. Any user input marks the end of the idle state.
  - **Start the task only if the computer is idle for**
    This condition will only start when the trigger condition was met AND the system has been idle for x time. Where x is the defined idle time.
    - Stop if the computer ceases to be idle
      When this option is enabled, the task will stop running when the system ceases to be idle.
      - Restart if the idle state resumes
        This option will cause the task to start running again when it was previously stopped because of the last option.
- **Power**
  - **Start the task only if the computer is on AC power**
    This means the task will not run when the system is on battery power.
    - Stop if the computer switches to battery power
      This will stop the task when a system switches to battery power.

- **Wake the computer to run this task**
  This condition will wake up the computer from sleep or hibernation to run a task. Waking up the computer may not automatically turn on the screen until user input is detected.

- **Start only if the following network connection is available**
  This condition allows you to define the named network where the task is supposed to run. The name of the network usually consists of the dns suffix on the specified network.

Settings

Task settings specify how a task is run, stopped, or deleted. A task's settings are displayed on the Settings tab of the Task Properties or Create Task dialog box. Most settings are new for Windows Vista.

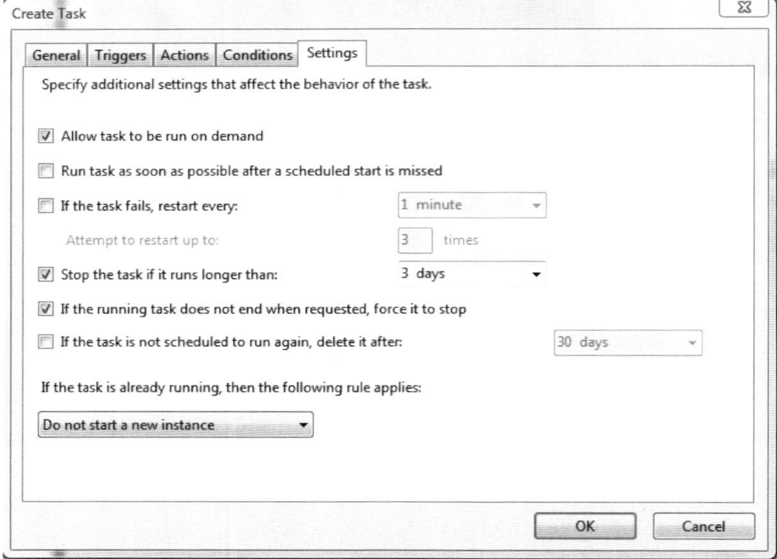

Figure 4-4 Configure task settings

The options here are:

- **Allow task to be run on demand**
  You can specify whether a task can be run manually, before or after it is scheduled to run, by allowing the task to be run on demand. The default setting allows a user to run the task at any time, on demand.

- **Run task as soon as possible after a scheduled start is missed**
  If this setting is checked, the Task Scheduler service will start the task if the task was scheduled to run at a certain time, but for some reason (for example, the computer was turned off or the Task Scheduler service was busy) the task was not activated. The Task Scheduler service will not start the task immediately after the task was missed. By default the service waits ten minutes before starting the missed task.

- **If task fails, restart every: <time period>**
  Use this setting to restart a task if the task fails to run (the last run result of the task is not a success). You specify the time interval that takes place between task restart attempts, and the number of times to try to restart the task.

- **If the task does not end when requested, force it to stop**
  If this setting is selected, the task will be forced to stop if the task does not respond to a request to stop.

- **If the task is not scheduled to run again, delete it after: <time period>**
  If this setting is selected, the Task Scheduler service will automatically delete the task if it is not scheduled to run again. The Task Scheduler service will wait for the specified time period before deleting the task. If this setting is not selected, the Task Scheduler service will not automatically delete the task. The task must include at least one trigger with an expiration date in order to select this setting.

- **If the task is already running, then the following rule applies:**
  - Do not start a new instance
    The Task Scheduler service will not run the new instance of the task and will not stop the instance that is already running.
  - Run a new instance in parallel
    The Task Scheduler service will run the new instance of the task in parallel with the instance that is already running.
  - Queue a new instance
    The Task Scheduler service will add the new instance of the task to the queue of tasks that the service will run, and the service will not stop the instance of the task that is already running.
  - Stop the existing instance
    The Task Scheduler service will stop the instance of the task that is already running, and run the new instance of the task.

4.3.4 Scripting the Task Scheduler

The task scheduler in Windows Vista contains a number of options, besides the options within the Task Scheduler GUI:

- Using the command prompt with AT.exe
  That's right. AT.exe is still there in Windows Vista for backwards compatibility. Just like in Windows XP, AT does not offer all available functionality of the new Task Scheduler service. It has even been cut down in functionality, as the /INTERACTIVE option has been disabled.
- Using the command prompt with SchTasks.exe
  SchTasks.exe is there to provide full access to the Task Scheduler Service from the command line. Probably the best solution when CMD-scripts or the command line are used to manage the Task Scheduler.

Schtasks examples	
`Schtasks /Query /S <hostname>`	List all tasks on remote system <hostname>
`Schtasks /Query /XML /TN <taskname> > taskname.xml`	Export task <taskname> to taskname.xml
`Schtasks /Create /TN <taskname> /XML taskname.xml`	Use taskname.xml to create a new task <taskname>
`Schtasks /Run /TN <taskname>`	Start task <taskname> now

- Using the Task Scheduler API in script
  The Task Scheduler API provides complete access to the Task Scheduler from script. The options for this functionality are almost endless. Here is a small example that shows the complete list of Tasks defined on a system:

Script: Listing all Tasks defined on a system

```
Set service = CreateObject("Schedule.Service")
service.Connect
Set rootFolder = service.GetFolder("\")
Set colTasks = rootFolder.GetTasks(0)

For Each task In colTasks
    Wscript.Echo task.Name
Next
```

4.4 Group Policy

Microsoft greatly expanded the possibilities of Group Policy in Windows Vista. The number of GPO settings increased massively to 2400+ settings. Besides numerous new settings, Vista introduces an new way of storing group policy templates. ADMX and ADML files take the place of what used to be ADM files in earlier versions of Windows. Also the way Windows Vista applies group policies has changed a bit. This provides better possibilities to make sure Group Policies get applied, even when network capacity is not that good.

4.4.1 What's new in Group Policy

Group Policy Client Service

GP processing in Windows Vista now runs in shared service host (SVCHOST) and is not just part of the Winlogon process anymore – the new service is called "Group Policy Client" (or GPSVC). This dedicated service is now responsible for applying settings configured by administrators for the computer and users. The service is hardened, requiring elevated privileges to stop the service (not even local administrators can stop the service by default) and the service restart configuration provides recovery on unexpected failures. All this will be 100% transparent to the user (from *http://www.windowsecurity.com/articles/Managing-Windows-Vista-Group-Policy-Part3.html*).

Network Location Awareness

Before Windows Vista, policies were applied to clients only at machine startup (computer settings), at user logon (user settings) and every 90 minutes, plus up to 30 minutes offset, also known as the background refresh interval (which can be changed from the default value).

Another issue was the fact that Slow Link Detection (SLD) relied on the Internet Control Message Protocol (ICMP), so PING/ECHO requests were sent to determine the network state between client and Domain Controller (DC). When administrators turned off/filtered the ICMP protocol in routers or firewalls, often for security reasons, policies were never applied because SLD determined the network was slower than 500Kbps (the default value).

Windows Vista uses Network Location Awareness (NLA) to solve these issues. NLA constantly monitors the network condition and introduces responsiveness to network changes and resource availability (subscribes to DC availability notification).

NLA is, among other things, aware of the presence of DCs; if the previous policy application cycle was skipped or failed, Vista will retry GP processing when a DC is available. The improved GP engine, based on GPSVC, will even initiate a background refresh over a VPN connection, updating both the machine and user policy. So there's no need to reboot or log off and back on, before connecting to the corporate network over a VPN connection.

With the access to resource detection and event notification capabilities in the OS, such as recovery from hibernation, moving in and out of wireless networks, successfully exiting quarantine and docking of a laptop, Windows Vista has very accurate indicators to GP, to ascertain whether the network is ready and reliable.

Unfortunately it is not possible to filter policies based on the network location. This is only possible for firewall settings that may differ, on the detected network profile.

Multiple local Group Policies

Windows Vista is capable of creating multiple local group policies (MLGPOs) for user settings on a system, thus making it possible to provide different possibilities for different users on the same system, with only local policies. Typically MLGPOs will be used in non-Active Directory environments where you have standalone or workgroup computers; MLGPO supports different policy configurations for "Administrators" and "Non-Administrators" ("limited users") and specific policy settings for individual users. If a given user is not a member of the "administrators" group, then the user is automatically considered a "non-administrator", which is actually not a security group in itself.

When a policy is about to be applied, Windows Vista checks to see if the user is a member of the Administrators group: if so, the "Administrator LGPO" is loaded; if not, the "Non-Administrators LGPO" is loaded. You can only load one of the two policies mentioned above, not both. After this, any specific user policy is processed and applied.

The Local Group Policy processing order is as follows:

1. The LGPO Computer Configuration (same as previous Windows Versions).
2. The LGPO User Configuration (same as previous Windows Versions).
3. Local group membership (either "Administrators" or "Non-Administrators" LGPO, not both).
4. Local users (individual/specific user policy).

Tip: Disabling local Policies

Windows Vista introduces a new policy setting: "Computer settings \ Administrative Templates \ System\Group Policy \ Turn off Local Group Policy objects processing". If you enable this policy setting, the system will not process and apply any Local GPOs. This setting will be ignored on stand-alone computers. A domain administrator can enable this policy to ensure that no other policies are applied to his/her domain users and computers.

New templates

Windows Vista uses a new file format to store registry settings for Group Policies in administrative templates. Instead of adm-files, Vista uses a combination of ADMX- and ADML- files that are both XML based. The new structure allows Windows Vista to easily support multiple languages, as the descriptions and names for the policies are all stored in ADML files.

Central templates store

ADMX and ADML files can be centrally stored in the domain, thus creating a single repository for all Group Policy settings in the enterprise.

4.4.2 New Group Policy Categories

Windows Vista introduces the following new categories for Group Policy settings:

- **Power Management Settings**
  Windows Vista now introduces the possibility to configure power management centrally, using Group Policy.
- **Blocking Device Installation**
  Windows Vista enables administrators to restrict which hardware can be introduced by users on their workstations. The introduction of devices such as USB drives, CD-RW drives, DVD-RW drives, and other removable media can now be centrally managed.
- **Assign printers based on locations**
  In Windows Vista, you can assign printers based on site location. When mobile users move to a different location, Group Policy can update their printers for the new location. Mobile users returning to their primary locations get to see their usual default printers.
- **Expanded Internet Explorer Settings**
  In Windows Vista, you can open and edit Internet Explorer Group Policy settings, without the risk of inadvertently altering the state of the policy setting based on the configuration of the administrative workstation. Unlike earlier versions of Windows, the settings on the management system don't have to be changed in order to configure Group Policy settings for Internet Explorer.
- **Windows Firewall Settings**
  Windows Vista allows Group Policy based management of the Windows Firewall and IPSec.

These and other extensions to Group Policies greatly enhance the possibilities when managing Windows Vista with Group Policies.

4.4.3 Group Policy Templates

Windows Vista introduces a new format for displaying registry-based policy settings. Registry-based policy settings (located in the Administrative Templates category in the Group Policy Object Editor) are defined using a standards-based, XML file format known as ADMX files. These new files replace the ADM files, which were based on a proprietary format. The Group Policy Object Editor and Group Policy Management Console remain largely unchanged. In the majority of situations, you will not notice the presence of ADMX files during your day-to-day Group Policy administration tasks.

ADMX files are accompanied by ADML files. ADML files represent the description of the defined policies per language. This enables one to change the language in which Group Policies are represented without changing the templates itself.

Unlike ADM files, ADMX files are not stored with individual GPOs. For domain-based networks, administrators can create a central store location of ADMX files, accessible by anyone with permission to create or edit GPOs. Group Policy tools will continue to recognize custom ADM files you have in your existing environment, but will ignore any ADM file that has been superseded by ADMX files: System.adm, Inetres.adm, Conf.adm, Wmplayer.adm, and Wuau.adm. Therefore, if you have edited any of the these files, to modify existing or create new policy settings, the modified or new settings will not be read or displayed by the Windows Vista–based Group Policy tools.

The Group Policy Object Editor automatically reads and displays Administrative Template policy settings from ADMX files that are stored either locally or in the optional ADMX central store. The Group Policy Object Editor will automatically read and display Administrative Template policy settings from custom ADM files stored in the GPO. You can still add or remove custom ADM files with the Add/Remove template menu option. All Group Policy settings currently in ADM files delivered by Windows Server 2003, Windows XP, and Windows 2000 will also be available in Windows Vista and Windows Server 2008 ADMX files.

The file location of Administrative Templates has changed with Windows Vista. In earlier Windows versions, ADM files were located in the directory *%WINDIR%\inf*; ADMX files are located in *%WINDIR%\PolicyDefinitions*, and corresponding ADML files are located in *%WINDIR%\PolicyDefinitions \<LanguageFolder>*. The <LanguageFolder> can be named \EN-US for U.S. English, \NL for Dutch, etc. - following the ISO-style language or 'Culture Name'.

In order to create a central ADMX Group Policy Template Store, create a folder *PolicyDefinitions* in *\\<FQDN>\SYSVOL\<FQDN>\policies*. Replace <FQDN>

with the fully qualified domain name of the Active Directory Domain. The full procedure for creating a central ADMX Group Policy Template store is explained in KB article 929841 at *http://support.microsoft.com/kb/929841*.

4.4.4 Group Policy Preferences

Group Policy Preferences (GPP) is a new feature of Windows Vista that has been introduced in the product with Service Pack 1. GPP allows you to define settings from Group Policy that used to be defined in logon scripts and default profiles. GPP settings are more flexible then the current Group Policies, because you can specify if settings are permanent or can be changed by the end user, and you can define the scope of each setting on the setting itself. This creates the option to define multiple settings for multiple target groups within the same GPO.

Here is a short overview of stuff you can define with GPP:

- Drive Mappings to shares.
- Creation, replacement and updating of Printers and printer connections, including the assignment of the default printer.
- Creation, replacement and updating of Environment Variables.
- Creation, replacement, updating and deletion of Files on the target system.
- Creation, replacement, updating, deletion and cleanup of Folders on the target system
- Creation, deletion and updating individual entries in INI-Files.
- Creation, deletion and updating of File Shares, including management of Access Based Enumeration.
- Creation, deletion and updating of any entry in the Registry for REG_SZ, REG_DWORD, REG_BINARY, REG_MULTI_SZ, and REG_EXPAND_SZ types.
- Creation, deletion and updating of Shortcuts to files, websites and Shell Objects like the Recyle Bin.
- Definition of all settings that you find in the Control Panel, including:
    - Definition of Data Sources for ODBC
    - Enabling and disabling of Devices
    - Definition of Folder Options (finally no more hidden extension for "known" apps)
    - Linking File Extensions to applications
    - Definition of Internet Settings for Internet Explorer (5, 6 and 7)
    - Configuration of Local Users and Groups
    - Definition of VPN and Dial-up connections

- (Easy) definition of Power Options
- Definition of Regional Settings, including UI language and time/data formatting
- Creation, deletion and updating of Scheduled Tasks
- Configuration of Services
- Configuration of the Start Menu

This is quite a list. Now consider that for each setting, you can define whether the user will be able to change it, and that you won't be needing SCRIPTING to do all this stuff!

What do you need to use Group Policy Preferences?

The administration tool for GPP is included in Windows Server 2008 and in the Remote Server Administration Tools (RSAT) that will run on Windows Vista with Service Pack 1. RSAT is a separate download on the Microsoft website.

The client side for GPP is already built-in in Windows Server 2008. A GPP Client Side Extension is available for the following operating systems:

- Windows XP with Service Pack 2
- Windows Server 2003 with Service Pack 1
- Windows Vista with Service Pack 1

The GPP client side extensions for Windows XP and Windows Server 2003 can be downloaded from the Microsoft website.

There is no need for Schema updates or changes in the configuration of Domain Controllers.

4.4.5 Troubleshooting Group Policy

Unlike previous versions of Windows, Windows Vista stores all information about Group Policy processing in the Eventlog. Previous versions of Windows only stored part of the GPO logging information in the eventlogs. Another problem with those logs was, that those logs were shared with other Windows components. To really find out what was going on with Group Policy processing you had to enable logging and wade through pages of irrelevant data in the *Userenv.log* file that was stored in *%windir%\Debug\UserMode*.

What's new in Group Policy logging

Windows Vista has a separate event source – Group Policy – solely for Group Policy processing. This makes it much easier to filter Group Policy events from the Event Log.

Windows Vista provides two types of Group Policy events:

- Administrative events
  Administrative events appear in the System event log. The events mainly consist of basic event messages reporting successful or unsuccessful processing of GPs. Each event (Information, Warning or Error) contains a relevant link to Knowledge Base (KB) articles at Microsoft's.
- Operational events
  The Group Policy operational events provide a view of what the Group Policy service does before and during Group Policy processing. Group Policy operational events replace the *userenv.log* file and provide more comprehensive and detailed event descriptions than its predecessor. Operational Group Policy events appear in the new "Applications and Services Logs" under Microsoft - Windows - GroupPolicy – Operation.

How to troubleshoot Group Policy

Troubleshooting Group Policy in Windows Vista starts in the System event log, where you will find the administrative events indicating Group Policy processing start and finish. Each event contains a number of fields telling what policy was being processed and how. Here are a few important fields found in administrative Group Policy events.

System\Correlation:ActivityID and EventData\PolicyActivityID

Each administrative event contains an ActivityID. The ActivityID represents one instance of Group Policy processing. The Group Policy service creates a unique ActivityID each time Group Policy refreshes. For example, a computer processes Group Policy during startup. At that moment, the Group Policy service assigns an ActivityID to that instance of processing. Further events logged during that instance use the same ActivityID, until that instance of Group Policy processing completes (Group Policy processing completes when the process ends either successfully or with errors). Users process Group Policy during the logon process. Again, the Group Policy service assigns a unique ActivityID to that instance of Group Policy processing and uses it until processing completes. This behavior is repeated for each new instance of Group Policy processing, which includes automatic and forced Group Policy refreshing. You can view this value on all Group Policy events.

EventData\PolicyApplicationMode

The Group Policy service records the type of Group Policy processing in the PolicyApplicationMode field. The PolicyApplicationMode field is one of three values. Those values are:

Value	Explanation
0	Background processing: The instance of Group Policy processing occurring after the initial instance of Group Policy processing. Background processing occurs when the Group Policy service refreshes. For example, the Group Policy service periodically refreshes Group Policy every 90 minutes.
1	Synchronous Foreground processing: Foreground processing is the instance of policy processing that occurs at computer startup and user logon. Synchronous foreground processing is when the processing of computer Group Policy must complete before Windows displays the logon dialog box, and user Group Policy processing, which happens during user logon, must complete before Windows displays the user's desktop.
2	Asynchronous Foreground processing: Asynchronous Foreground processing is the instance of Group Policy processing that occurs at computer startup and user logon. However, Windows does not wait for computer Group Policy processing to complete before displaying the logon dialog box. Additionally, Windows does not wait for user Group Policy processing to complete before displaying the user's desktop.

EventData\PolicyProcessingMode

The PolicyProcessingMode field is used to determine the presence of loopback processing, and whether loopback processing is in Merge or Replace mode.

Value	Explanation
0	Normal Processing mode: Loopback is not enabled.
1	Loopback Merge mode: Loopback processing is enabled. The Group Policy service merges user settings within the scope of the computer with user settings within the scope of the user.
2	Loopback Replace mode: Loopback processing is enabled. The Group Policy service replaces user settings within the scope of the user with user settings within the scope of the computer.

EventData\ProcessingTimeInMilliseconds

The ProcessingTimeInMilliseconds field is used to determine the amount of time, in milliseconds, that the described event has used to complete the operation.

EventData\DCName

The Group Policy service records the name of a domain controller in the DCName field. The name found in this field is the domain controller the Group Policy service uses when communicating with Active Directory.

EventData\ErrorCode and EventData\ErrorDescription

These two fields appear only on error events. The ErrorCode field provides a value, represented as a decimal, which the described event encountered. The ErrorDescription field provides a short description of the ErrorCode value.

How to start troubleshooting

Now it is time to find out what really went wrong. It is probably good to start by getting your information organized, by creating a custom view containing only information about the Group Policy processing instance you are currently investigating. A computer often has more than one instance of Group Policy processing. Having a view of only relevant events may makes life much easier.

Use the following procedure to create a custom view of a Group Policy instance. You can do this by using an Event Viewer query. This query creates a filtered view of the Group Policy operational log for a specific instance of Group Policy processing.

Create a custom view of a Group Policy instance

1. Start the **Event Viewer**.
2. Right-click **Custom Views**, and then click **Create Custom Views**.
3. Click the **XML** tab, and then select the **Edit query manually** check box. The Event Viewer displays a dialog box that explains that editing a query manually, prevents you from modifying the query using the Filter tab. Click **Yes**.
4. Copy the Event Viewer query (provided at the end of this step) to the clipboard. Paste the query into the **Query** box.

```
<QueryList><Query Id="0" Path="Application">
<Select Path="Microsoft-Windows-
GroupPolicy/Operational">
*[System/Correlation/@ActivityID='{INSERT ACTIVITY ID
HERE}']
</Select>
</Query></QueryList>
```

5. Copy the ActivityID you previously saved from the "To Determine an instance of Group Policy processing" procedure to the clipboard. In the Query box, highlight "**INSERT ACTIVITY ID HERE**" and then press **CTRL+V** to paste the ActivityID over the text.
   Note: Be sure not to paste over the leading and trailing braces ({ }). You must include these braces for your query to work properly.
6. In the **Save Filter to Custom View** dialog box, type a name and description significant to the view you created. Click **OK**.
7. The name of the saved view appears under **Custom Views**. Click the name of the saved view to display its events in the Event Viewer.

Investigating events of a Group Policy instance

Most of the events in the Group Policy operational log appear in pairs. For each start event, there is an end event. End events can be successful, warning, or error events. Usually these events share the last two digits in their event id's. For example, a 4017 event appears in the event log, which represents a Group Policy component starting a specific action. If the action is successfully completed, then the Group Policy service records a 5017 event. If the action completes with errors or fails then the Group Policy service records a 6017 or 7017 event, respectively. Policy processing events use the same numbering scheme for warning and error eventmessages in the 8000–8007 range for Group Policy success events. You can use these numbering patterns to quickly identify warning and failure events in the Group Policy operational log.

The best way to troubleshoot Group Policy processing is to break the process down into three phases. Within each phase of the process there is a subset of processing scenarios. When processing Group Policy, the Group Policy service iterates through each scenario as it runs through each phase. The phases of Group Policy processing are:

1. **Preprocessing phase**

   The preprocessing phase indicates the starting instance of Group Policy processing and gathers information required to process Group Policy. This phase includes the following actions:

   - Start policy processing
     This occurs at computer startup, user logon, network change, or policy refresh.
   - Retrieve account information
     The Group Policy service must retrieve the location of the user or computer object in Active Directory before it can apply Group Policy.
   - Domain controller discovery
     The Group Policy service reads Group Policy objects from Active Directory. Therefore, the service must discover a domain controller.
   - Computer Role discovery
     The computer role determines if the current computer is a standalone workstation or a server; a domain member computer, which supports directory services; a domain controller; or a domain member computer, which does not support directory services. The Group Policy service requires this information to apply Group Policy based on the computer's role.
   - Security principal discovery
     The Group Policy service must discover if the current security principal is a user or a computer, in order to apply the correct policy settings.
   - Loopback processing mode discovery
     Group Policy loopback processing changes how the Group Policy service applies user policies. Depending on the mode, loopback processing merges or replaces the user policy settings with user policy settings included in Group Policy objects within the scope of the computer object.

- GPO discovery
  The Group Policy service discovers a list of Group Policy objects applicable to the computer or user. When the service has the list, it checks the accessibility of each Group Policy object by reading the gpt.ini file. The Group Policy service records this activity with a series of start and end-trace events (event ID 4017). You can use the corresponding end-trace event to determine the success or failure of each attempt to read the gpt.ini file.
- Slow link detection
  The Group Policy service is responsible for detecting and estimating bandwidth between the computer and the domain controller. The Group Policy service compares the result of the estimated bandwidth to the slow link threshold (configured by Group Policy). A value below the threshold, results in the Group Policy service flagging the network connection as a slow link. This value triggers various client-side extensions and determines whether or not they should be applied.
- Nonsystem GP Extension discovery
  The Group Policy service runs in a shared service host process with other components included with Windows Vista. The service operating in this shared service host increases its performance. However, third party developers can extend Group Policy by providing additional extensions, which are processed during Group Policy processing. The Group Policy service detects non-system extensions during the pre-processing phase of Group Policy processing. The service reconfigures itself to run in a separate service host process when it detects non-system extensions, also known as standalone mode.

2. **Processing phase**

The processing phase uses the information gathered in the preprocessing phase to cycle through each Group Policy extension, which applies policy settings to the user or computer.

3. **Post-processing phase**

The post-processing phase reports the end of the policy processing instance and records if the instance ended successfully, was processed with warnings, or failed. This is logged with a single event.

4.5 Print Management

Print Management is a snap-in in Microsoft Management Console (MMC) that enables you to install, view, and manage all of the printers in your organization from any computer running the snap-in. The Print Management snap-in is available in a full featured version in both Windows Vista and Windows Server 2003 R2. Print Management is available for Windows XP (x86 and x64), with the following exceptions: property pages are not supported (e.g. Printer/Ports/Driver/Form properties and Server properties), and the feature "Automatically Add Network Printers" on the local server is not supported.

Print Management provides almost real time details about the status of printers and print servers on the network. The Print Management MMC can be used to install printer connections to a group of client computers simultaneously. The Print Management MMC can help to easily locate printers that have an error condition by using filters. It can also send e-mail notifications or run scripts when a printer or print server needs attention. On printer models that provide a Web page, Print Management has access to more data, such as toner and paper levels.

Together with Group Policy, Print Management can automatically make printer connections available to users and computers in your organization. In addition, Print Management can automatically search for and install network printers on the local subnet of your local print servers.

4.5.1 Security requirements

To take full advantage of Print Management, you must be logged on as a member of the Administrators group on the print servers you are managing. Print Management can also be used to monitor any print server and printer without administrative privileges[4]. However, certain functions will not be available, such as adding and deleting printers and printer drivers.

4.5.2 Print Management

The Windows Print Management console was introduced with Windows Server 2003 R2. The Print Management Console provides centralized management for print servers running Windows Server. With the Print Management console you can centrally:

---

[4] When running as an administrator with reduced privileges, the MMC cannot be started without elevated privileges.

- Add/Remove printer drivers on remote print servers
- Manage forms on print servers
- Create, delete, and configure printer ports
- Create, delete, and configure printers

Print Management is an MMC snap-in that is installed with Windows Vista. The snap-in can be executed from the Start Menu or using Printmanagement.msc.

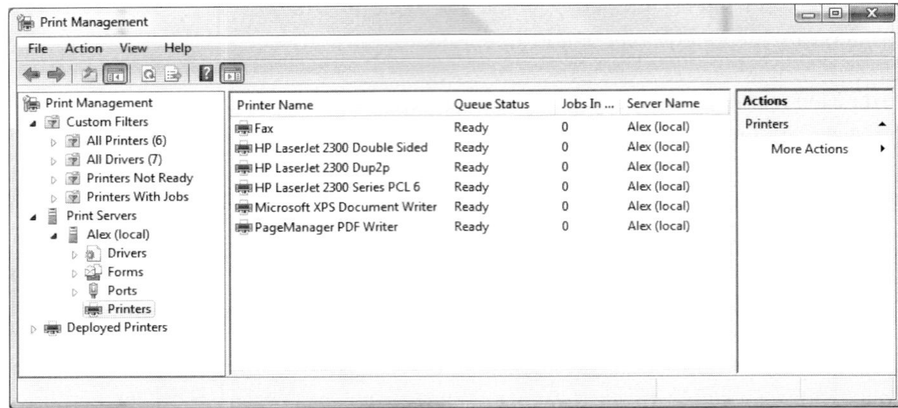

Figure 4-5 Print Management Console

Add Print Servers

The following procedure describes how to add network print servers to the console.

Add a print server to Print Management

1. In the Print Management tree, right-click **Print Management** or **PrintServers**, and then click **Add/Remove Servers**.
2. In the **Add/Remove Servers** dialog box, under Specify print server, in **Add server** field, do one of the following:
  • Type the name of the print server you want to manage.
  • Click **Browse** to locate and select the print server.
3. Click **Add to List**.
4. Add as many print servers as you like, and then click **OK**.

Viewing Printers

The Print Management tree contains three places where printer information is stored: **Custom Printer Filters**, **Print Servers**, and **Deployed Printers**. The Custom Printer Filters folder contains the following nodes:

- All Printers
- Paused Printers
- Printers Not Ready
- Printers With Jobs

The All Printers node displays a dynamic view of all of the printers on all of the servers available for managing with Print Management. You can also create your own custom views or filters. Those will also be stored in the Custom Printer Filters folder.

Network printer servers that you add to Print Management are stored in Print Servers. Every printer server automatically gets four objects that serve as filters for information about that server:

- Drivers
- Forms
- Ports
- Printers

To quickly access the Print Server Properties dialog box, right-click the Drivers, Forms, or Ports object, and then click Manage Drivers, Manage Forms, or Manage Ports.

The Deployed Printers node contains a list of all the printers located in Print Management that are managed by Group Policy objects. Later on in this chapter you will learn more about Print Management and Group Policy.discussed

Offline Print Servers

If a server goes offline, the printer server icon will change and (Offline) will be appended to the server name. All of the printers on that server will be hidden from all views. The Drivers, Forms, Ports, and Printers objects will also be hidden from view until the server comes back online.

Printer Details

The details for each printer are displayed in the results pane of the console. The results pane contains columns with values such as the printer name, queue status, jobs in queue, and server name. You can add and remove columns to show only certain characteristics of the printers, and you can filter among all the print servers in your organization to display only printers with specific criteria in the columns. In any view, you can sort the results according to one criterion by clicking on the heading of one of the columns.

Print Management can also show an extended view, which displays more details about the queue and provides access to the printer's Web page, if one is available. You can add, remove, and sort columns in both the standard and extended view.

To add and remove columns

1. In the Print Management tree, under a print server, right-click **Printers**, point to **View**, and then click **Add/Remove Columns**.
2. In the **Add/Remove Columns** dialog box, select the name of the column, and then click **Add** or **Remove**.

The chosen columns will be the same in all of the Printers objects and all of the custom views. These columns will only be in effect the next time you open Print Management if you save the MMC file.

Extended View

Extended view enables Print Management to display more information about the status of a print job, its owner, the number of pages, the size of the job when it was submitted, its port, its priority, and so on.

In addition, when the printer has a Web page, extended view enables access to this page by exposing an additional tab. The Web page displays details about the physical properties of the printer and its specifications, and sometimes allows remote administration.

When extended view is enabled, it is enabled for all Printer objects under all print servers and custom views.

Filtering Views

The filtering feature may be used to create custom views of printers; for example, it might be helpful to filter for printers with certain error conditions, or those printers of a specific type, regardless of the print server they use. Each view is dynamic. This ensures the data is always up to date. All filtered views are stored in the Printers folder in the Print Management tree.

An example of a filter that may be useful is shown in Figure 4-6. This custom view displays all printers on the specified print server that have a queue status other than Ready, and containing one or more jobs in the print queue.

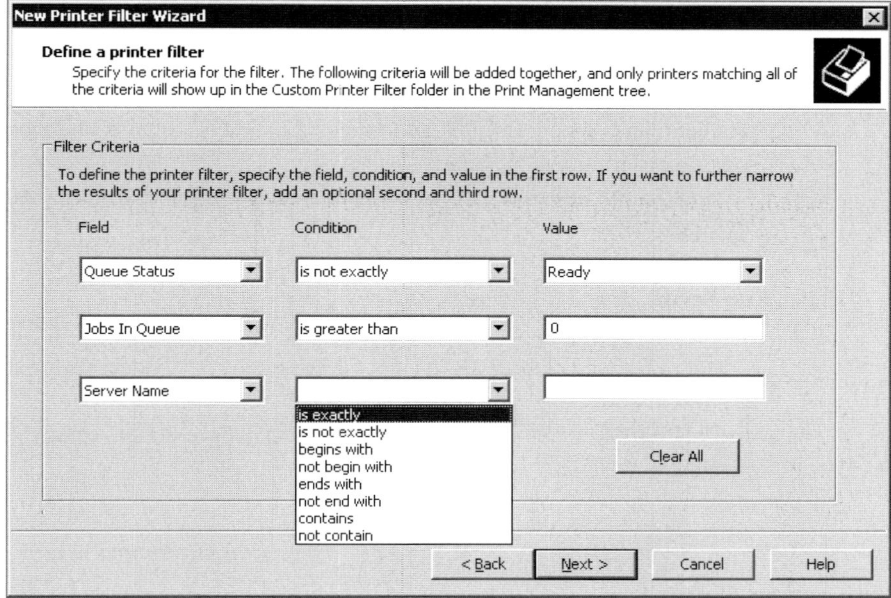

Figure 4-6 Defining a printer filter

When creating a filtered view, you have the option to set notifications by e-mail or to run a script. This opens great opportunities for systems management to get notified when something goes wrong with printers in the network.

To set up and save a filtered view

1. In the **Print Management** tree, right-click **Custom Filters**, and then click **Add New Printer Filter**. This will launch the New Printer Filter Wizard. Under Printer Filter Name and Description, do the following:
2. Type a name for the printer filter. The name will appear in **Custom Filters** in the Print Management tree.
3. Type a description that helps you recall the difference between this and other printers filters. The description is displayed when you choose **Properties** for a filter.
4. Click **Next**.
5. Under **Define a printer filter**, do the following:

a. In the **Field** list, click the print queue or printer status characteristic.
b. In the **Condition** list, click the condition.
c. In the **Value** box, type a value.
d. Continue adding criteria until your filter is complete, and then click **Next**.

6. Under **Set Notifications (Optional)**, do the following:
   a. Select the **Send e-mail notification** checkbox and type one or more recipient and sender e-mail addresses. An SMTP server must be specified to route the message.
   b. To create a New Printer Filter with no e-mail notification, clear the checkbox.
   c. Click **Next**.
7. Under **Run Script**, do the following:
   a. Select the checkbox and then type the path where the script file is located. To add more arguments, type them in the **Additional arguments** box.
   b. To create a New Printer Filter without specifying a script, clear the checkbox.
8. Click **Finish**.

Managing Printers

Print Management is perfectly capable to manage all of the printers in the enterprise, including printers in branch offices. Print Management provides a single interface with which you control how printers are shared, update drivers, and control print queues. There is no need to navigate to the individual folders for each printer on each printer server.

4.5.3 Group Policy to configure printer connections

The option to add printer connections to the client from Group Policy was introduced with Windows Server 2003 R2. Previous versions of Windows had to run PushPrinterConnections.exe at startup or logon to get printer connections configured through group policy. Windows 2000 only allowed the connection of printers to the user. From Windows XP onwards, printers can be connected to the user or to the computer. Windows Vista has no need for *PushPrinterConnections.exe*, since the functionality is fully integrated in the OS.

When you deploy printer connections through Group Policy, the client reads the configuration information from the Group Policy, and adds the deployed printer connections for each printer defined in the Group Policy object to the user or computer that is affected by the policy.

When adding printer connections to Group Policy with the Print Management console, you must be a member of the Administrators group on the print server and have the privileges to edit the Group Policy object that will contain the deployed printer connections.

When using the following procedure, first create the OU for the users or computers that will be affected and the Group Policy that will contain the deployed printers.

Deploying printer connections through Group Policy

1. Open the **Administrative Tools** folder, and then double-click **Print Management**.
2. In the Print Management tree, under the appropriate print server, click **Printers**.
3. In the results pane, right-click the printer you want to deploy, and then click **Deploy with Group Policy**.
4. In the Deploy with Group Policy dialog box, click **Browse**, and then choose a Group Policy object.
5. Click **OK**.
6. To assign the printer connection setting to the GPO, do one or both of the following:
    - As a per-user setting, select the users that this GPO applies to (per user) check box.
    - As a per-machine setting, select the computers that this GPO applies to (per machine) check box.
7. Click **Add**.
8. Repeat steps 3 to 6 to add the printer connection setting to another GPO.
9. Click **OK**.

4.6 Backup/Restore

Windows Vista contains a set of completely new backup and restore tools. The tools available in Windows Vista are:

- File backup and restore
- Complete PC Backup and Restore
- Shadow Copy
- System Restore

All the tools target specific needs and user profiles.

NTBackup support

As you probably have already noticed, NTBackup has left the scene in Windows Vista. NTBackup.exe is still available for Windows Vista in a “Read-only” version. This version can only be used to restore a backup you made earlier with a previous version of Windows. You must download NTBackup for Windows Vista from the Microsoft website when needed.

4.6.2 File Backup and Restore

File Backup and Restore is aimed at the “simple” user of Windows Vista. It is a consumer or home user solution that is stripped from all possible complexity that comes to mind when you think of backups.

File Backup and Restore only performs backups of user data. This means the following data will not be backed up:

- System files
  Executables and DLL’s belonging to the operating system will not be backed up.
- Temporary files
  Temporary files and search indexes will also not be part of the backed up data.
- EFS encrypted files
  EFS encrypted files **cannot** be backed up using Windows Vista File Backup. This is due to a technical issue that might possibly be solved in an upcoming update of Windows Vista.

A few things to consider:

- Backup device support.
  Windows Vista's built-in file backup will backup to optical media like CDs and DVDs, hard disks and file servers. Tapes are no longer supported by the built-in tool. Tape drives are still supported for 3rd party backup solutions.
  NB: Backup to a file server is not supported on Windows Vista Home Basic Edition.
- Volume Shadow Copy Service (VSS)
  The Volume Shadow Copy Service first appeared in the Windows OS in Windows Server 2003. The service creates a snapshot of the disk, which can then be used to create a backup. VSS enables a point-in-time backup of all files on a disk without having to consider "open" files that are not available for backup. VSS also guarantees a consistent backup of all files meaning that a restored file should never be corrupt because it was in an "inconsistent state" (being changed) during backup. VSS is not used in the Home Standard and Home Premium versions of Windows Vista.
- UDF on optical media
  When optical media is used to create a backup, Windows Vista will always use the UDF file format. This makes it possible to use the CD or DVD (or anything newer) as a standard disk and add data in a later stadium.
- Backup media format
  When using a hard disk to store the backed up data, Windows Vista File backup only supports NTFS formatted volumes.
- Backup Target
  Backups can only be made on a volume different from the volume being backed up. It is recommended that the location is based on a different physical disk.

How Windows Vista File Backup works

Extension based backup

You cannot select files or file locations when backing up files with Windows Vista File Backup and Restore. You can only select a category or file type to backup. Windows Vista File Backup will backup all data of the specified category from the selected system, regardless of its location.

Scheduling backup

Windows Vista File Backup has the option to schedule backup creation at a fixed time in the future. The schedule is set up in such a way that it will try to catch up when a scheduled backup was missed, because, for instance, the system was turned off at the scheduled time or the system was running on batteries at the scheduled time.

NB: Scheduled backups are not available on Windows Vista Home Basic Edition.

Zip files

Windows Vista File Backup stores the backed up data in zip files with a size of up to about 200MB. This ensures that the files are readable by a number of applications on numerous operating systems. Windows Vista File Backup will create a new zip file with every backup operation. It will not reopen pre-existing zip files to add data in a second backup operation.

Catalog

The catalog is a file that is used to store information on which files are backed up, and where. This enables fast location of files in case of a restore operation. The catalog is saved in two locations:

- On the disk that is being backed up
  This is the central or global catalog file containing all information of every file that was ever backed up on the system.
- On the disk where the backed up data is stored
  A copy of the catalog is stored with the data being backed up on the backup location. This comes in handy in case the original disk is not available anymore.

User privileges

Only members of the local Administrators group can create or schedule a backup of a system. In order to create a backup you must at least have the "Back up files and directories" privilege (SeBackupPrivilege). This privilege enables a user to read data for creating a backup regardless the user rights specified in the ACL of the file or folder.

Users don't need administrative privileges in order to restore their own data on the system from where the files were backed up.

When restoring data to another system than the one that was used to create a backup, the user must be a member of the local administrators group, or have the "Restore files and directories" privilege (SeRestorPrivilege).

Backup caretaker notifications

The First time a backup is created using Windows Vista File Backup, it will schedule a number of actions to notify users about actions that should be taken regarding the backups. Most common notifications are:

- Backup errors
  When a backup failed, a notification will tell the user about it.
- New "Full Backup" required
  Window Vista File Backup will create a "Full Backup" the first time it runs. On subsequent runs it will only backup the changed files in a so called "Incremental Backup". Based on built-in heuristics in Windows Vista, the backup program will determine when it is appropriate to start a new "Full Backup", due to the number of media being used, or the amount of changed files since the last "Full Backup".
- More than 30 days since last backup
  Window Vista File Backup will keep track of when the latest backup took place and warn the user when a period of more than 30 days has gone by since the latest backup was performed.

4.6.3 Complete PC Backup and Restore

Complete PC Backup and Restore is a backup feature in Windows Vista that is meant for disaster recovery of complete systems. It is supported in Windows Vista Enterprise, Business, and Ultimate Editions. Complete PC Backup and Restore creates a backup of a complete volume and stores it in a VHD file. Complete PC Backup uses the Volume Shadow Copy Service to overcome problems with open files when backing up the system.

Complete PC Backup only backs up the complete system. There is no option to select which parts of the system must be backed up. The backup can be stored on an external hard disk, internal disk partition, or a set of DVDs. When the target location for the backup is selected, you will see files in the destination drive in a folder named *WindowsImagebackup\COMPUTERNAME\Backup YYYY-MM-DD*.

The backup is created in a VHD file. This is the same Virtual Hard Disk file format used by Virtual Server and Virtual PC. The VHD file can be mounted in a Virtual Machine with one of the programs mentioned above, in order to inspect its contents. Another option to inspect the contents of a Complete PC Backup or even restore parts of it, is the VHDMOUNT utility that is provided with Virtual Server 2005 SP2. VHDMOUNT enables one to mount a VHD file as a drive letter and use its contents as if it w a local drive. The VHD file created by Complete PC Backup cannot be used to boot as a Virtual Machine.

A partial restore of a Complete PC Backup is not a feature of the utilities delivered with Windows Vista. Complete System Restore is the only option. Complete System Restore can be executed in two ways:

- From the running system in the Backup and Restore Center
  This option restarts the PC with WinRE in order to proceed restoring the complete PC configuration.
- From the Windows Recovery Environment (WinRE) on the Windows Vista installation DVD
  When booting from the DVD, select the language first, and then select the Repair your computer option in the second screen. When you get to the Windows Recovery Environment screen, as shown in Figure 4-7, select the Complete PC Restore option and follow the prompts to restore the system.

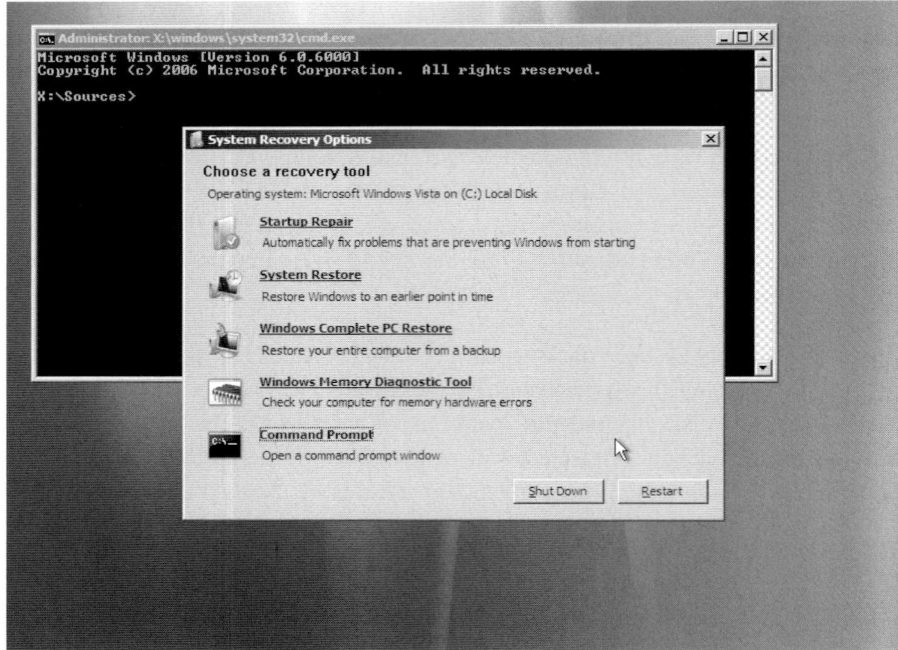

Figure 4-7 Starting Complete PC Restore from WinRE

4.6.4 Shadow Copy or Previous Versions

Windows Vista is the first desktop version of Windows that contains the Volume Shadow Copy Service. It is supported in Windows Vista Enterprise, Business and Ultimate editions. As mentioned before, this service creates a point-in-time snapshot of the data contained in the volume. This enables an easy consistent backup of all files in case of a File backup. VSS also provides the possibility to have a "do-it-yourself" easy file recovery option available for end-users.

How Previous Versions works

In order to keep track of previous versions of files on a disk, the Volume Shadow Copy service creates a snapshot daily at 4:00 AM, or, when the system is not running at the time, a dozen minutes after the system becomes idle. VSS then stores the current status of the data in the same volume. Previous versions doesn't store the whole contents of every file every time it creates a snapshot, but only stores the changes in each file. All snap-shots together should occupy no more than 15% of the volume size. Older snapshots will be deleted to free up space for new ones, when necessary.

Users can access previous versions of their data by right-clicking a file or folder and selecting "Restore previous versions." It enables the user to go back in time and access files and folders as they were on previous dates. Users can preview each file in a read-only version to determine which file to restore. Then, to fully restore it, they can just drag the file to a folder, or select it and click "Restore" to restore it to its original location. As shown in the picture, the previous versions UI also shows files backed up using Windows Vista File Backup. In order to successfully restore those files, the backup media must be provided.

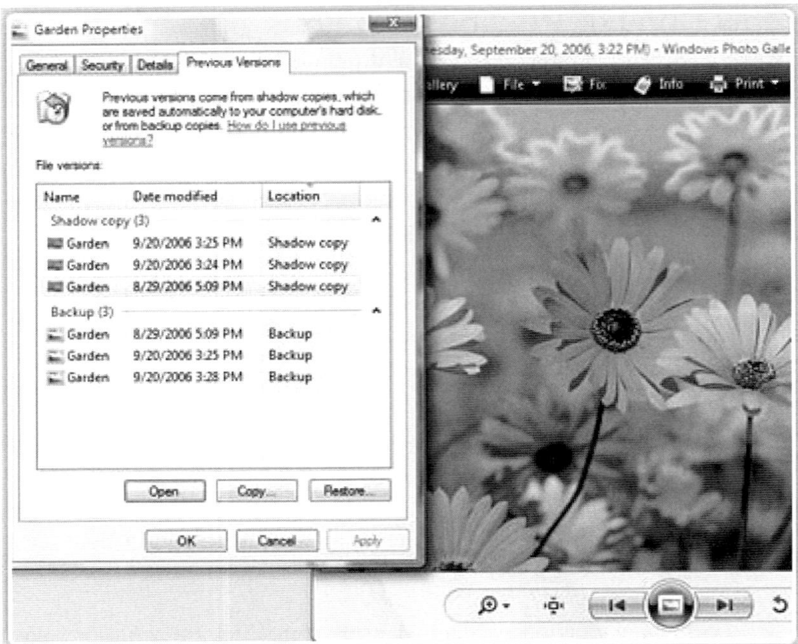

Figure 4-8 Previous versions UI

The Previous Versions feature works on single files as well as whole folders. When restoring a file, all previous versions that are different from the live copy on the disk are shown. When accessing a previous version of a folder, users can browse the folder hierarchy as it was in a previous point in time.

4.6.5 System Protection

System Restore was introduced in Windows XP, to enable people to restore their computers to an earlier state without losing data. Functionally nothing really changed in the concept, except that System Protection in Windows Vista uses the Volume Shadow Copy service under the hood.

Restore Points

Just like Windows XP, Windows Vista uses Protection Points to store previous states of a system. The technical implementation is different, because Windows Vista uses VSS to provide this functionality. A protection point is a VSS snapshot of a collection of disks containing the system state at a certain time.

Configuring System Protection

System Protection in Windows Vista is enabled on a per volume basis. In the UI this can be done by going to the Control Panel>System and choosing "Advanced System Settings" - this will open the System Properties dialog. Then click on the "System Protection" tab. In the box "Available disks:", select the disks to be protected.

To manually create a protection point, click on the "Create…" button on the "System Protection" tab. You should then see an information dialog stating the protection point is being created, followed by one stating that the protection point has been created successfully.

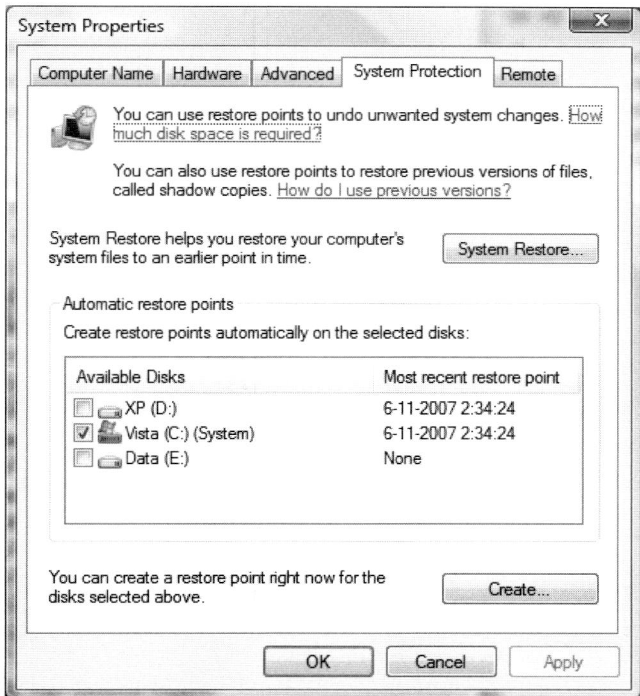

Figure 4-9 Configure System Protection

Restoring a computer to an earlier state

System Restore can be accessed from the System Protection Tab used above by clicking on the "Click here to roll back unwanted system changes" link, or alternatively, through Start>All Programs>Accessories>System Tools>System Restore.

When the System Restore Dialog opens you will be presented with two choices which will differ, depending on whether you have previously restored the system state or not. The first choice will be either to restore to the most recent protection point, or to undo the latest system restore. The second choice will allow you to choose a protection point from a list.

Figure 4-10 System Restore UI

Change the disk space used for System Restore

System Restore by default will take up to 15% of the volume size. This space can be customized.

Use an elevated command prompt to type the following:

```
vssadmin resize shadowstorage /on=<Volume>:
/For=<Volume>: /MaxSize=<Number>GB
```

Where <Volume> stands for the drive letter to be customized and <Number> stands for the number of Gigabytes to be used for System Restore.

4.7 Reliability and Performance snap-in

The Reliability and Performance snap-in in Windows Vista is a new performance reporting and troubleshooting tool, that replaces Performance Monitor and adds some new functionality that makes life a lot easier when troubleshooting performance and reliability issues with Windows Vista.

4.7.1 Resource Overview

When you start the tool, you first enter the Resource Overview. Resource Overview is my Task Manager on steroids. It shows resource use of CPU, Disks, Network and Memory in a single view. At the same time, it allows you to zoom in on each of these on the process level, to find out what process is stressing the particular resource. Use the column headers to sort the processes based on any column in the table. Locating a process and file that, for example, stresses the disk a little bit too much, is a breeze this way.

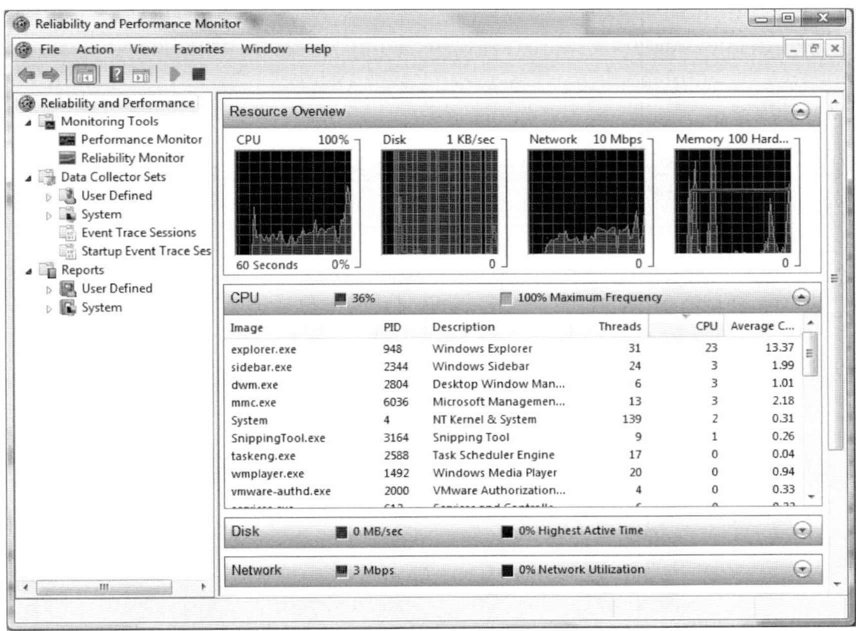

Figure 4-11 Reliability and Performance Monitor default view

4.7.2 Performance Monitor

Good old Performance Monitor is still there in Windows Vista. Only now it is part of the Reliability and Performance Monitor. Its functionality is still the same, though you will find a number of new performance categories when you start adding counters to the output graph or report. A custom view in Performance Monitor can be exported as a Data Collector Set for use with performance and logging features in the Reliability and Performance Snap-in.

4.7.3 Reliability Monitor

Reliability Monitor is a new tool in Windows Vista, that provides a system stability overview and trend analysis about events that possibly affect system stability. These events include hard- and software installation, operating system updates and hardware failures. Reliability Monitor calculates the System Stability Index that reflects whether unexpected problems reduced the stability of the system. The graph that shows the Stability Index over time, provides a quick overview of the moment when problems began to occur, and what might have been the cause of those problems. The System Stability Report in the bottom of the screen gives detailed information about each failure or software install event.

The graph, in combination with the System Stability Report, provides an excellent combination of information to view how system changes may have impacted the overall stability of Windows Vista.

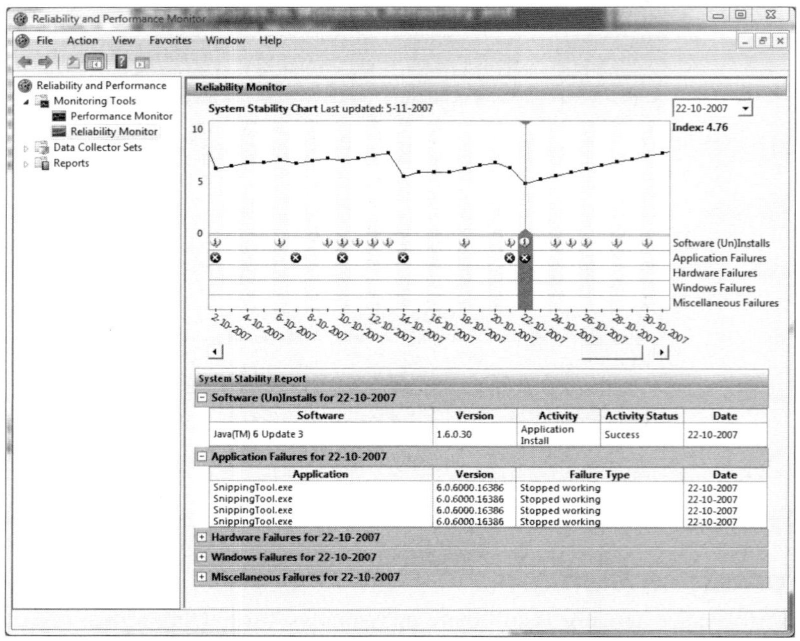

Figure 4-12 Reliability Monitor

4.8 Windows Recovery Environment (WinRE)

Windows Recovery Environment (WinRE) is a recovery solution based on Windows PE. WinRE has two main functions:

- Automatic repair of boot problems.
- Central platform for advanced recovery tools. Namely:
  - System Restore
  - Complete PC Restore
  - Windows Memory Diagnostic Tool
  - Windows PE command prompt with tools like DISKPART

WinRE replaces the recovery console in Windows XP. WinRE is available on the Windows Vista install DVD. Choose repair from the start screen to start WinRE.

WinRE can also be started from the network, using WDS, or from the local hard disk as a repair option. In order to do this, you first have to build your own WinRE image.

Building the WinRE image

1. Create a local WinRE image folder. For instance *C:\WinRE*

```
MD WinRE
```

2. Extract WinRE from boot.wim on the Windows Vista product DVD:

```
imagex /export /boot d:\sources\boot.wim 2
c:\WinRE\WinRE.wim "Windows Recovery Environment"
```

3. Create a mount folder to customize *WinRE.wim*:

```
MD c:\WinRE\Mount
```

4. Mount WinRE.wim to the mount folder:

```
imagex /mountrw c:\winre\WinRE.wim 1 c:\WinRE\Mount
```

5. Create a text file *winpeshl.ini* in *C:\WinRE\Mount\Windows\System32* with the following contents:

```
[LaunchApp]
```

```
AppPath=x:\sources\recovery\recenv.exe
```

6. Inject required drivers in WinRE:

```
peimg /inf=c:\drivers\driver.inf c:\WinRE\Mount\Windows
```

7. Copy extra required tools to *c:\WinRE\Mount* or one of the subfolders.
8. Unmount the *WinRE.wim* storing all changes:

```
imagex /unmount /commit C:\WinRE\Mount
```

The resulting file *WinRE.wim* can be used to boot from the network using WDS.

Note: Windows AIK does not support the creation of a Windows RE solution using the base Windows PE image (Windows PE.wim).

You can also create an ISO and burn it to CD using oscdimg. This procedure is described in chapter 3.5.6 Booting Windows PE from a USB stick or CD ROM

When installing WinRE on the local hard drive, you should follow a number of guidelines:

- WinRE must not be installed in the OS partition with Windows Vista. This is to make sure that WinRE can still boot when booting the OS is no longer possible.
- The WinRE partition should be hidden in order to prevent accidental deletion or corruption by the end user.
- It is best practice to create the WinRE partition before the OS partition. Hidden partitions created after the OS partition may interfere with advanced volume management functionalities like dynamic partitions.

A hidden partition for WinRE should be assigned a special type:

- On a MBR disk, the partition should be assigned type 0x27.
- On a GPT disk, the partition should be assigned type {DE94BBA4-06D1-4D40-A16A-BFD50179D6AC}.

In the following procedure we assume you are installing WinRE on a clean system.

Creating the WinRE partition on a clean system

1. Open a command prompt in Windows PE.
2. Start **DISKPART** and type the following commands to create the first partition:

```
SELECT DISK 0
CLEAN
CREATE PARTITION PRIMARY SIZE=1500
ASSIGN LETTER=R
ACTIVE
FORMAT FS=NTFS QUICK
```

3. Now type the following commands to create the OS Partition:

```
CREATE PARTITION PRIMARY
ASSIGN LETTER=C
FORMAT FS=NTFS QUICK
EXIT
```

Now make sure the required files for booting WinRE are in place.

Copy the required files to the WinRE partition

1. Copy WinRE.wim to the WinRE partition.

```
copy c:\WinRE\WinRE.wim R:\
```

2. Copy *boot.sdi* from *C:\Program Files\Windows AIK\Tools\PETools\x86\boot*.

```
copy C:\Program Files\Windows
AIK\Tools\PETools\x86\boot\boot.sdi R:\
```

With all files in place, we only have to make sure Windows knows where to locate WinRE in case of an emergency. Windows AIK provides a script that will do just that.

Configure the system for WinRE

1. Open a Command prompt with administrative privileges.
2. Use *SetAutoFailover.cmd* in *C:\Program Files\Windows AIK\Recovery*.

```
SetAutoFailover.cmd /target R: /wim /hide
```

Note: This command will hide the WinRE partition. If you don't want to hide this partition, use /nohide for the last parameter.

WinRE is now ready to run. All we have to do now, is tell the system to boot WinRE:

Testing WinRE

1. Restart the computer.
2. Press **F8** when the system starts booting, just after BIOS initialization.
3. Select the first item in de menu "**Repair your computer**".
4. This will start WinRE.

4.9 Remote Desktop and Remote Assistance

Windows Vista Remote Desktop is based on the next version of the Remote Desktop Protocol. RDP 6.0 contains a number of security enhancements that must overcome some obvious shortcomings of Terminal Services, or Remote Desktop in Windows XP and Windows Server 2003. A new version of the Terminal Server Client software is launched together with the server side component. The new terminal server client is available both in Windows Vista out-of-the-box and for Windows XP and Windows Server 2003 as a downloadable component.

4.9.1 What's new in Remote Desktop

Terminal Services in previous versions of Windows, somehow did not really feel safe when the remote desktop was published to the Internet. In a certain sense it always felt like you were putting a keyboard, monitor and mouse on the streets for anybody to give it a try. The answer to this is Network Level Authentication, or NLA. With Network Level Authentication, the server side of a Terminal Server session proves its authenticity using a computer certificate. After the server has proven authenticity, the client provides the user credentials. When the user is positively authenticated, the server creates a new session for the user to logon. In the default configuration, the user will now automatically logon to the session.

NLA provides the following security enhancements:

- Two way authentication
  Before the client provides the user credentials for the session, the server must first prove its identity to the client. In this way it is much less probable that the user credentials are provided to a rogue system. The creation of a secure session also prevents a man-in-the-middle attack from taking place.
- Session creation after user authentication
  With NLA, the new session is only created after user authentication. This prevents the unnecessary creation of sessions. In theory, an attacker of an old style terminal server on Windows XP or Windows Server 2003, can possibly create a Denial of Service attack through creating numerous sessions on a terminal server, and thus effectively draining available resources. The creation of a new session after user authentication prevents this kind of attack.

When configuring Remote Desktop on Windows Vista, you will see the following options:

- **Don't allow connections to this computer**
  This option prevents anyone from connecting to your computer using Remote Desktop or Remote Programs.
- **Allow connections from computers running any version of Remote Desktop**
  This option allows any version of Remote Desktop or Remote Programs to connect to your computer. This is what you need when working in a mixed environment where not all clients support NLA.
- **Allow connections only from computers running Remote Desktop with Network Level Authentication**
  This option allows only NLA-supported connections to Remote Desktop. Remote Desktop Connection clients without NLA-support will be denied access.

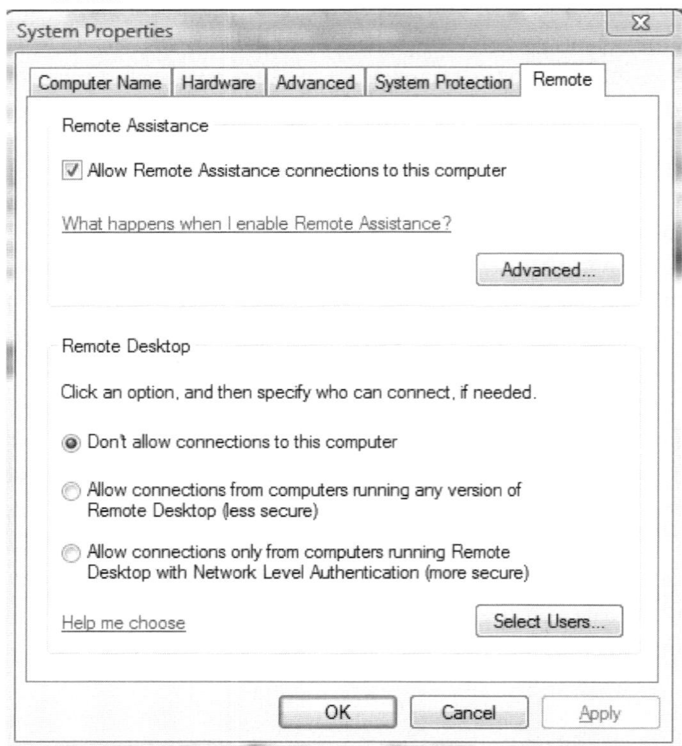

Figure 4-13 Remote Desktop configuration

4.9.2 Remote Desktop Client 6.x

Windows Vista has Remote Desktop Client 6.x built-in. Remote Desktop client 6.x provides the following new features:

- Support for Network Level Authentication
- Support for dual monitor setup
- Support for seamless applications (remote programs)
- Cached credentials for remote sessions
- Support for the Terminal Services Gateway Server

Except for the new features, the new client has also changed its behavior in certain common situations.

- The pre-populated username used to be the last username used in any remote connection. In Remote Desktop client 6.x it is the last username used when connecting to the specific system. This means that every first time a connection is setup to a system, the username will be blank.
- There is no Domain Name field in the logon screen. Just like Windows Vista, the domain name field is no longer available in the logon dialog box. Usernames must be specified with the domain name as USERDOMAIN\USERNAME or USERNAME@userdomain. When only the username is specified, the client will assume that the user is defined in the computer name specified in the connection string. As a result of this assumption, the client will change the username to 127.0.0.1\USERNAME when connecting to 127.0.0.1.

The following paragraphs discuss the new features, and how they can be used.

Support for Network Level Authentication

Remote Desktop Client 6.x supports Network Level Authentication. Network Level Authentication is available for remote computers running Windows Vista or Windows Server 2008. Windows Server 2003, Windows XP and earlier operating systems don't support Network Level Authentication.

There are three authentication options available:

- Always connect, even if authentication fails (least secure)
  With this option, even if Remote Desktop Connection cannot verify the identity of the remote computer, it connects anyway. This option will be

commonly used when connecting to systems that don't support Network Level Authentication.

- Warn me if authentication fails (more secure)
  With this option, Remote Desktop Connection warns you when it cannot verify the identity of the remote computer, so that you can choose whether to proceed with the connection or not.
- Do not connect if authentication fails (most secure)
  With this option, Remote Desktop Connection will only connect when it is able to verify the identity of the remote computer.

The default setting in Windows Vista is: "Warn me if authentication fails." To save another setting for future use, select the appropriate authentication level, and then, on the General tab, click Save or Save As to save the settings to a .rdp file.

Support for Dual Monitor Setup

When working on a dual monitor system, you can start a Remote Desktop session that spans both monitors. The monitors must be the same height, and aligned side by side. To start a session that spans both monitors, type mstsc /span.

Use CTRL-ALT-BREAK to toggle in and out of full-screen spanned mode.

Support for seamless applications (remote programs)

Remote programs is a feature of the next version of Terminal Services running on Windows Server 2008. Remote Programs enables starting an application in a Terminal Server session without a remote desktop. This makes the remote program look like it is running on the local system.

Cached credentials for remote sessions

Remote Desktop Client 6.x remembers usernames per connected system. Optionally, Remote Desktop Client 6.x also stores the password used to logon to the session. This option can be controlled through Group Policy. Both on the user level and computer level there is a setting "Do not allow passwords to be saved", under "Windows Components\Terminal Services\Remote Desktop Connection Client". Enabling this setting disables the possibility to save user credentials for Remote Desktop Client.

Besides disallowing password caching on the client side, administrators on the server side can also force the logon screen to appear whenever the Remote Desktop Client connects. The server administrator can do this in two ways:

1. By selecting the "Always prompt for password" setting on the server. This setting is located in the Terminal Server Configuration administrative tool (tscc.msc) on the tab "Logon Settings" in the "RDP-Tcp Properties" dialog box. On Windows 2000 systems, this setting is enabled by default.
2. Windows Server 2003 has a Group Policy setting "Always prompt client for password upon connection", under "Administrative Templates\Windows Components\Terminal Services\Terminal Server\Security". Enabling this setting will force all systems to prompt for a password after the remote desktop session is created, regardless of which version of the Remote Desktop Client is running.

Support for Terminal Services Gateway Server

A Terminal Services Gateway (TS Gateway) server enables tunneling RDP through a Secure Sockets Layer (SSL) tunnel. As RDP port 3389 is almost always blocked on firewalls connecting to the Internet, it is often hard or impossible to connect to a remote desktop session from a corporate network. With a TS Gateway, the firewall cannot distinguish the Remote Desktop session from an ordinary https connection. The TS Gateway is a new feature for Windows that will be made available on Windows Server 2008. Windows Server 2003 does not provide a TS Gateway Server.

A TS Gateway server can be configured on the Remote Desktop Client as follows:

1. Start mstsc.exe.
2. Click Options, click the Advanced tab, and then, under Connect from anywhere, click Settings.
3. Select Use these TS Gateway server settings and then type the server name (ask your network administrator for this information).
4. Select one of the three available logon methods:
    a. Allow me to select later. This option lets you select a logon method when you connect.
    b. Ask for password (NTLM). This option prompts you for a password when you connect.
    c. Smart card. This option prompts you to insert a smart card when you connect.
5. Select or clear the Bypass TS Gateway server for local addresses check box. Selecting this check box prevents traffic to and from local network addresses from being routed through the TS Gateway server, which can make your connection faster.

Configuration of a TS Gateway server can be prevented through Group Policy. User settings for TS Gateway are defined under "Windows Components\Terminal Services\TS Gateway".

4.9.3 Remote Assistance

Windows Vista also has the Remote Assistance functionality of Windows XP. In Remote Assistance, a User can get help from an Expert. When this happens, both users involved are looking at the same desktop with the same logon credentials and can share control of the desktop. With Remote Desktop, when the remote user logs in, the interactively logged on user is logged out.

Just like Remote Desktop, Remote Assistance is based on the RDP protocol. The big difference with Windows XP is that in Windows XP, Remote Assistance uses TCP port 3389 (the same port as Remote Desktop). Windows Vista uses a dynamic port in the range of TCP/UDP 49152-65535.

New features for remote assistance in Windows Vista are:

- NAT Traversal
  Remote Assistance creates a peer-to-peer connection between the helper and user PC. Windows Vista uses IPv6 Teredo technology to traverse NAT routers between the two systems.
- Command line features
  Windows Vista features a new command line program msra.exe to create RA request files or offer RA as an Expert.
- UAC integration
  RA is completely aware of UAC. When the user is not an admin on the local system, the Expert will not be able to see the consent UI or respond to it[5]. When the user is an Admin, he or she can configure whether the expert will be able to respond to UAC prompts.
- Encrypted request files
  Windows Vista encrypts information in the RA file so that the hostname or IP address of the requesting host cannot be extracted by untrustworthy parties.

Initiating Remote Assistance

Remote Assistance or RA can be initiated in several ways:

---

[5] Windows Vista Service Pack 1 offers the option to enable the UAC prompt for the Helper when the user is not a member of the Administrators Group.

Initiated by the user:

- Using the Remote Assistance program
- From the command line using msra.exe
- From MSN Messenger

Initiated by the expert:

- Using the Remote Assistance program
- From the command line using msra.exe
- From MSN Messenger

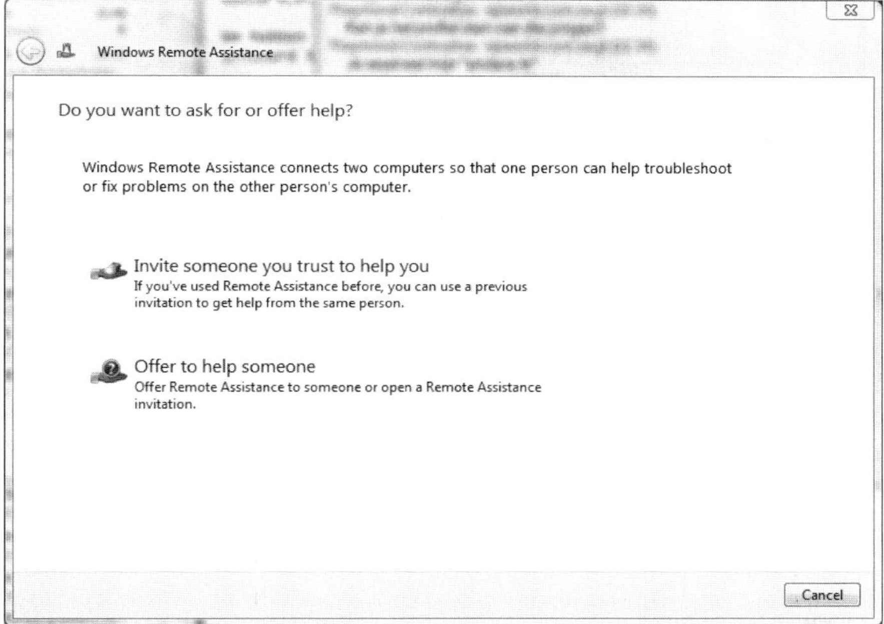

Figure 4-14 Windows Remote Assistance wizard

Users can create an invitation for remote assistance using the Remote Assistance program in the start menu, or from the command line using *MSRA.EXE*. The invitation can be stored in a file or sent by e-mail. The default request file is compatible with Windows XP. Compatibility with Windows XP can be disabled in Group Policy. Windows Vista-only invitations can be encrypted to hide information like the users' IP address and computer name.

MSRA.EXE is used to initiate RA sessions from the command line. Here is a list of common operations with *MSRA.EXE*:

Command	Task
`Msra /novice`	Open the RA program in the novice page that allows the user to use e-mail to send an invitation, or save the invitation as a file.
`Msra /expert`	Open the RA program in the expert page that allows to enter an invitation file or type the IP address or name of the user system.
`Msra /offerRA <computer>`	Offer RA as an expert using DCOM and open RA on the user's computer to accept the session.
`Msra /saveasfile <path> <password>`[6]	Save a RA request file in <path> and protect it with the password <password>.
`Msra /openfile <path> <password>`[6]	Open a RA request file in <path> with the password <password> to setup an RA session as an expert.

Remote Assistance Network configuration

Remote Assistance can use IPv6 and Teredo to provide NAT-traversal between the helper and the user. This enables scenarios where one or both are located behind NAT routers. You may remember that NAT traversal was also possible with Windows XP, using UPnP. That is true, but Windows Vista also traverses NAT through non-UPnP NAT routers, with one restriction: the NAT routers must not be symmetric NAT routers. Remote Assistance will not work when the router is configured to block all UDP traffic.

Remote Assistance also integrates with Windows Firewall with Advanced Security in Windows Vista. The networking chapter describes the three network profiles of the new firewall in Windows Vista. By default, only the Private profile allows the

[6] The password must be six characters or more.

use of RA. In order to use RA in a corporate environment, RA must be specifically allowed by the system administrator.

Offering Remote Assistance

With offered Remote Assistance, the Remote Assistance session is initiated by the helper using DCOM. In order to offer remote assistance, the following requirements apply:

- You can only offer Remote Assistance from a system running Windows Vista to another system running Windows Vista. Windows XP uses a different authentication mechanism for offered remote assistance, which is not compatible.
- You must know the hostname, or FQDN, or the IP address of the user's computer.
- Your account, or the designated group that you are a member of, must be configured in Group Policy as Helpers who are allowed to offer Remote Assistance.

Windows Firewall must be configured to allow Offered Remote Assistance. This is the default for the Private firewall profile, but not for other profiles.

Remote Assistance between Vista and Windows XP

Remote Assistance in Windows Vista is backwards compatible with Windows XP, with the exception of the operations in the following list:

- Offer RA from XP to Vista
  It is not possible to offer RA from a system running XP to a user running a Windows Vista system. Offering RA requires that the expert is running Windows Vista.
- Voice support is not available in Vista
  This feature is removed from RA in Windows Vista.
- Offer RA from Messenger
  Offering RA from Live Messenger is a new feature of Windows Vista and not supported in Windows XP.
- Use Teredo for NAT traversal
  Using Teredo to traverse NAT routers is only available when RA is used between two systems running Windows Vista.

5 Securing Windows Vista

5.1 User Account Control

User Account Control or UAC is probably the most discussed feature of Windows Vista ever. It is the typical example of how security often hurts user-friendliness in IT. If you have ever worked for a large company with a fully-fledged IT Risk Management (IRM) department, you know what I mean. If you haven't, here is a little bit of theory behind the fact that so many people hate UAC.

5.1.1 The security triangle

Whenever you design an IT infrastructure, you will have to make choices. These may be choices about features offered to end-users, or restrictions on whatever they need to do on a system. When security is involved, you will also find out very soon that whatever you want to do to increase the level of security, you will always hurt somebody, somewhere. This is the natural trade-off between usability and security. There must have been lots of discussions going on in the UAC product team at Microsoft about how intrusive the feature is supposed to be, and where it will or will not hurt usability. The basis for all this pain still is this simple triangle that you will also meet when you implement a new infrastructure, and have to keep security in mind.

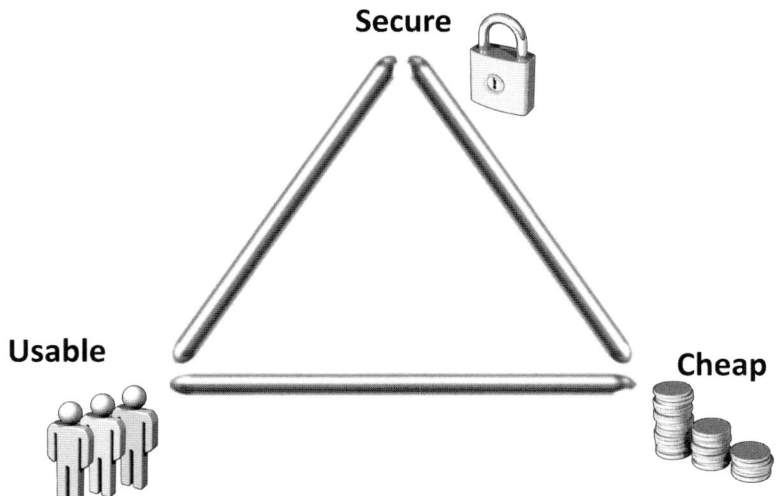

Figure 5-1 Security Triangle

Whenever you start designing, you must choose two of these items. When you decide that security is not important at all, you might just leave Windows Vista and move on while using Windows ME ;-)

5.1.2 What is UAC about?

Before you will be able to understand how UAC actually works, it is good to have a fundamental understanding of how Windows defines your possibilities on a system. When you logon to a system, a security token is created for your account. The token consists of the groups you are a member of and the privileges you have. Every time you try to access something in Windows, like a file or a registry key, Windows will view your token to check if you have the correct group membership or right to access the specific object, or perform the requested action. In Windows XP and previous NT based versions of Windows, this created potentially harmful situations when you logged on as an Administrator. Your token contained the group memberships and rights to do about everything you can think of (even when you didn't want to do it). That's why it has been best practice for a while not to use a privileged account for you daily work. This is sometimes hard, because there is so much you cannot do when you use a standard user account. Even the run as command does not offer a solution, because that starts a process as a DIFFERENT user.

Looking at alternative operating systems, you see quite the same issues. One way of solving the issue is by logging on without the powerful privileges and then adding those when needed. Let's say Microsoft did not exactly invent the wheel with UAC. The fact is, this is exactly what's happening.

When you logon to a default Windows Vista system with an administrator account, you actually get two tokens:

- One with all the group memberships and privileges you have. This is the same token you would get on any pre-Vista system. This token is called the "administrator access token".
- The second token is the stripped token. It is called the "standard user access token". "Standard user" stands for a user without administrative group memberships and privileges. Windows XP used to have something like this, but that was called a "restricted user" at that time.

The default mode for UAC in Windows Vista is called "administrator in Administrative approval mode". Being in this mode means that Windows Vista will ignore the administrator access token when you logon. Even when you are an administrator it will treat you as if you are a standard user. That is to say, until you start doing something that might need administrative privileges. At that moment, Windows Vista will present you with the “Consent UI”. Around this time you probably start thinking: “(beeped), wasn’t I already logged on as an admin?” Well you are, but Windows is now warning you, saying: “If you are sure you want to move on doing this with your administrator token, click Continue.” Now your administrator access token kicks in and you will be able to do what you want to do as an administrator.

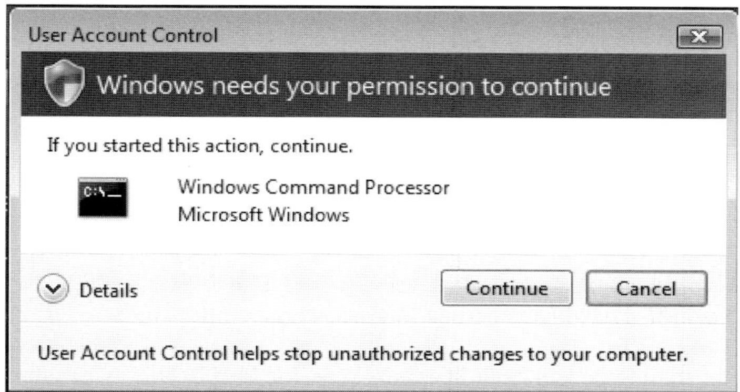

Figure 5-2 Consent UI

In larger organizations, most users probably don't logon on their system as an administrator. In those cases the impact of UAC will be much less than for home users who log on as administrator all the time. I suppose there still is a benefit for UAC in a corporate environment, where administrators who still use privileged accounts for daily use at least don’t turn off UAC, and will notice when they unintentionally change the configuration of their environment through malware.

5.1.3 What does UAC strip from the access token?

When you logon to a Windows system, your access token is created in RAM. The access token on a Windows Vista system will consist of the following items:

- The user SID
- The SIDs of the groups you're a member of
- Your privileges
- Your Windows integrity level

You can tell what your access token looks like, using the following command:

```
Whoami /all
```

The User SID

The user SID or Security ID is the representation of your account in Windows. When Windows looks for an account, it will always look for the SID and not for a user name. Every user in Windows has a unique user SID. The user account SID in Windows looks like:

S-1-5-21-domainID-relativeID

DomainID is a 96-bit number that identifies the user database where the account is located. This can be a domain or the local SAM of a workstation. The relative ID or RID defines the location of the account in the database. For non-built in accounts the RID counter starts at 1000. A very well known RID for a built-in account is 500, which is used for the built-in administrator account. Knowing this, you can always tell that S-1-5-54321-500 stands for the built in administrator account of a system, while S-1-5-54321-1234 is an account that was created afterwards.

The user SID will be maintained in both access tokens for UAC. This is because this SID represents your account in Windows, and actually, the user SID is you.

Group SIDs

After the user SID, the token consists of a list of groups that you're a member of. These groups can be:

- Domain Local Groups
- Global Groups in the domain
- Universal groups in the domain
- Built-in local groups
- Normal local groups

Groups are also listed as SIDs. Group SIDs are slightly different from user SIDs, as not all of them start with S-1-5-21. Built-in SIDs do not contain a DomainID and may look like S-1-5-32-544 (this is the Built-in Administrators group). There are also a couple of special groups whose membership depends on the way you logged on, like Interactive (S-1-5-4) or Everyone (S-1-1-0).

When logging on to Windows Vista, UAC only looks at four built-in groups and strips those from the access token, to create the standard user access token. All other group memberships will remain unchanged from the original administrator access token. The four groups stripped from the access token are:

1. BUILTIN\Administrators

2. BUILTIN\Backup Operators

3. BUILTIN\Power Users

4. BUILTIN\Network Configuration Operators

Don't be surprised when you see that your membership of the Domain Administrators group continues to remain in the standard user access token.

Privileges

Besides SIDs that are used to evaluate whether or not to give access to objects, users get privileges or rights to perform certain tasks. Rights refer to the way that Windows controls whether you can or can't log onto something, so the ability to "log onto this machine locally" or "deny access to this machine over the network" are rights. All other abilities are called "Privileges".[7]

Windows Vista defines 34 different user privileges and 10 different user rights. You find them in the "Security Settings" section of the Group Policy Editor as User Rights. In the Group Policy Editor you will see nice-looking names like "Change the system time" or "Debug programs". Programmers and internal Windows structures will usually refer to more cryptic names like SeSystemTimePrivilege or seDebugPrivilege. Those are different names for the same thing. I will not discuss all 44 privileges and rights in this chapter. Let's see what the new ones are and which ones are important for UAC.

New privileges and rights:

- Access Credential Manager as a trusted caller
- Change the time zone

---

[7] Taken from "Administering Windows Vista Security – The Big Surprises" by Mark Minasi

UAC has a list of nine potentially dangerous privileges. It is this list of privileges that UAC will strip from your account when you logon to Windows Vista.

1 Create a token object (SeCreateTokenPrivilege)
2 Act as part of the operating system (SeTcbPrivilege)
3 Take ownership of files and other objects (SeTakeOwnershipPrivilege)
4 Load and unload device drivers (SeLoadDriverPrivilege)
5 Back up files and directories (SeBackupPrivilege)
6 Restore files and directories (SeRestorPrivilege)
7 Impersonate a client after authentication (SeImpersonatePrivilege)
8 Modify an object label (SeRelabelPrivilege)
9 Debug Programs (SeDebugPrivilege)

Windows Integrity level

The Windows Integrity level is a completely new concept for Windows Vista. For those who have studied security concepts, it is Microsoft's first implementation of a mandatory access control system. I guess it will be worked out in more detail in upcoming versions of Windows after the release of Windows Server 2008. The Windows Integrity Level is a way of describing to what extent the operating system will trust a process. There are six levels of Windows Integrity. The Windows Integrity level is shown in the access token as an SID. It looks like S—1-116-*value*. Usually you will see four of these in Windows Vista.

Mandatory Level	SID	Description
Low	S-1-16-4096	The Low Mandatory Level is used to run less trusted processes. Everything from the Internet including Internet Explorer in protected mode will run at the low mandatory level.
Medium	S-1-16-8192	The Medium Mandatory level is given to all processes running as a standard user.
High	S-1-16-122288	The High Mandatory level is given to processes running with the administrator access token.
System	S-1-16-16384	The System Mandatory level is only given to system processes that have unrestricted access to all system resources.

The main idea behind Windows Integrity, is that some "thing" with a low integrity level is never able to start messing around with something at a higher integrity level. As everything from the Internet is now running at the low integrity level, it is much harder for a downloaded piece of software to start changing stuff without at least triggering UAC and requesting the user if this is supposed to happen.

In Windows Vista the Administrator access token contains the High Mandatory Level SID (S-1-16-12288) and the Standard user access token contains the Medium Mandatory Level SID (S-16-8192).

5.1.4 When does the Consent UI kick in?

While working with Windows Vista, you will find that in a lot of cases you experience that increased privileges will be needed before even starting the program you just tried to initiate. In fact, besides just defining a program to always "Run as administrator" Windows will use some "intelligence" to determine whether or not you need administrative powers to run a certain program. Windows Vista will look at the following aspects of a program in order to decide to fire up the consent UI:

- The Manifest with or in an exe-file
  The manifest is a description of how a program is supposed to be executed for successful operation. The Manifest can for example be used to define which privilege level is needed. The Manifest can be in the file (internal), or it can be a .manifest file in the same folder as the executable (external). Based on the manifest, Windows Vista decides if administrative privileges are needed and shows the consent UI.
- The file name
  When the filename contains “setup” or “install”, Windows Vista will think the program will need administrative privileges and show the consent UI.
- Program compatibility Assistant
  Windows Vista keeps an eye on executed programs. When a program ends unexpectedly with an error, the Program Compatibility Assistant may come to the rescue and try elevated operation of the program for successful execution.
- Vista's internal compatibility database
  Windows Vista has an internal database with information about how certain programs must be executed. For instance, this can be the requirement for a program to run with elevated privileges. The internal compatibility database can be edited with the Application Compatibility Toolkit 5.0.

5.1.5 UAC Group Policy options

UAC is managed in Group Policy as a part of the Security Configuration Options. These are found under: **Computer Configuration | Windows Settings | Security Settings | Local Policies | Security Options**

Here is the list of configurable options:

Policy	Security Setting
User Account Control: Admin Approval Mode for the Built-in Administrator account	Disabled
User Account Control: Allow UIAccess applications to prompt for elevation without using the secure desktop	Disabled
User Account Control: Behavior of the elevation prompt for administrators in Admin Approval Mode	Prompt for consent
User Account Control: Behavior of the elevation prompt for standard users	Prompt for credentials
User Account Control: Detect application installations and prompt for elevation	Enabled
User Account Control: Only elevate executables that are signed and validated	Disabled
User Account Control: Only elevate UIAccess applications that are installed in secure locations	Enabled
User Account Control: Run all administrators in Admin Approval Mode	Enabled
User Account Control: Switch to the secure desktop when prompting for elevation	Enabled
User Account Control: Virtualize file and registry write failures to per-user locations	Enabled

Figure 5-3 User Account Control settings in Group Policy

- Admin Approval Mode for the Built-in Administrator Account
  This option enables the UAC for the built-in Administrator account. This account is disabled by default, just like the policy.
- Allow UIAccess applications to prompt for elevation without using the secure desktop
  This option enables an expert to use UAC for elevation during a Remote Access session.
- Behavior of the elevation prompt for administrators in Admin Approval Mode
  This option controls what UI will be presented to members of the local Administrators group when elevation is needed. The options here are:
  - Elevate without prompting
  - Prompt for credentials
  - Prompt for consent (default)
- Behavior of the elevation prompt for standard users
  This setting controls the UI presented to standard users, when elevation is needed. The options are:
  - Prompt for credentials (default)
  - Automatically deny elevation requests
- Detect application installations and prompt for elevation
  Enable the heuristic detection of install programs by Windows so that an installation is detected beforehand and elevated.
- Only elevate executables that are signed and validated

Enforces that executables are signed with a valid certificate before elevation is allowed.

- Only elevate UIAccess applications that are installed in secure locations
  When this setting is enabled, UAC will only allow elevation for UIAccess authorized programs that are located in %windir%, %programfiles% and their subfolders.
- Run all administrators in Admin Approval Mode
  Setting this policy removes the possibility for a member of the local Administrators group to disable UAC.
- Switch to the secure desktop when prompting for elevation
  The secure desktop ensures that only approved system components can access the consent UI. In some circumstances this causes issues (mostly with display operation). This setting disables the secure desktop and may therefore lower the security level of the system.
- Virtualize file and registry write failures to per-user locations
  Use this setting to control the operation of File and Registry virtualization

5.2 File and Registry Virtualization

With Windows Vista, Microsoft is seriously trying to change the landscape of users running applications on a workstation, by removing their administrative privileges by default. The fact that users without administrative rights cannot write to certain areas of the file system and registry is not new to Window Vista. Actually, Windows XP disallowed writing to %SystemRoot%\, %windir% and %ProgramFiles% by default, just like it did to HKEY_LOCAL_MACHINE in the registry. Only Windows XP did not take away the administrative privileges by default.

Vista being stricter regarding the fact that you actually log on as a non-administrator, required Microsoft to put some compatibility fixes in the operating system to ease the pain for the users that still use software that wasn't written with those security aspects in mind. And that wasn't only 3rd party software. Even Microsoft's own Visual Studio Express tries to store new projects in its Program Files directory.

5.2.1 What is File and Registry virtualization?

When Microsoft developed Windows Vista, they realized that just taking away administrative privileges from users would break a lot of applications. That's why they needed a fix to make sure that for the time being those old applications - that do not behave according to windows security best practices - keep working on the new operating system. File and Registry virtualization is the fix for these applications.

File and Registry virtualization will make a "misbehaving" application – running as a standard user - think it is still allowed to write to one of the well known "no go areas", while the data is actually stored in a different location that is fully accessible for a standard user account. So when an application tries to write data to HKLM\Software, it is redirected to another location in HKCU instead of being presented an "Access Denied" message. The same thing happens when an application tries to write data to let's say C:\. Without the user being confronted with an "Access Denied" message, the data is written to a per-user alternative location. The consecutive read action also gets redirected to the alternative location, so that the application gets back the data that was redirected earlier.

Windows File and Registry virtualization is a temporary workaround that is planned to be removed from the version of Windows following Windows Vista.

5.2.2 When are files and registry entries virtualized

Windows File and Registry Virtualization will only kick in under the following circumstances:

- When the user is logged on as a standard user or administrator in Administrator approval mode
- When the application is not a part of Windows Vista
- When the application is not a 64-bit application
- When UAC is enabled
- When the application tries to write to a specific file or registry location where it has no write permissions
- The user running the application is logged on locally
- When the registry key is not marked as "dont_virtualize" (see chapter 5.2.4)

5.2.3 How File virtualization works

File Virtualization only virtualizes the following folders:

- %windir% and its subfolders
- \Program Files and its subfolders
- \Program Files (x86) and its subfolders

This list cannot be extended.

All redirected files are stored in the following location:

- *%USERPROFILE%\AppData\Local\VirtualStore*

When a virtualized application tries to store a file in *C:\Windows*, for instance, the write action gets redirected to:

- *C:\Users\username\AppData\Local\virtualStore\Windows.*

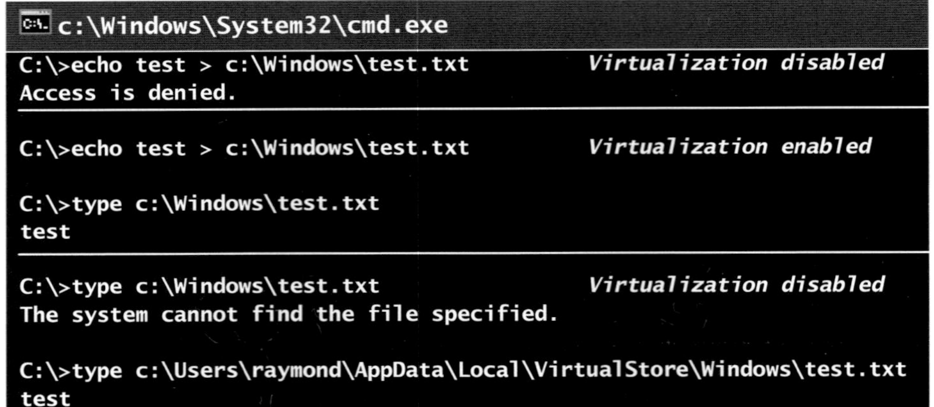

Figure 5-4 The effect of file virtualization

To subsequently read the correct version of the file, Windows must do something special when this application tries to read the file it did just store using file virtualization. The fact is, that Windows uses an alternative scheme for reading files when file virtualization is active. Windows will **first** look in the VirtualStore folder to see if the file is there before looking in the protected folder the application is trying to read.

By default all programs that belong to Windows Vista are not virtualized. This means programs like CMD.exe and Notepad.exe will not be virtualized. X64 applications will also never be virtualized. Virtualization is enabled by default for all other applications on Windows Vista. You can see in the Task Manager if an application is virtualized by adding the Virtualization column in the Processes tab.

You can also use Windows Task Manager to change the Virtualization status of a process: just right-click the process and click Virtualization to toggle the Virtualization status of the process.

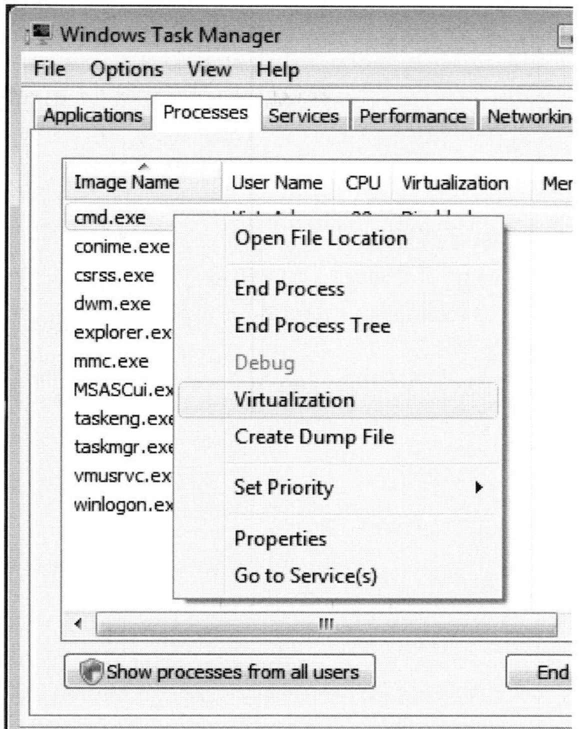

Figure 5-5 Manually enabling Virtualization per process

5.2.4 How Registry virtualization works

Registry virtualization follows the same approach as File Virtualization does. Only now, it is the registry that is being protected.

Registry Virtualization protects a single registry key and its subkeys:

- HKEY_LOCAL_MACHINE\Software

All redirected registry entries are stored in a registry key that is new for Windows Vista:

- HKEY_CURRENT_USER\Software\Classes\VirtualStore\MACHINE\SOFTWARE

Just like in File Virtualization, the number of protected registry keys cannot be extended. But the list can be shortened by excluding specific keys from being virtualized. The reg.exe application enables this. Reg.exe uses the following syntax to exclude a key <keylocation> from being virtualized:

```
reg <keylocation> dont_virtualize [/s]
```

The optional /s stands for: "also make this change for subkeys".

5.2.5 Investigating Virtualization

When you try to find out if and what File and Registry Virtualization did actually virtualize on your system, you can simply browse to the %USERPROFILE%\AppData\Local\VirtualStore folder or the HKCU\Software\Classes\VirtualStore\MACHINE\SOFTWARE key in the registry and see what's in there.

Besides viewing those locations, you need to know that the Event Viewer contains a log dedicated to File Virtualization. This log can be found in the Event Viewer at:

- Applications and Services logs \ Microsoft \ Windows \ UAC-FileVirtualization

Here you will find an event for each time File Virtualization occurred on the system in events with event ID 4000. Keep in mind that the most valuable data is found when examining the XML view of the event. Information about which application caused File Virtualization to kick in, can only be found in the advanced view of these events.

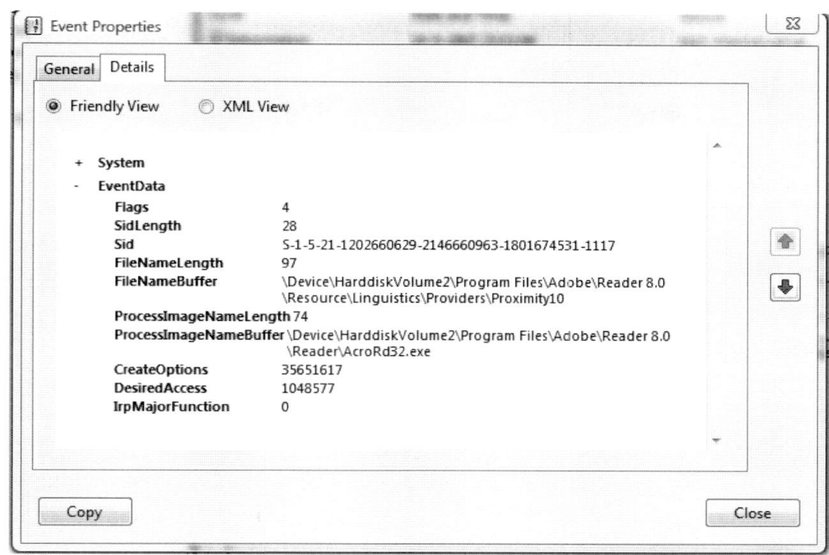

Figure 5-6 Event Properties Friendly View

5.2.6 Possible issues with File and Registry Virtualization

File and Registry Virtualization may solve a number of possible issues with applications that try to store data in protected areas. It may also cause new problems. Suppose, for example, an old application that is used by multiple users on a single system stores shared data in an ini file located in \Program Files\BadApp. When the ini-file is virtualized, it is now stored in a per user location and no longer shared among the users logging on to the system. This might also happen when an administrator tries to create initial settings for this application in the ini-file from the application, and does not notice the file is being redirected. This is only one example of a case where things may go wrong. There are many more cases you can think of.

Microsoft has created a Knowledge Base article about issues that may occur with File and Registry Virtualization at *http://support.microsoft.com/?id=927387*. The contents of the article are not shown here because I expect it will grow in time.

5.2.7 Controlling File and Registry Virtualization using Group Policy

Group Policy contains two security settings that can be used to completely turn of File and Registry Virtualization:

- "User Account Control: Run all administrators in Admin Approval Mode" When this setting is disabled, UAC is disabled, including File and Registry Virtualization.
- "User Account Control: Virtualize file and registry write failures to per user locations"
  When disabled, this setting will only disable File and Registry Virtualization.

5.3 Internet Explorer in Protected Mode

By default, Windows Vista will run Internet Explorer 7 in Protected Mode. This means that Internet Explorer will be running with far less privileges than a standard user process does. Running Internet Explorer in Protected mode should reduce the risk of Internet Explorer running malicious code that silently writes, alters or destroys data on the user's machine, or of malicious software being installed.

Internet Explorer in Protected Mode uses three security features in Windows Vista to enable tighter security:

- User Account Control
- Windows Integrity Control
- User Interface Privilege Isolation

User Account Control must be enabled in order to run Internet Explorer in Protected Mode.

Figure 5-7 Internet Explorer Protected Mode

5.3.1 Windows Integrity control and Internet Explorer Protected Mode

Internet Explorer in Protected Mode leverages the newly introduced integrity levels that were described earlier in paragraph 5.1.3. Internet Explorer in Protected Mode is running at the Low integrity level. A normal user process runs at the Medium integrity level. All existing files and registry keys by default are protected with an ACL that prevents them from modification by processes at a lower integrity level than Medium. This prevents Internet Explorer to modify any of these files or registry keys.

In order not to completely shut off Internet Explorer, some folders have a low integrity mandatory label. This enables Internet Explorer in Protected Mode – or any other process running at the low integrity mandatory level – to store data in these folders. Data created by processes at the low integrity mandatory level is automatically assigned a low integrity mandatory label.

In Protected Mode, Internet Explorer writes/reads special Low versions of the cache, TEMP folder, Cookies and History:

- Cache: *%userprofile%\AppData\Local\Microsoft\Windows\Temporary Internet Files\Low*
- Temp: *%userprofile%\AppData\Local\Temp\Low*
- Cookies: *%userprofile%\AppData\Roaming\Microsoft\Windows\Cookies\Low*
- History: *%userprofile%\AppData\Local\Microsoft\Windows\History\Low*

Child processes started by a process running at low integrity mandatory level are by default also running at the low integrity mandatory level. When a low integrity process tries to start a process at a higher mandatory level, this must be accomplished through a broker process. Starting a broker process by default causes a warning for the user, saying a program will open outside of Protected Mode. The registry key HKLM\Software\Microsoft\Internet Explorer\Low Rights \ElevationPolicy provides the possibility of defining processes that are allowed to be started by Internet Explorer outside of Protected Mode without a warning. Whenever Microsoft determines that an application in this list presents a danger to the system, Windows Vista (probably Defender) will remove the suspected entries from the ElevationPolicy hive.

5.3.2 User Account Control and Internet Explorer Protected Mode

Internet Explorer uses two higher privilege broker processes to perform elevated operations. Broker processes are processes separate from Internet Explorer that run in their own context. They interact with Internet Explorer using inter-process communication. You could say that Internet Explorer sends commands to other processes in order to execute tasks that it cannot accomplish running at low integrity mandatory level. In most cases, the broker processes will only perform the required actions when given user consent (through UAC).

The two broker processes used by Internet Explorer are:

- IEUser.exe
  IEUser.exe is the user privilege broker process. It provides a set of functions that enables a user to save files to areas outside of low integrity mandatory level areas.
- IEInstal.exe
  IEInstall.exe is the administrator privilege broker process. It allows Internet Explorer to install ActiveX controls.

5.3.3 IE User Interface Privilege Isolation

Internet Explorer in protected mode also uses a security feature called "User Interface Privilege Isolation", or UIPI. UIPI limits the possibilities for lower integrity level processes to send window messages to higher integrity processes. This prevents Internet Explorer from sending potentially harmful window messages to processes running at a higher integrity level.

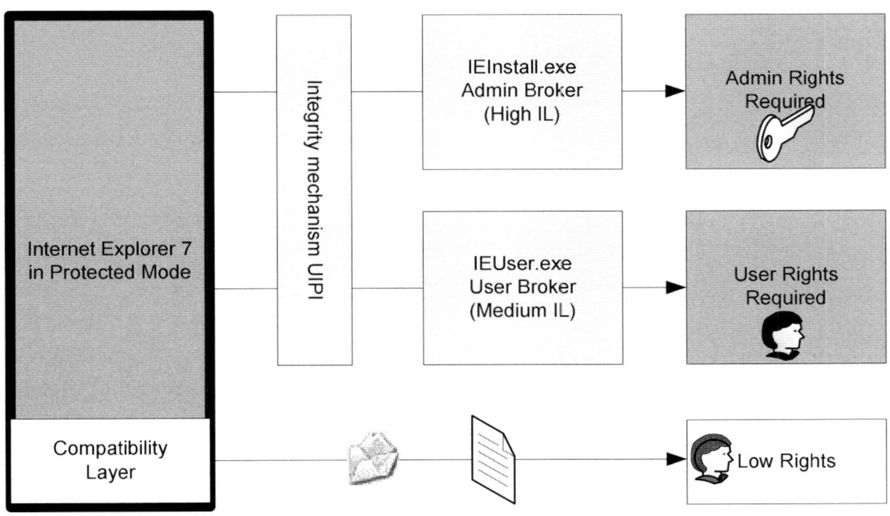

Figure 5-8 Internet Explorer protection architecture

5.3.4 Internet Explorer Compatibility Layer

Internet Explorer Compatibility Layer provides Internet Explorer with its own virtualization layer. Just like UAC virtualization, the Compatibility Layer enables certain write operations for Internet Explorer in Protected Mode. These operations appear to be successful while they are in fact being redirected to an alternative location in the file system or registry.

The Compatibility Layer in Internet Explorer Protected Mode is fairly restricted in its operations, compared to UAC virtualization. Compatibility Layer will only intercept write operations to user specific areas like the "Documents" folder or HKCU in the registry. Write operations to system locations like the Program Files folder or HKLM in the registry will just generate an "Access Denied" message.

Internet Explorer Compatibility Layer will redirect operations meant for user-specific areas to the following low integrity locations:

- %USERPROFILE%\AppData\Local\Microsoft\Windows\Temporary Internet Files\Virtualized
- HKCU\Software\Microsoft\InternetExplorer\InternetRegistry

5.4 Session 0 isolation

Session 0 isolation is a new feature of Windows Vista. In Windows, a session is basically the representation of the desktop with its applications presented to the user. The session presented on the physically connected monitor and controlled by the physically connected keyboard and mouse, is also known as the console session. Windows Servers running Terminal Services allow multiple sessions with remotely connected monitors, keyboards and mouse devices. The set of a monitor, keyboard and mouse is also known as a terminal. In a Terminal Services setting, the terminal can be both locally (console session) or remotely connected.

In previous versions of Windows, the first session represented on the local console was always running in Session 0. This provided an easy way for developers when creating messages supposed to be sent to the console session. In Windows Vista, session 0 no longer belongs to the console. Session 0 is now a special session, only to be used by services and device drivers. When a user logs on to Windows Vista, the user terminal will be connected to Session 1 or higher (with fast user switching). By isolating the services in session 0, Windows Vista removes the possibility for services running with high privileges to interact with user level processes through the UI.

Now that session 0 no longer belongs to the console, applications must use different methods to make sure that output is actually presented in the console session. When a service running in session 0 needs to present output in the user session, it must use a separate process running in the user's context.

5.5 File System Security

Windows Vista uses the same NTFS version as Windows XP with SP2 (NTFS 5.2). So there virtually are no new features in the file system. Still, there are a few things to take notice of.

5.5.1 Owner ACL

In Vista the owner no longer has implicit rights to a file or registry object. In Windows XP the owner of any object always has two absolute rights:

- The right to change the Access Control List (ACL) of the object
- The right to provide access rights to the object

There was no way to take away these rights in Windows XP, unless you'd take away the ownership of the file. In Windows Vista this has changed. If you are the owner of an object, but there is an Access Control Entry (ACE) for the OWNER RIGHTS SID, the rights for OWNER RIGHTS will supersede the fact that you are the owner. If the ACE provides you with enough rights, you can still edit the ACL, but being the owner does not provide you with extra rights anymore, just because you are the owner.

The OWNER RIGHTS SID applies to whoever happens to own the file or folder at the time it is accessed.

If I have a folder that grants modify to OWNER RIGHTS and I am the owner, I do NOT have the right to modify the ACL on that folder. The OWNER RIGHTS SID supersedes my right as the owner to modify the ACL. In order to do so I have to change ownership back to the Administrators group, and then elevate to a member of that group, in which case I have that right.

Here is an Example:

The User Profile folder in *C:\Users* is owned by the user who created the folder at first login. By default access is granted to the specific user, Administrators and System. Each user that created a folder *%username%* in *C:\Users* is able to change its ACL and grant other users access to their folder structure or deny System or Administrators access. By adding the OWNER RIGHTS SID to the ACL for the Users folder, users can be restricted in their ability to change the ACL for their own *%username%* folder. Use the following command-line to accomplish this scenario:

```
icacls c:\Users /grant OWNER RIGHTS:(OI)(CI)(IO)M
```

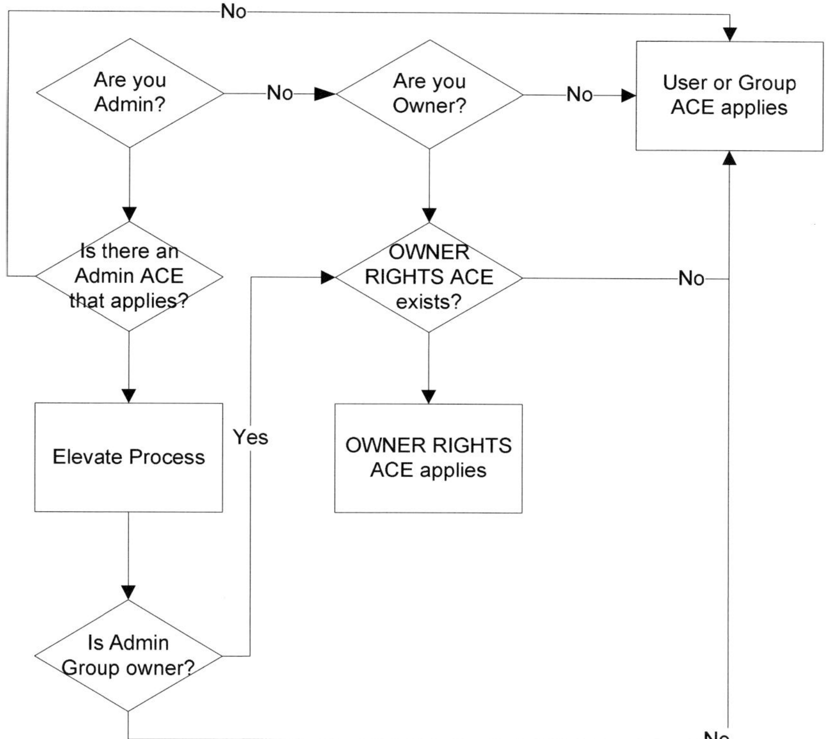

Figure 5-9 How OWNER RIGHTS impacts file system security

OWNER RIGHTS are reset when you give or take ownership.

For example, you own a folder and can therefore change ownership on it. When you do so, the inheritance (apply to:) bit for the OWNER RIGHTS ACE is set to Nothing. In other words, the ACE for OWNER RIGHTS now applies to nothing. If it did not, there could be a catch-22 situation where the ownership can change, but the new owner still cannot modify the ACL.

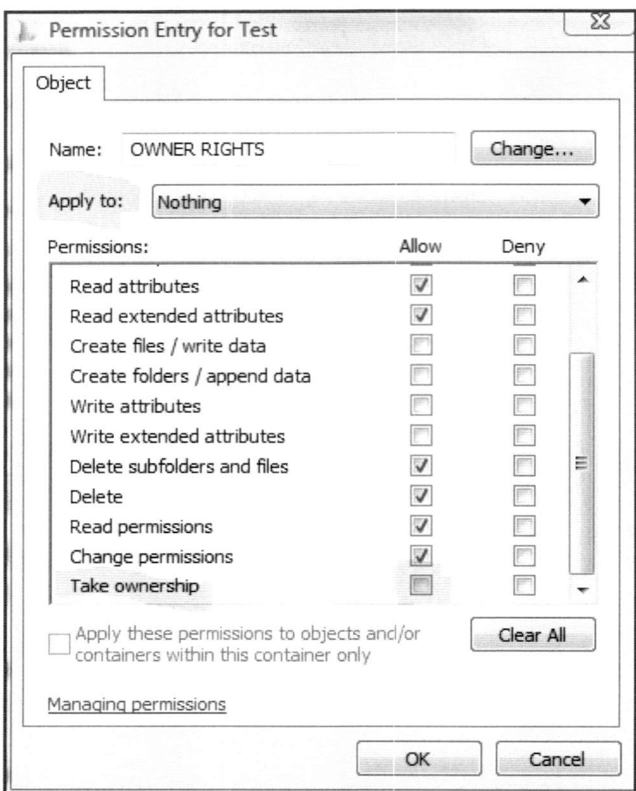

Figure 5-10 OWNER RIGHTS ACE after Take Ownership

5.5.2 TrustedInstaller

When you look into the ACLs of the system files that are part of Windows Vista, you will find a new significant change compared to previous versions of Windows. In those versions of Windows we got used to the fact that all files in *%windir%* and its subfolders were owned by SYSTEM or Administrators and that both SIDs had full control access to those files. Now look at this:

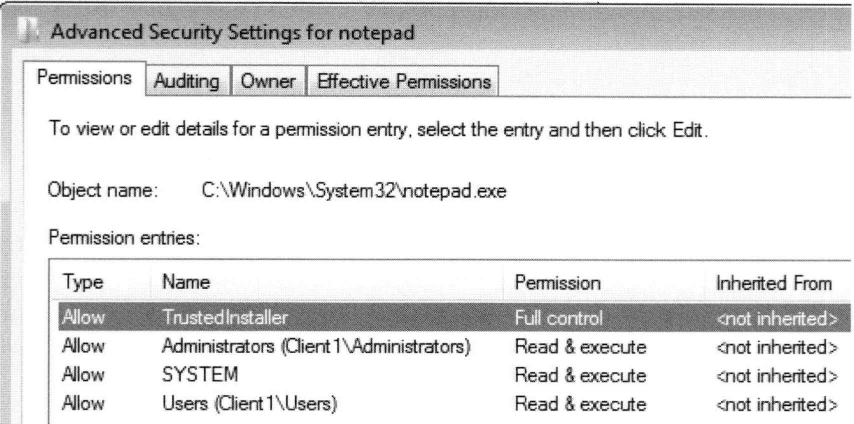

Figure 5-11 Default ACL for system files in Windows Vista

You probably think: "who or what on earth is TrustedInstaller?".

TrustedInstaller is the new owner of all operating system files of Windows Vista. TrustedInstaller is also the only SID with full control access to those files; SYSTEM and Administrators only get Read & Execute rights by default. TrustedInstaller is the implementation of a new security feature of Windows Vista. Windows Vista allows each service to get its own SID. Therefore the Windows Installer service has its own SID in Vista and this SID has the friendly name of TrustedInstaller in the Security properties dialog box of Windows Vista.

The new ACL and new permissions for SYSTEM and Administrators create an extra hurdle when processes running as system try to modify parts of the operating system. In order to change those files, processes running in the context of SYSTEM must first take ownership and change the ACL before it is possible to actually change their contents.

Windows Installer Service is part of Windows Resource Protection (WRP). WRP is the functional successor of Windows File Protection (WFP) in Windows XP. WRP is there to prevent unauthorized actions on your system from leading to unsupported changes of critical parts of the operating system. WRP protects both files and parts of the registry. In Windows Vista, only the Windows Installer service (TrustedInstaller) is allowed to make changes to files that are part of the operating system.

Windows Installer service is responsible for the following actions:

- Installation of Windows Service Packs
- Installation of Hotfixes
- Installation of other operating system upgrades
- Patches and installations by Windows Update

When applications or installers try to change WRP-protected files without using Windows Installer, this will usually cause an "Access Denied" message to that process. But that is not true in all cases. When this happens with a "well known" installer, these messages will be suppressed and Windows Vista will pretend that the unauthorized action took place (change or replacement of system files or registry keys). The installer will think that everything worked out fine, while in fact those changes did not take place.

When adding TrustedInstaller to an ACL (with the Windows Vista object picker or ICACLS.EXE), use "NT Service\TrustedInstaller" when referring to the Windows Installer Service.

5.5.3 What happened to the Documents and Settings folder?

When you first look at the C-root folder, you will see that the "Documents and Settings" folder is missing from the list. Probably you already noticed it is still there, but hidden as an Operating System Folder. What you will also notice – and will probably make you frown – is the fact that the folder is empty. It is empty because Microsoft decided to move the user specific data stored in this folder to a different place for Vista. From now on, you will find the user profile data in *C:\Users*. This is more convenient when you write code or scripts, because a folder name without spaces is much easier to code, than one with spaces.

So, what's the purpose of the empty "Documents and Settings" folder? Well, this folder is a so-called symbolic link. Not a real folder, but a link to the Users folder in the same volume. It is supposed to fool programs written to look in "Documents and Settings" into thinking that the data is there to be used. You can see the concept in action when you type the following in the Windows Explorer address bar: *C:\Documents and Settings\%username%*. This will take you to your profile folder, while just double clicking the "Documents and Settings" folder will only present you an "Access Denied" dialog box.

New locations for common folders

Documents and Settings is not the only folder that has changed places in Windows Vista. Here is a short list of folders that have got a new location in Windows Vista.

Was	Now
Application Data	AppData\Roaming
Cookies	\AppData\Roaming\Microsoft\Windows\Cookies
Local Settings	\AppData\Local
My Documents	\Documents
NetHood	\AppData\Roaming\Microsoft\Windows\Network Shortcuts
PrintHood	\AppData\Roaming\Microsoft\Windows\Printer Shortcuts
Recent	\AppData\Roaming\Microsoft\Windows\Recent
SendTo	\AppData\Roaming\Microsoft\Windows\SendTo
Start Menu	\AppData\Roaming\Microsoft\Windows\Start Menu
Templates	\AppData\Roaming\Microsoft\Windows\Templates

5.6 BitLocker

BitLocker is Microsoft's implementation of full disk encryption for protecting system files and data. BitLocker prevents a thief who boots another operating system or runs a software hacking tool, from breaking Windows Vista file and system protections or viewing offline the files that are stored on the protected drive. BitLocker is available in Windows Vista Enterprise and Ultimate Editions and will be available in Windows Server 2008.

BitLocker ideally uses a Trusted Platform Module (TPM) 1.2 to protect user data and to ensure that a PC that is running Windows Vista has not been tampered with while the system was offline. BitLocker provides enhanced data protection if a system is lost or stolen and secures data deletion when those assets are decommissioned.

BitLocker enhances data protection through two major sub-functions: drive encryption and integrity checking of early boot components.

Drive encryption protects data by preventing unauthorized users from breaking Windows file and system protection on lost, stolen, or inappropriately decommissioned computers. This protection is achieved by encrypting the entire Windows volume. With BitLocker, all user and system files are encrypted, including the swap and hibernation files. BitLocker uses AES 128 or 256 to encrypt the data. This is configurable from Group Policy.

Integrity checking of the early boot components helps to ensure that data decryption is performed only if those components appear unmolested, and that the encrypted drive is located in the original computer.

5.6.1 BitLocker pre-requisites

In addition to running the right version of Windows Vista, BitLocker requires the following in order to function properly.

- **Two partitions**
  Because at least some of the Windows boot process after the BIOS load needs to be unencrypted to boot, BitLocker requires a separate active, system volume. This volume must be at least 1.5 GB. It will NOT be encrypted by BitLocker. The boot code will be protected for machines with a TPM 1.2.

- **Preferably a Trusted Platform Module (TPM) 1.2**
  BitLocker can operate with a TPM or a USB key to store the encryption key material. The TPM is a microcontroller that stores keys, passwords and digital certificates. It typically is affixed to the motherboard of a PC. The nature of this silicon ensures that the information stored there is made more secure from external software attack and physical theft. Security processes, such as digital signature and key exchange, are protected through the secure TCG subsystem. Access to data and secrets in a platform can be denied if the boot sequence is not as expected. Critical applications and capabilities such as BitLocker drive encryption are thereby made much more secure.
- **Compatible BIOS**
  Even when a system is equipped with a TPM 1.2, it might not work with BitLocker until the BIOS has been updated. The BIOS must support the Trusted Computing Group (TCG) Static Root of Trust Measurement (SRTM) and the Microsoft-specific calls that are made during the boot with the TPM, to perform the static root of trust. Once BitLocker unlocks the protected OS volume, a filter driver in the Windows Vista file system stack transparently encrypts and decrypts data as it is written to and read from the protected volume.

When a USB key is used in conjunction with or as a replacement for TPM based BitLocker deployment, the system must support access of the USB Mass Storage Device Class 2 directly from the BIOS before Windows is booted.

5.6.2 Limitations of BitLocker

BitLocker in Windows Vista has the following limitations:

- BitLocker is not supposed to be used on removable media. The way BitLockers stores it's key material (in the TPM) makes it hard to exchange the key to unlock the data on the encrypted volume.
- By license restriction, BitLocker is not licensed for use on virtualized systems.
- BitLocker is only available as an option with the Enterprise and Ultimate versions of Windows Vista.
- There is no support for smart card based strong authentication for release of the BitLocker encryption key.

5.6.3 How BitLocker works

BitLocker includes integrity checks on critical early boot components. BitLocker uses the TPM to collect and store measurements from multiple sources within the boot process to create a sort of system "fingerprint". This fingerprint remains the same, unless the boot system is tampered with. BitLocker relies on the TPM to restrict access to the root secrets, based on these measurements. After the integrity of the boot process is proven, BitLocker uses the TPM to unlock the rest of the data. The system then continues startup, and system protection becomes the responsibility of the running operating system.

The main function of BitLocker, as shown in Figure 11, is to protect user data on the operating system volume of the hard drive. To achieve this, disk sectors are encrypted with a (Full Volume Encryption Key) FVEK, which is always encrypted with the (Volume Master Key) VMK, which, in turn, is encrypted by the TPM.

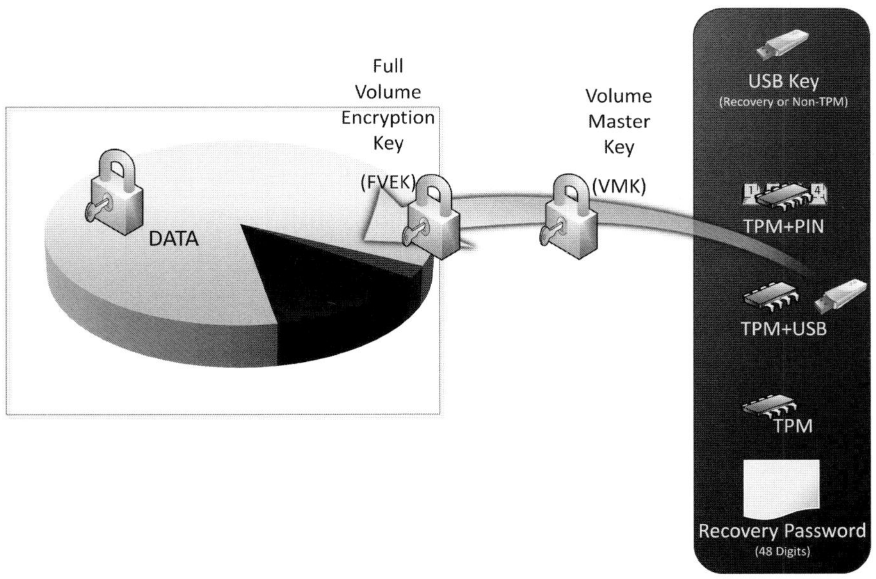

Figure 5-12 - How BitLocker uses the encryption keys

Figure 5-12 shows how volume contents are encrypted with a full-volume encryption key (FVEK), which in turn is encrypted with a volume master key (VMK). Securing the VMK is an indirect way of protecting data on the disk volume. The addition of the VMK allows the system to be rekeyed easily when keys upstream in the trust chain are lost or compromised. This saves the expense of decrypting and re-encrypting the entire disk volume.

After BitLocker authenticates access to the protected operating system volume, a filter driver in the Windows Vista file system stack encrypts and decrypts disk sectors transparently as data is written to and read from the protected volume. When the computer hibernates, the hibernation file is saved encrypted to the protected volume. Resume from hibernation is treated almost exactly the same as the boot process: this saved file is decrypted when the computer resumes from hibernation. The performance penalty for encryption and decryption should be about 4 to 7% and transparent under most circumstances.

5.6.4 BitLocker key scenarios

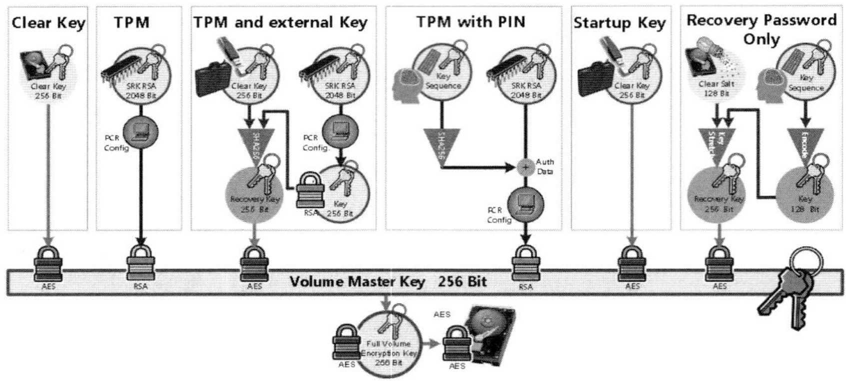

Figure 5-13 - Bitlocker key scenarios

While the TPM-supported way, absolutely is the preferred method to deploy BitLocker, it is not the only way BitLocker stores its key material. Figure 5-13 shows all different options for accessing a BitLocker encrypted Volume in Windows Vista.

Clear Key

In the clear key scenario, the VMK is stored in the clear on the system boot volume. In this situation the system is effectively unsecured. BitLocker secured systems are usually put in this state to perform automated maintenance.

TPM only

This is the least intrusive BitLocker scenario where the user will not notice that the system is BitLocker encrypted and will not require any passwords or keys to boot the system. The TPM will check for boot integrity and provide the VMK to enable

Windows Vista to boot. When an attacker takes the disk out of the system, it is encrypted and its data unavailable on another system.

TPM and External Key
In this scenario, the TPM requires a key from a removable storage device before providing the VMK. The TPM integrity check and the external key together form the VMK that enable decryption of the data.

TPM with PIN
In the TPM with PIN scenario, the TPM acts like most smartcards do. It will only provide the requested operation after the user has entered the correct PIN code.

Startup Key
This is the TPM-less scenario, where the key material is stored on a removable storage device. This scenario lacks the boot integrity check that can only be performed by a TPM.

Recovery Password
The Recovery Password scenario is put in place to rescue the poor guy who gets in the undecryptable hard drive situation. When the hard disk is moved to another system, the TPM is replaced with the motherboard, or the user has forgotten the PIN, there is no other way to get to the data than by using the recovery key.

5.6.5 Key recovery and management

In BitLocker, recovery consists of decrypting a copy of the volume master key BLOB that has been encrypted with a recovery key that is stored on a pluggable USB flash drive, or with a cryptographic key that is derived from a recovery password. The TPM is not involved in any recovery scenarios, so recovery is possible if the TPM fails boot component validation, malfunctions, or disappears.

To recover a volume, the user may use any of the recovery mechanisms that were set up at initialization time. The user can use either a recovery password or a recovery key (a machine-readable equivalent of the recovery password).

Recovery Password
The recovery password is a 48-digit, randomly generated number that was created during BitLocker setup. It can be managed and copied after BitLocker is enabled. Through the interface, the recovery password can be printed or saved to a file for future use.

The domain administrator can configure Group Policy to automatically generate recovery passwords and transparently back them up to Active Directory as soon as

BitLocker is enabled. Furthermore, the domain administrator may choose to prevent BitLocker from encrypting a drive unless the computer is connected to the network and Active Directory backup of the recovery password is successful.

5.6.6 Storing BitLocker recovery information in Active Directory

By default, BitLocker does not backup recovery information. Administrators can configure Group Policy settings to enable backup of BitLocker or TPM recovery information. Before configuring these settings, as a domain administrator you must ensure that the Active Directory schema has been extended with the necessary storage locations, and that access permissions have been granted to perform the backup.

You should also configure Active Directory before configuring BitLocker on client computers. If BitLocker is enabled first, recovery information for those computers will not be added to Active Directory.

Required files

The following sample scripts and LDF file, available from Microsoft, are required to configure Active Directory for backing up recovery information:

- Add-TPMSelfWriteACE.vbs
- BitLockerTPMSchemaExtension.ldf
- List-ACEs.vbs
- Get-TPMOwnerInfo.vbs
- Get-BitLockerRecoveryInfo.vbs

The files can be downloaded at *http://go.microsoft.com/fwlink/?LinkId=78953*.

Domain Controller requirements

Make sure all Domain Controllers in the domain are running Windows Server 2003 with SP1 or later. Earlier versions of Windows lack the Active Directory confidential flag feature used to protect access to BitLocker and TPM recovery information.

The confidential flag is a feature available in Windows Server 2003 with SP1 and later. With this feature, only domain administrators and appropriate delegates have Read access to attributes marked with the confidential flag. The BitLocker and TPM schema extension marks selected attributes as "confidential" using the "searchFlags" property. Domain Controllers running earlier versions of Windows, will expose confidential information regarding BitLocker when recovery information is stored in the directory.

Extend the Active Directory Schema with BitLocker and TPM attributes:

1. Log on with a domain account in the Schema Admins group.
2. Check if your Windows Server installation enables schema updates.
3. Check if you have access to the Schema Operations Master.
4. Review *BitlockerTPMSchemaExtension.ldf.*
5. Run the following command:
   ```
   ldifde -i -v -f BitLockerTPMSchemaExtension.ldf -c "DC=X" "dc=example,dc=local" -k -j .
   ```
   a. The trailing period (".") is part of the command(!)
   b. The use of -k suppresses "Object Already Exists"-errors if the portions of the schema already exist. The use of -j . saves an extended logfile to the current working directory.

BitLocker objects in Active Directory

Backed-up BitLocker recovery information is stored in a child object of the Computer object. That is to say, the Computer object is the container for a BitLocker recovery object.

Each BitLocker recovery object includes the recovery password and other recovery information. More than one BitLocker recovery object can exist under each Computer object, because more than one recovery password can be associated with a BitLocker-enabled volume.

The name of the BitLocker recovery object incorporates a globally unique identifier (GUID), and date and time information, for a fixed length of 63 characters. The form is:

<Object Creation Date and Time><Recovery GUID>

For example: 2005-09-30T17:08:23-08:00{063EA4E1-220C-4293-BA01-4754620A96E7}

The common name (cn) for the BitLocker recovery object is ms-FVE-RecoveryInformation. Each ms-FVE-RecoveryInformation object has the following attributes:

- ms-FVE-RecoveryPassword
  This attribute contains the 48-digit recovery password used to recover a BitLocker-encrypted disk volume. Users enter this password to unlock a volume when BitLocker enters recovery mode.
- ms-FVE-RecoveryGuid
  This attribute contains the GUID associated with a BitLocker recovery password. In BitLocker's recovery mode, this GUID is displayed to the user so that the correct recovery password can be located to unlock the volume. This GUID is also included in the name of the recovery object.
- ms-FVE-VolumeGuid
  This attribute contains the GUID associated with a BitLocker-supported disk volume. While the password (stored in ms-FVE-RecoveryGuid) is unique for each recovery password, this volume identifier is unique for each BitLocker-encrypted volume.
- ms-FVE-KeyPackage
  This attribute contains a volume's BitLocker encryption key secured by the corresponding recovery password.

With the key package and the recovery password (stored in ms-FVE-RecoveryPassword), you can decrypt portions of a BitLocker-protected volume if the disk is corrupted. Each key package will work only for a volume that has the corresponding volume identifier (stored in ms-FVE-VolumeGuid). You must use a specialized tool to make use of this key package.

Setting Permissions for backing up BitLocker password information

The following procedure adds an access control entry (ACE), so that backing up TPM recovery information is possible.

A Windows Vista client can back up BitLocker recovery information under the Computer object's default permission. However, a Windows Vista client cannot back up TPM owner information unless this additional ACE is added. The ACE is an inheritable permission that allows SELF (the computer itself) to write to the ms-TPM-OwnerInformation attribute for Computer objects in the domain.

Use the following procedure to allow TPM recovery information to be backed up:

1. Review *Add-TPMSelfWriteACE.vbs*, the sample script containing the permission extension.
2. Type the following at a command prompt, and then press ENTER:

```
cscript Add-TPMSelfWriteACE.vbs
```

5.6.7 Installing BitLocker

IT administrators can configure BitLocker locally and remotely, through the wizard or with the interfaces exposed by the Windows Vista *Win32_EncryptableVolume* Windows Management Instrumentation (WMI) provider. Interfaces include management functionality to begin, pause, and resume encryption of the disk volume, and to configure how the disk volume's encryption key (FVEK) is protected. The wizard by default does not provide the possibility to use only a USB key to store BitLocker encryption keys. This possibility can be activated by enabling BitLocker Drive Encryption Advanced Startup Options in Group Policy.

Preparing the TPM

When you are configuring BitLocker on a system with a version 1.2 TPM, you must first prepare the TPM. Preparation of the TPM consists of four steps:

1. Enable the TPM in the BIOS
   When the TPM is enabled, it is visible by the OS. An enabled TPM is required for use with BitLocker.
2. Clear the TPM
   When the TPM has been used before, you must clear the TPM before you can own it.
3. Activate the TPM
   Activation of the TPM generates a unique key pair in the TPM. Activation can be done both from the BIOS and from within Windows Vista. It is transparently executed by the wizard or can be manually triggered using the –TurnOn option of manage-bde.wsf.
4. Take ownership of the TPM
   When taking ownership of the TPM, a password is configured on the TPM for future access.

Partitioning a Hard Disk for BitLocker

As stated earlier, BitLocker must have two partitions on a disk to properly function. The first partition, that we will label S, is the active boot partition (it contains the boot information), which is unencrypted and has a minimum size of 1.5 GB. The second partition is the operating system volume and will be labeled C. This volume is encrypted and contains the operating system.

On a system with no operating system installed, the following must be done in order to create the required partitioning scheme:

1. Create a new 1.5 GB primary partition.
2. Set this partition as active.
3. Create a second primary partition using the rest of the space on the disk.
4. Format both new partitions so they can be used as Windows volumes.
5. Now don't reboot and start setup.exe to install Windows Vista on the larger volume (drive C).

Partitioning a disk for BitLocker

1. Start the computer from the Windows Vista product DVD.
2. In the initial Install Windows screen, choose your Installation language, Time and currency format, and Keyboard layout, and then click **Next**.
3. In the next **Install Windows** screen, click **System Recovery Options**, located in the lower left side of the screen.
4. In the **System Recovery Options** dialog box, choose your keyboard layout, and then click **Next**.
5. In the next **System Recovery Options** dialog box, make sure no operating system is selected. To do this, click in the empty area of the Operating System list, below any listed entries. Then click **Next**.
6. In the next **System Recovery Options** dialog box, click **Command Prompt**.
7. Use Diskpart to create the partition for the operating system volume. At the command prompt, type:

   ```
   diskpart
   ```

   press **ENTER**.
8. Now type the following commands in the Diskpart console:

   ```
   SELECT DISK 0
   CLEAN
   CREATE PARTITION PRIMARY SIZE=1500
   ASSIGN LETTER=S
   ACTIVE
   FORMAT FS=NTFS QUICK
   CREATE PARTITION PRIMARY
   ```

```
ASSIGN LETTER=C
FORMAT FS=NTFS QUICK
LIST VOLUME
```

9. You will now see a listing of each volume, with volume numbers, letters, labels, file systems, types, sizes, status, and information. Check that you have two volumes and that you know the label used for each volume.
10. Type **EXIT** to leave the diskpart application.
11. Type **EXIT** to leave the command prompt.
12. In the **System Recovery Options** window, use the "close window" icon in the upper right corner (or press **ALT+F4**) to close the window to return to the main installation screen. (*Do not click Shut Down or Restart*).
13. Click **Install** now and proceed with the Windows Vista installation process. Install Windows Vista on the larger volume, C: (the operating system volume).

On a system where Windows Vista is already installed, the procedure is a bit different:

1. When the current Windows Vista partition covers the whole disk, shrink the partition to create at least 1.5 GB of disk space.
2. Create a new volume in the free disk space.
3. Set this volume as active.
4. Format the new partition.
5. Create the BCD in the new partition.

Repartitioning Vista for Bitlocker

1. Open the Command prompt with administrative privileges.
2. Use BCDEDIT to backup a copy of the BCD:

```
BCDEDIT /export c:\temp\bcd_backup.bcd
```

3. Start DISKPART and type the following commands:

```
SELECT DISK 0
SELECT PARTITION 1
SHRINK REQUIRED=1500
CREATE PARTITION PRIMARY
FORMAT FS=NTFS QUICK
```

```
ASSIGN LETTER=S
ACTIVE
EXIT
```

The system is now unbootable because it is missing the BCD on drive S:, which is active now.

4. First copy the Boot Manager to drive S:

```
xcopy /h C:\bootmgr S:
```

5. Now create the BCD on S: with the backup we made in step 2.

```
BCDEDIT /import C:\Temp\bcd_backup.bcd
```

6. Edit the BCD to reflect its new location:

```
BCDEDIT /set {bootmgr} device partition=S:
BCDEDIT /set {memdiag} device partition=S:
```

7. Reboot the system.

Activating BitLocker drive encryption with a TPM

Use the following procedure to activate BitLocker Drive Encryption:

- Log on as an administrator.
- Eventually you can configure a printer to print BitLocker recovery passwords.

Activating BitLocker Drive Encryption with a TPM

1. Click **Start**, click **Control Panel**, click **Security**, and then click **BitLocker Drive Encryption**.
2. If the User Account Control message appears, verify that the proposed action is what you have requested, and then click **Continue**.
3. On the **BitLocker Drive Encryption** page, click **Turn On BitLocker** on the operating system volume.
   If your TPM is not initialized, you will see the Initialize TPM Security Hardware wizard. Follow the directions to initialize the TPM and restart your computer.
4. On the **Save the recovery password page**, you will see the following options:

a. **Save the password on a USB drive**. This saves the password to a USB flash drive.
b. **Save the password in a folder**. This saves the password to a network drive or other location.
c. **Print the password**. This prints the password.

Use one or more of these options to preserve the recovery password. For each option, select the option and follow the wizards' steps to set the location for saving or printing the recovery password.
When you have finished saving the recovery password, click Next.

5. On the Encrypt the selected disk volume page, confirm that the **Run BitLocker System Check** checkbox is selected, and then click **Continue**. Confirm that you want to restart the computer by clicking **Restart Now**. The computer restarts and BitLocker verifies if the computer is BitLocker-compatible and ready for encryption. If it is not, you will see an error message alerting you to the problem.
6. If the computer is ready for encryption, the Encryption in Progress status bar is displayed. You can monitor the ongoing completion status of the disk volume encryption by dragging your mouse cursor over the BitLocker Drive Encryption icon in the tool bar at the bottom of your screen.

5.6.8 Managing BitLocker

A management script (manage-bde.wsf), available with Windows Vista and Windows Server 2008, provides IT administrators with a simple way to manage and check the disk status. This script is based on the available WMI providers and can be easily modified to help build custom solutions for different enterprise administrative needs.

Here are a few examples of what you can do with manage-bde.wsf

Activate the TPM

```
Cscript %windir%\system32\manage-bde.wsf -tpm -TurnOn
```

Take ownership of the TPM

```
Cscript %windir%\system32\manage-bde.wsf -tpm -
TakeOwnership <TpmPwd>
```

Enable BitLocker with a TPM

```
Cscript %windir%\system32\manage-bde.wsf -on -
recoverypassword C:
```

Enable BitLocker without a TPM

```
Cscript %windir%\system32\manage-bde.wsf -on C: -
startupkey <USBDrive>: -recoverypassword -recoverykey
<recovery drive>:
```

<USBDrive> is the drive used to store the startup-key on a USB stick

<recovery drive> is the drive used to store the recovery key

Display the BitLocker status

```
Cscript %windir%\system32\manage-bde.wsf -status
<drive>:
```

Create a new Recovery Password

```
Cscript %windir%\system32\manage-bde.wsf -protectors -
delete C: -type RecoveryPassword
Cscript %windir%\system32\manage-bde.wsf -protectors -
add C: -rp
```

Restore the startup information in the TPM after a BIOS change.
This prevents the request for the Recovery Key at startup.

```
Cscript %windir%\system32\manage-bde.wsf -protectors -
disable C:
Cscript %windir%\system32\manage-bde.wsf -protectors -
enable C:
```

5.7 Removable Device Control

Device Control is one of those long anticipated features of Windows Vista that created a good market for 3rd party developers on Windows XP, especially for customers who could not wait for Microsoft to come up with a feature that controls how users connect and use removable devices to their systems.

Windows Vista seems to have quite a complete feature set to control removable devices. One of the main advantages of the built-in solution is that it is just a part of the standard set of Group Policy settings. This makes it very flexible to manage and easy to use if you know how to use Group Policies in Windows.

Windows Vista removable Device Control consists of two options:

- Device Installation
  Device Installation control defines which devices can and cannot be installed by users on a system. This enables administrators to define a set of allowed devices that can be connected and used on their systems.
- Removable Storage Access
  Removable Storage Access defines how removable storage can be accessed when it is connected to the system. For example, this enables an administrator to declare all USB storage devices Read Only. Removable Storage Access can also define access policies for CD/DVD, Tape drives, WPD Devices (cellular phones, media players, auxiliary displays and CE devices), Floppy Drives and Custom Devices defined by the administrator.

Two entries in Group Policy control removable device behavior.

5.7.1 Device identification

To understand Device Installation Control, one must first have some understanding of hardware identification. Each device connected to a Windows system is identified by a number of ID's:

- Hardware ID
  The Hardware ID identifies the hardware connected to the system. The hardware ID consists of multiple levels. Each level is a bit more specific in the definition of the device. At its most specific level, the Hardware ID describes everything about the connected device including manufacturer, device model, and revision level. On lower levels less detail is specified in the hardware ID. The lowest level may not specify more than the device class. This could for instance be "Display Adapter".

- Compatible ID

  Some devices also have a compatible ID. This is an optional device ID defining device ID's that use drivers compatible with the connected device. This creates extra options for the system when selecting a driver for the device.
- Class ID

  The Class ID is a high level ID defining what type of device is connected to the system. The first level of devices shown in the Device Manager MMC sort of consists of all class IDs connected to the system. When specifying the class ID for removable device IDs, the GUID of the class ID is used to identify the class. Multi-function devices carry multiple Class IDs. A multi-function printer device for instance may be a printer, scanner and fax device at the same time. In order accommodate all those functions the Class IDs are organized in a tree. The device will have a parent Class ID for the multi-function printer and multiple child Class IDs for its various functions.

5.7.2 The Device identification process

Whenever a new device is connected to the system, Windows tries to locate the driver that best fits the detected device. Therefore it compares the device IDs of the drivers in the driver store with the devices' Hardware and Compatible IDs. When a match is found, the match is "ranked". The lower the rank, the better the match. When a driver is found that matches the most specific ID-string of the Hardware ID, it will be ranked 0. When all available drivers are scored, the lowest rank is selected as the driver for the connected device.

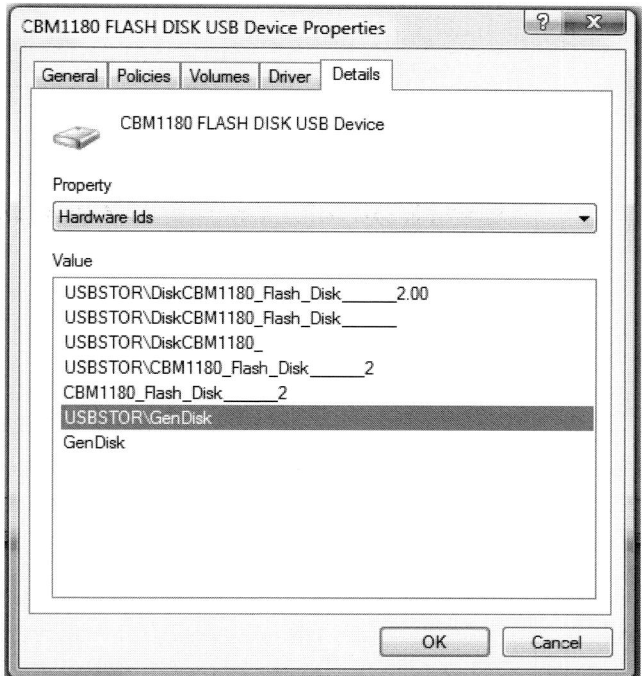

Figure 5-14 Plug-and-Play hardware IDs

For example, when we connect a USB thumb drive to a computer, all hardware IDs are gathered. Then the OS starts searching for a driver matching the hardware IDs of the thumb drive. The OS will rank each 'hit' for a Hardware ID or Compatible ID, and then choose the driver with the lowest rank. In this case there will probably be no driver from the specific hardware vendor. The best matching driver will be a generic USB storage driver (USBSTOR/GenDisk). This is reported in the hardware properties as the Matching Device ID.

Figure 5-15 Matching Device ID for Plug-and-Play device

5.7.3 Restricting Device Installation

Device Installation control is defined in Group Policy as a Computer Policy and therefore applies to all users connected to the system. Device installation offers the possibility to define which devices can be installed on a system. This only applies to devices that do not already have a driver associated in the Device Manager. When a device already has an associated driver in the Device Manager, one can disassociate the driver by uninstalling the device from the Device Manager.

The following Group Policy settings are available to restrict Device Installation for Windows Vista:

Computer \ Administrative Templates \ System \ Device Installation \ Device Installation Restrictions.

Setting
Allow administrators to override Device Installation Restriction policies
Allow installation of devices using drivers that match these device setup classes
Prevent installation of devices using drivers that match these device setup classes
Display a custom message when installation is prevented by policy (balloon text)
Display a custom message when installation is prevented by policy (balloon title)
Allow installation of devices that match any of these device IDs
Prevent installation of devices that match any of these device IDs
Prevent installation of removable devices
Prevent installation of devices not described by other policy settings

Figure 5-16 Device installation restrictions in Group Policy

A common strategy when implementing a policy that only permits installation of well known devices, is to enable "Prevent installation of removable devices" and then define the permitted devices in "Allow installation of devices that match any of these device IDs". These two settings permit only installation of devices defined in the second policy. When the policy must be overridden by support personnel, one can enable "Allow administrators to override Device Installation Restriction policies". This enables members of the local Administrators group to install devices regardless of other policies restricting device installation.

Permitting a single type of USB stick with Device Installation Restriction Policies

1. Insert the permitted USB stick in the machines USB port.
2. Start the Device Management MMC using **devmgmt.msc**.
3. Browse to the USB device under "**Disk Drives**".
4. Double click the device to open its properties.
5. Click on the "**Details**" tab and select "**Hardware IDs**".
6. Select the row that specifies the device without the revision level (for example *USBSTOR\DiskCBM1180_*) and click Ctrl-C to copy the line to the clipboard.
7. Start the Group Policy Editor using **gpedit.msc**.
8. Browse to "**Computer \ Administrative Templates \ System \ Device Installation \ Device Installation Restrictions**".
9. Double click "**Prevent installation of removable devices**", select **Enable** and click **OK**.
10. Double click "**Allow installation of devices that match any of these device IDs**".
11. Click Show... .
12. In the dialog "**Show Contents**" click **Add**…
13. Paste the contents of the clipboard in the line "**Enter the item to be added**" and click **OK** three times.
14. Close the Group Policy Editor.
15. Start an elevated Command Prompt.
16. Type **Gpupdate** and press **Enter**.
17. Now insert a USB device of a different type that has not been used on the system before[8].
18. Watch the message saying device installation for this device is denied.

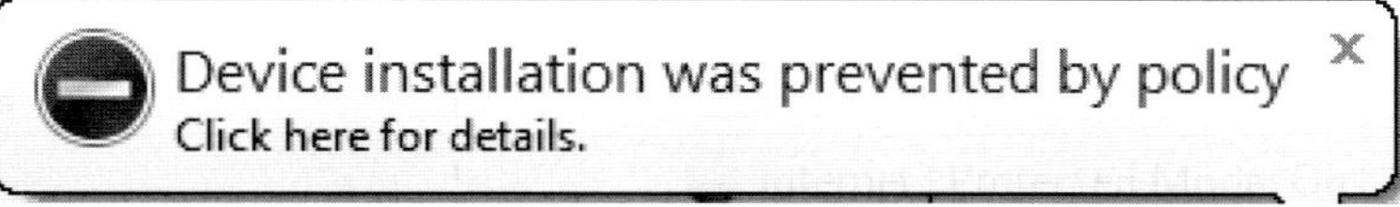

Figure 5-17 Device installation prevented by policy

[8] If the device was already used on the system, uninstall the device from the Device Manager MMC and reboot the system.

5.7.4 Device driver installation by non-admins

By default only users with administrative privileges are able to install new device drivers in Windows Vista. This prohibits standard users for example to install a driver for their new printer at home on their corporate laptop, when the driver is not already in the local driver store.

A system administrator can allow a standard user to install new device drivers on their systems based on the device class. This enables users without administrative privileges to install new device drivers only for those devices that are approved by their system administrator.

The following Group Policy setting allows users without administrative privileges to install new device drivers for a specific device class:

Computer \ Administrative Templates \ System \ Driver Installation\

Allow non-administrators to install drivers for these device classes

Use the GUID of the device class to define what type of devices can be installed. Here are a few common classes:

Device class	GUID
Printer	{4D36E979-E325-11CE-BFC1-08002BE10318}
Scanner	{6BDD1FC6-810F-11D0-BEC7-08002BE2092F}
Pen Tablets and pointing devices	{4d36e96F-E325-11CE-BFC1-08002BE10318}

5.7.5 Controlling Removable Storage Access

Removable Storage Access is the other half of controlling the way removable storage can be used on Windows Vista Systems. Removable storage access control defines if reading and/or writing is allowed on removable storage devices. Removable storage can consist of the following items:

- USB sticks and hard drives
- Rewritable optical media like DVD's and CD's

- Floppy Disks
- Tape Drives
- WPD Devices
  WPD (Windows Portable Devices) are devices running a portable version of Windows, like PDA's, Smartphones and Media Players.
- Custom Class Devices
  Custom Class Devices prepare Windows Vista for the future. Devices that we might not have heard of before can be future storage media. Custom Class Devices enable administrators to select any device class and manage its storage access through Group Policy.

Removable Storage Access can be managed both on the computer level and on the user level. When both levels are configured and cause a conflict, computer level takes precedence over user level.

The following Group Policy settings are available to restrict controlling Removable Storage Access:

Computer Configuration
Administrative Templates
System
Removable Storage Access

User Configuration
Administrative Templates
System
Removable Storage Access

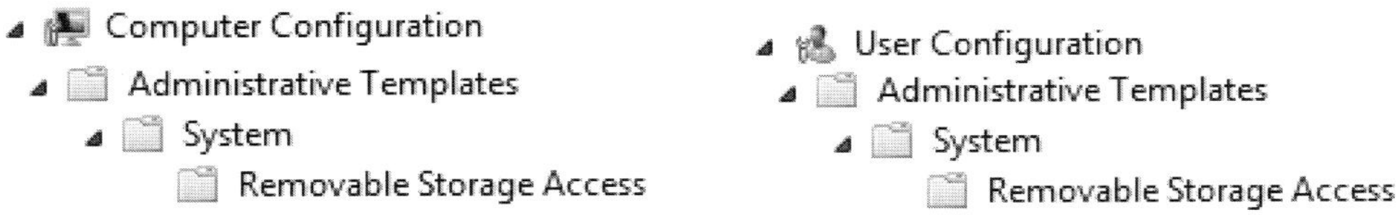

Figure 5-18 Removable Storage Access in Group Policy

Setting
Time (in seconds) to force reboot
CD and DVD: Deny read access
CD and DVD: Deny write access
Custom Classes: Deny read access
Custom Classes: Deny write access
Floppy Drives: Deny read access
Floppy Drives: Deny write access
Removable Disks: Deny read access
Removable Disks: Deny write access
All Removable Storage classes: Deny all access
All Removable Storage: Allow direct access in remote sessions
Tape Drives: Deny read access
Tape Drives: Deny write access
WPD Devices: Deny read access
WPD Devices: Deny write access

Figure 5-19 Restricting access to removable media in Group Policy

Changes to Removable Storage Access rights will not take effect until the system is restarted. A restart of the system can be forced using the policy "Time (in seconds) to force reboot".

The policy "All Removable Storage classes: Deny all access" overrules any individual removable storage policy settings. When enabled, the setting disables all access to any removable storage class device. When this setting is disabled or not configured, write and read access is allowed to all removable storage classes.

6 Windows Vista Networking

Windows Vista includes an updated implementation of the TCP/IP stack known as the Next-Generation TCP/IP stack. Development of the Next-Generation TCP/IP stack was targeted to address the following goals:

- Increase scalability
- Leverage new hardware
- Provide better performance on low latency and congested networks
- Provide more control over connectivity

This chapter describes some of the most obvious changes in Windows networking in Vista. In the next chapters the following subjects will be discussed:

- New stack architecture
- Performance Enhancements
- Network Discovery
- Network Location Awareness
- IPv6
- Name Resolution
- Wireless Networking
- IPSec Enhancements
- Policy based QoS
- Windows Firewall with Advanced Security

6.1 The new stack

Microsoft completely rewrote the network stack for Windows Vista and Windows Server 2008. When you look at its topology you see a quite familiar stack with a few things that differ from previous versions of Windows.

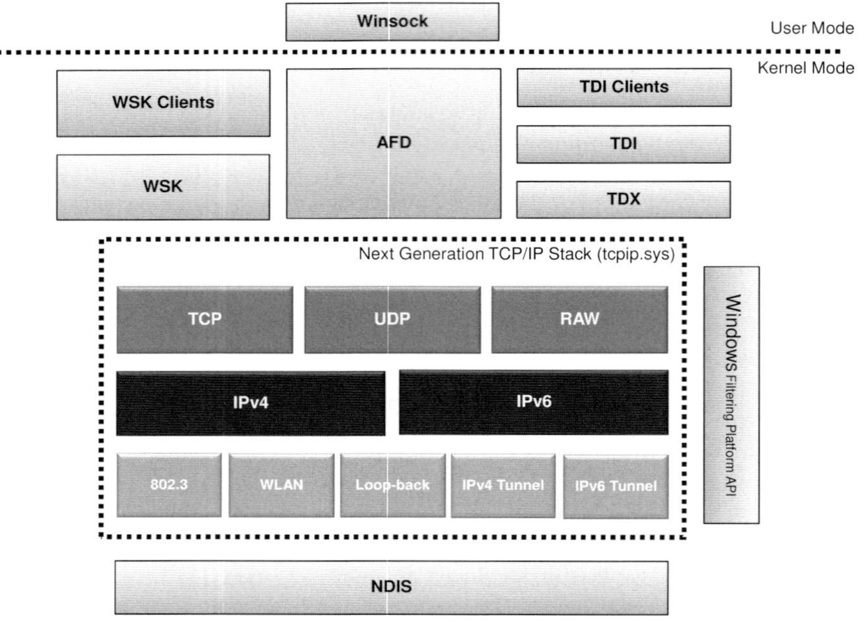

Figure 6-1 The Next Generation Network Stack

First of all, there is native availability of both IPv4 and IPv6. IPv6 is clearly the future of IP-based communication, providing a lot of advantages over IPv4 that is the standard at present. Positioning IPv6 next to IPv4 in the stack enables the protocols to operate completely independent from each other. So in the future you may even disable IPv4 completely. Today there is a bigger chance that you have to disable IPv6 in your network. It is not possible to uninstall IPv6.

Another new element in the stack is the Windows Filtering Platform API. This API provides a common interface for solution providers building antivirus or firewall software. These vendors no longer have to create their own obscure hooks in the system to get access to the traffic that flows through the network stack.

6.2 Performance enhancements

Under the hood, the Next Generation IP stack contains a number of features provided to enhance performance. Especially on networks that don't have the almost ideal characteristics of Ethernet.

TCP Receive Window Auto-Tuning

TCP Receive Window Auto-Tuning is aimed at optimizing network utilization on high bandwidth, high latency networks. The TCP Receive Window is the amount of data that a computer can accept without acknowledging the sender. If the sender has not received an acknowledgement for the first packet it sent, it will stop and wait. If the time waiting exceeds a certain limit, it may even retransmit. Even if there is no packet loss in the network, TCP windowing can cause a limit for the throughput. Because TCP transmits data up to the window size before holding the packets, full bandwidth of the network may not always get used. This is especially the case on high bandwidth satellite connections. Windows XP uses a fixed TCP Receive Window of 64Kb. With this TCP Receive Window size on a 100 Mbps network with a latency of 100ms, the bandwidth of a Windows XP system never passes beyond 5 Mbps. Windows Vista with TCP Receive Auto-Tuning uses a variable TCP Receive Window size that can scale up to 16Mb. When Vista sets up communication, it will tune the size of the TCP Receive Window in order to optimize utilization. In our example this can bump up the speed of communication up to 80Mbps when transferring large files.

Compound TCP (CTCP)

Compound TCP (CTCP) is what Receive Windows Auto-Tuning does on the sending end of the communication channel. For TCP connections with a large TCP Receive Window size and a large bandwidth-delay product (the bandwidth multiplied by the latency of the connection), Compound TCP (CTCP) in the Next-Generation TCP/IP stack aggressively increases the amount of data sent at one time by monitoring the bandwidth-delay product, delay variations, and packet losses. CTCP also ensures that its behavior does not negatively impact other TCP connections.

Explicit Congestion Notification support

Explicit Congestion Notification support or ECN support is another technology meant to deal with congestion in a network connection. With Explicit Congestion Notification (ECN) support on both TCP peers and in the routing infrastructure, routers experiencing congestion mark the packets as they forward them. TCP peers receiving marked packets lower their transmission rate to ease congestion and prevent segment losses. Detecting congestion before packet losses are incurred increases the overall throughput between TCP peers. Windows Vista supports ECN but it is disabled by default.

Server Message Block 2.0

Server Message Block 2.0 is the new version of the protocol used for file access over the network. SMB has been the standard for accessing file shares in Windows ever since Windows entered the market. SMB 1 was originally designed by IBM and was used by various operating systems besides Windows. With SMB 2.0 Microsoft introduces a number of improvements with the goal to improve performance and reliability of the protocol. Most significant improvements are:

- The notion of "durable file handles" allow SMB connections to survive brief network outages, such as occur with wireless networks.
- Support for symbolic links.
- The ability to compound multiple actions into a single request, reducing the number of roundtrips the client needs to make to the server.

SMB 2.0 is used when two Windows Vista systems access each other's file shares or when Windows Vista accesses a file share on Windows Server 2008. One of my own tests comparing SMB-based large file transfer from Windows Vista with Windows Server 2003 displayed much better performance when the files where copied from Windows Vista. On the other hand, FTP for instance may show much less gain compared to previous versions of Windows.

6.3 Network Discovery

Network Discovery allows Windows Vista to locate and advertise computers and shared resources on the network. Windows Vista uses the following protocols, which are new for Windows, for Network Discovery:

- Link Layer Topology Discovery (LLTD)
- Web Services for Devices (WSD)
- Function Discovery (FD)

Enabling network discovery greatly increases broadcast traffic on the network. For this reason, Windows Vista disables network discovery when connected to the corporate network. For security reasons, Network Discovery is disabled on public networks.

Windows Vista still uses the good old Computer Browser Service and NetBIOS broadcasts in order to locate computers running earlier versions of Windows.

6.3.1 Link Layer Topology Discovery

LLTD enables Windows Vista to create a very nice looking network map showing discoverable network components. LLTD is a non-routable protocol that depends on LLTD responders in order to locate available resources on the network. As previous versions of Windows do not support LLTD, they will not appear in Windows Vista's network map. Microsoft released an LLTD responder for Windows XP that can be downloaded via KB article 922120. Windows XP systems running the LLTD responder will show up in the Window Vista network map.

LLTD is not a secure protocol. Rogue systems on the network may create invalid or non-existing entries in the network map. Windows Vista creates network maps on a per user basis, because each user can have a unique set of network profiles.

In order to create a network map, the LLTD Mapper Service must be running on the computer creating the map. This service is configured to start manually and should only be disabled when network mapping is not desired. In order to appear in the map, computers must have the Mapper I/O (LLTDIO) Driver enabled. Both the mapper and the responder can be managed through Group Policy. Use the following policies to manage LLTD mapping in a domain environment:

Computer Configuration \ Administrative Templates \ Network \ Link-Layer Topology Discovery

- Turn on Mapper I/O (LLTDIO) driver
- Turn on Responder (RSPNDR) driver

Use the following procedure to view the network map in Windows Vista:

1. Open the **Network and Sharing Center**
2. Click **View full map** in the upper right of the dialog box

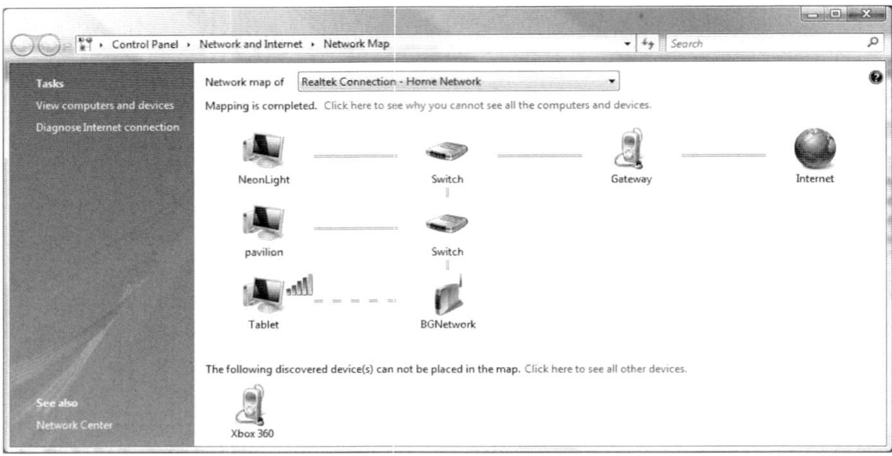

Figure 6-2 Network Map in Network and Sharing Center

6.3.2 Web Services for Devices and Function Discovery

Web Services for Devices uses the Function Discovery Provider Host service (FDPS) and Web Services Dynamic Discovery (WS-Discovery) to locate available services on the network. Function Discovery Resource Publication (FDRP) Service, on the other hand, is responsible for announcing available resources like shared folders and printers on the network. Web Services for Devices is primarily intended for home networks. Corporate networks offer more efficient methods like Active Directory for resource publication.

WS-Discovery

WS-Discovery is a multicast protocol developed by Microsoft, BEA, Canon, Intel and webMethods. A Windows Vista computer sends out a multicast request for one or more target services, such as shared folders or printers. Any computer which offers services to match the request will respond. In order to minimize the traffic caused by WS-Discovery, every newly published resource announces itself on the network. This process is described in the next paragraph.

Function Discovery Resource Publication

The Function Discovery Resource Publication is responsible for announcing available resources on systems acting as a server on the network. The announcement of a resource or HELLO message includes the following information:

- Name
- Description
- If the computer is member of a workgroup or domain
- Computer type (Desktop, laptop, tablet, media center or server)
- If Remote Desktop is enabled
- Folder and printer shares with at least Read Access for Everyone and accessible through Windows Firewall. The following information is included for each share:
    - Path
    - Folder type (documents, pictures, music or videos)
    - Share permissions assigned to everyone

FDPS and FDRP may cause a lot of network traffic when used on large networks. For that reason both services are disabled in a domain environment.

6.3.3 Protocols used for Network Discovery

When investigating Windows Firewall, you will notice a large number of protocols changing when controlling Network discovery. After reading the previous paragraphs, most protocols should at least ring a bell after reading this chapter.

Protocol	Description	Protocol	Port
LLMNR	Link Local Multicast Name Resolution	UDP	5355
NB Datagram	NetBIOS Datagram	UDP	138
NB-Name	NetBIOS Name Resolution	UDP	137
Pub WSD	WS-Discovery Function Discovery	UDP	3702
SSDP	Simple Service Discovery Protocol	UDP	1900
UPnP	Universal Plug and Play	TCP	
WSD Events	WSDAPI Events via Function Discovery	TCP	5357
WSD EventsSecure	Secure WSDAPI Events via Function Discovery	TCP	5358

6.4 Network Location Awareness

Windows Vista is well prepared for mobile computers that often connect to different networks. Windows Vista will change its network configuration based on the network it is connected to. This enables new possibilities to provide better security and leverages applications to adjust to the systems connectivity.

6.4.1 Manually selected network locations

Whenever you connect a Windows Vista system to a new network, it will request what kind of network it is connected to. The network can be:

- Home
- Work
- Public

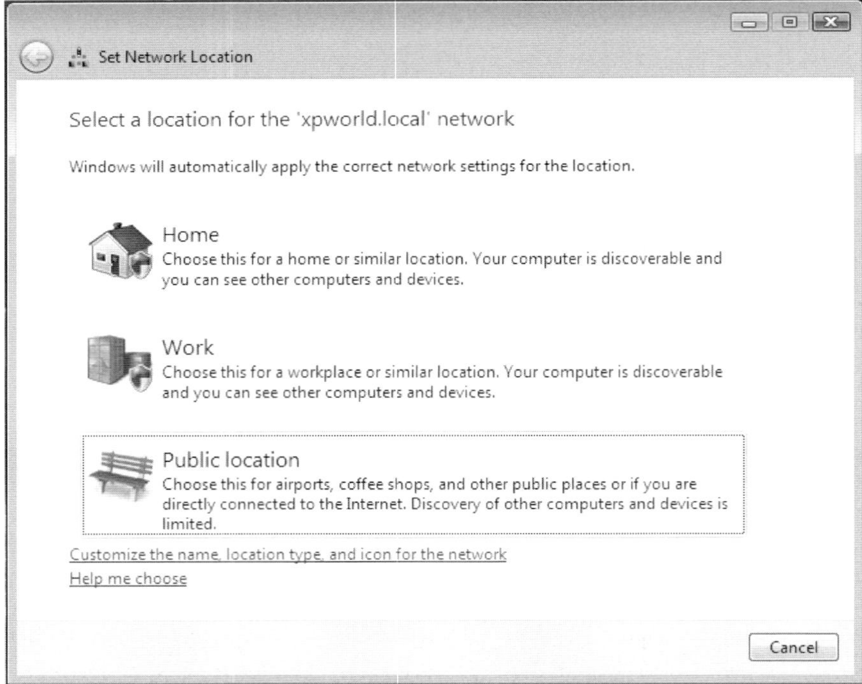

6-3 Selecting a network location

You must have elevated rights to change the network to Work or Home. Essentially Home and Work are treated the same by Windows Vista. Both networks are trusted networks where certain features like Network Discovery will be enabled by default.

The next time the system connects to this network, it will remember which location was chosen. The network will be identified both by the DNS settings and IP range used on the network.

To disable the Set Network Location Wizard, right-click the network icon in the system tray and click "Turn off notification of new networks". From now on every new connected network is a "Public location", unless the system automatically detects the network as a Domain Network (see the next paragraph).

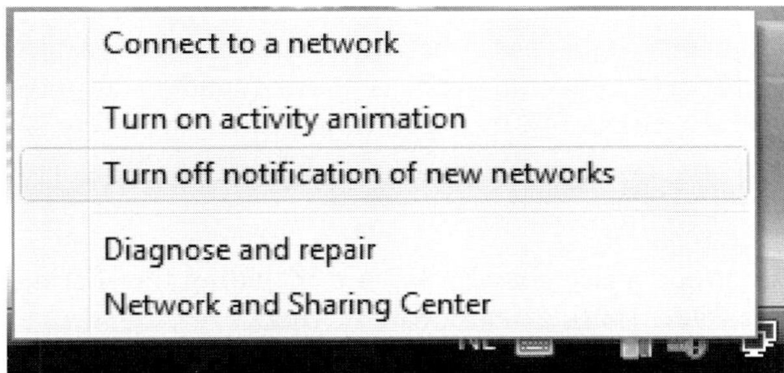

6-4 Configure notification of new networks

6.4.2 Location types

One may think that the chosen location in the previous paragraph has a one-to-one relation to the location types used to configure Windows Firewall. Unfortunately this is not true. After selecting the network location, Windows Vista will map the network to one of the following location types:

Private

The computer is connected to a network that has some level of protection from the Internet and contains known or trusted computers. Examples are home networks or small office networks that are located behind an Internet gateway device that provides firewalling against incoming traffic from the Internet. A network will only be categorized as private if a user or application has identified the network location as Home or Work. Only networks located behind an Internet gateway device should be identified as Home or Work. To designate a network as Home or Work, the user must have administrator privileges. When connected to a private network, the following settings automatically apply:

- Windows Firewall is turned on.
- Network discovery is turned on.

- All forms of file and printer sharing are turned off, including file sharing, printer sharing, public folder sharing, and media sharing.

Domain

The Domain location type is automatically selected when the computer is connected to a network that contains a domain controller for the domain to which the computer is joined. An example is an organization intranet. When connected to the domain network, the following settings automatically apply:

- Windows Firewall is turned on by default and configured by Group Policy settings downloaded from the Active Directory domain.
- Network discovery is turned off.
- All forms of file and printer sharing are turned off, including file sharing, printer sharing, public folder sharing, and media sharing.

Public

The computer is connected to a network that has a direct connection to the Internet. Examples are public Internet access networks such as those found in airports, libraries, and coffee shops. When connected to a public network, the following settings automatically apply:

- Windows Firewall is turned on.
- Network discovery is turned off.
- All forms of file and printer sharing are turned off, including file sharing, printer sharing, public folder sharing, and media sharing.

If you change the default settings for a specific location type, the new settings will be applied to every network with the specified location type. From the Network and Sharing Center, you can change a network from the Private to the Public location type, or vice versa.

The following table shows a summary of the differences between the default firewall settings for all location types in Windows Vista.

	Windows Firewall	**Network Discovery**	**File & Printer Sharing**
Private	☑	☑	☐
Domain	☑	☐	☐
Public	☑	☐	☐

Note: With Windows Firewall enabled in all network locations, it is not possible to ping Windows Vista clients in their default configuration. In order to enable ping, Windows Firewall must be configured to allow ICMP ping. The following command line will enable ping replies on Windows Vista clients:

```
netsh firewall set icmpsetting 8 enable
```

6.5 IPv6

Internet Protocol version 6 is the designated successor of IPv4, the current version of the Internet Protocol. The main improvement brought by IPv6 is a much larger address space that allows greater flexibility in assigning addresses. IPv6 can support up to 2^128 (about 3.4x10^38) addresses. The extended address length eliminates the need to use Network Address Translation (NAT) and avoids the potential exhaustion of the IPv4 address space that currently already hurts upcoming economies.

In Windows Vista Next Generation network stack IPv6 and IPv4 share common Transport and Framing layers. IPv6 is now supported by all networking components and services. In IPv6 mode, Windows Vista can use new name resolution protocols like LLMNR and PNRP (see paragraphs 6.6.1 and 6.6.2). IPv6 can also be used over PPP-based VPN and dial-up connections. IPv6 can be used in situations where full native IPv6 support is not available. ISATAP and Teredo provide solutions in those situations.

- ISATAP
  ISATAP enables IPv6 connectivity over IPv4 routers by placing an ISATAP router in every subnet. The ISATAP router can be implemented on Windows Server 2003 or Windows Server 2008. ISATAP assigns globally routable IPv6 addresses to Windows Vista clients on its subnet.
- Teredo
  Teredo is an IPv4/v6 transition technology that enables IPv6 connectivity between nodes over the Internet behind NAT connections.

6.5.1 IPv6 Addressing

IPv6 addresses are 128 bits long, whereas IPv4 addresses are 32 bits long. IPv6 addresses are typically composed of two logical parts: a 64-bit (sub-) network prefix, and a 64-bit host part, which is either automatically generated from the interface's MAC address or assigned sequentially.

IPv6 addresses are normally written as eight groups of four hexadecimal digits. For example, 2001:0db8:85a3:08d3:1319:8a2e:0370:7334 is a valid IPv6 address. If a four-digit group is 0000, the zeros may be omitted and replaced by two colons(::). For example, 2001:0db8:0000:0000:0000:0000:2510:07af can be shortened to 2001:0db8::2510:07af. Leading zeros in a group can also be omitted (as in ::1 for localhost). Having more than one double-colon abbreviation in an address is invalid, as it would make the notation ambiguous.

IPv6 networks are defined using CIDR (Classless Inter Domain Routing) notation. In IPv4 the network 169.254.0.0/16 stands for all addresses from 169.254.0.0 to 169.254.255.255. The same way 2001:db8::/64 stands for all addresses from 2001:db8:0000:0000:0000:0000:0000:0000 to 2001:db8:FFFF:FFFF:FFFF:FFFF:FFFF:FFFF.

Here is a short list of special addresses used with IPv6:

Address	Meaning
::1/128	Local host.
2001:db8::/32	Prefix used for all IPv6 example addresses mentioned in documentation.
fe80::/10	Link local prefix. This prefix specifies that the address is valid only on the local network. It is analogous with the APIPA address 169.254.0.0/16 in IPv4.
Ff00::/8	Multicast prefix used for multicast addresses.

6.5.2 Disabling IPv6 components

IPv6 is now a native part of the operating system. This also means there is no way to uninstall IPv6 when you don't want to make use of it. In those cases you can disable parts of IPv4 by configuring the registry. The following instruction shows how to disable certain parts of IPv6 in Windows Vista.

Disabling IPv6 features in Windows Vista	
Create and set the following registry value: HKLM\System\CurrentControlSet\Services\Tcpip6\Parameters Name: DisabledComponents Value (DWORD): *bitmask*	
0	All IPv6 tunnel interfaces, including ISATAP, 6to4 and Teredo tunnels disabled
1	All 6to4 based interfaces disabled

2	All ISATAP based interfaces disabled
3	All Teredo based interfaces disabled
4	IPv6 over all non-tunnel interfaces, including LAN and PPP interfaces disabled
5	Modifies the preference order to prefer IPv4 over IPv6 when attempting connections

The default value of *DisabledComponents* is 0.

Here is a list of common values for *DisabledComponents*:

Value	Result
0xffffffff	Disable all IPv6 components except the IPv6 loopback interface and prefer IPv4 over IPv6 when attempting connections
0x20	Prefer IPv4 over IPv6 when attempting connections
0x10	Disable all native IPv6 interfaces
0x01	Disable all tunnel IPv6 interfaces
0x11	Disable all IPv6 components except the IPv6 loopback interface

6.6 Name Resolution

Previous versions of Windows relied on the following main name resolution protocols:

- DNS
- NetBIOS name resolution
- Hosts file

In Windows Vista, Windows is clearly moving away from the NetBIOS name resolution protocol. The protocol is known for its hunger for bandwidth in large networks, and is not compatible with IPv6. Especially the last issue provides a good reason to look for new alternatives in name resolution. Windows Vista contains two additional name resolution protocols that will be discussed in the remainder of this chapter:

- Link Local Multicast Name Resolution (LLMNR)
- Peer Name Resolution Protocol (PNRP)

6.6.1 Link-Local Multicast Name Resolution (LLMNR)

LLMNR is a new naming resolution protocol for serverless name resolution for both IPv4 and IPv6. The protocol is in competition with the mDNS protocol, developed by Apple and widely used in the Open Source community. mDNS and LLMNR are not compatible, and both protocols offer quite the same functionality. The main difference is that LLMNR is defined as a standard in RFC4795 and mDNS is not.

LLMNR provides name resolution in networks without a DNS server. Usually those are home and ad-hoc networks. Ad-hoc networks are also supported for wireless networks connected without an Access Point.

An LLMNR client on a TCPv4 network sends out a multicast LLMNR Name Query Request message to the IPv4 multicast address of 224.0.0.252. The addressed host will respond to this message using a LLMNR Name Query Response message sent from UDP port 5355. The LLMNR Name Query Request message on IPv6 is sent to the IPv6 multicast address of FF02::1:3. Both on IPv4 and IPv6 networks, the multicast address is scoped so that the packets won't pass any multicast enabled routers on the network.

According to RFC4795, LLMNR works both on TCP and UDP. Windows Vista's implementation of LLMNR only operates on UDP for the LLMNR Query Response messages.

During system startup, an LLMNR host sends out a name request for its own name as a single label name (the name without the DNS suffix) and the Fully Qualified Domain Name (FQDN). These names are also called the authoritative names of the host. Whenever another host responds to the initial LLMNR Name Request Queries, the initiating host will report a naming conflict and will not respond to any name queries for its name. The host will retry the LLNMR Name Request Query for its own name every 15 minutes, to find out if the conflicting host is still on the network. When the conflicting host is removed from the network the new LLMNR host will start responding to LLMNR name queries.

With the introduction of LLMNR the name resolution scheme for Windows has changed a bit. The new name resolution order when resolving a single label name in Windows Vista is now as follows:

1. Hosts file (*%WINDIR%\System32\drivers\etc\hosts*)
2. DNS name resolution
    a. With the default search suffix
    b. With all additional search suffixes
3. Single label name LLMNR Name Resolution Request on IPv4 and IPv6
4. NetBIOS Name Query Request messages (if NetBT is enabled)

Windows Vista will stop sending name query requests as soon as one of the name resolution methods produces a successful result.

Note: As LLMNR hosts are only authoritative for the single label host name and its FQDN, an LLMNR host will not respond to queries with different domain suffixes.

6.6.2 Peer Name Resolution Protocol (PNRP)

PNRP or Peer Name Resolution Protocol is a distributed name resolution protocol used by IPv6 Peer-to-Peer applications, in order to identify network entities with changing IP addresses without using a name server. A network entity is identified as a Peer Name and can consist of a computer, user, device, group, server, or anything else that can be identified by an IPv6 address and port.

PNRP ID's or Peer Names are 32-bytes long and exist in two types:

- Unsecured names
  Unsecured names can be spoofed and are thus not secure and not to be trusted.
- Secured names
  Secured names are derived from a public/private key pair owned by the publisher of the peer name. These names cannot be spoofed.

PNRP uses groupings of computers called clouds. PNRP clouds correspond to two scopes of IPv6 addresses:

- Global Clouds
  Every system is connected to a single global cloud. When connected to the Internet, this cloud is Internet-wide. When located behind a firewall in a corporate network, the global cloud is network-wide.
- Link-local Clouds
  Link-local clouds are limited to the subnet or network link. Each node within a subnet or network link is connected to the same Link-local cloud.

Peer Names in a cloud are stored distributed across peers within a cloud. Each peer then contains part of the available names in the cloud in its cache.

When an issuing peer tries to locate the name of a requested peer, PNRP name resolution works as follows:

- The issuing peer will first consult its own cache. When this does resolve, the peer contacts the peer that most closely matches the requested peer.
- If the queried peer finds a closer match (numerically closer to the requested peer), it returns this information to the issuing peer, which will continue its quest with the new information.
- If the queried peer does not find a closer match, it returns this information to the issuing peer that will now turn to the next closest match in its cache to query for the requested peer. This process continues until the name is found or not, which means it is no longer present in the network.

6.7 Wireless Networks

In previous versions of Windows, a wireless network interface was implemented as an emulated wired connection. The lack of pure wireless support in Windows created a far from ideal situation where hardware vendors were forced to develop quite a large part of the wireless interfaces because Windows did not have them available. In Windows Vista, a Wireless Network is just another topology next to Ethernet. This allows implementation of wireless specific features, such as larger frame sizes and optimized error recovery procedures. It is now also easier for the hardware vendors to develop drivers for wireless network adapters in Windows Vista, because Windows offers a much more complete framework, so that drivers can be smaller than before.

A few improvements for wireless networks in Windows Vista are:

- It is now much easier to locate wireless networks that do not advertise their Service Set Identifier (SSID).
- EAP-TLS is now the default authentication mode.
- WPA2 is also available in ad-hoc mode when creating peer-to-peer connections.
- Fast roaming service allows the user to move from one access point to another.
- Pre-authentication allows a wireless client to perform an 802.1X authentication with other wireless APs in its range while it is still connected to its current wireless AP. If the wireless client roams to a wireless AP with which it has pre-authenticated, access time is substantially decreased.
- **Netsh wlan** command shell allows command-line management of wireless networks.

6.7.1 Managing Wireless Networks with Group Policy

Besides management from the GUI, wireless networking in Windows Vista can be managed from Group Policy. In Windows Server 2003, you must download 802.11Schema.ldf and the instructions from *http://go.microsoft.com/fwlink/?LinkId=70195*, and update the Active Directory Schema to implement Group Policy support for wireless networks in Windows Vista. Windows Server 2008 has this functionality built-in. With the schema update installed, Group Policy supports the creation of two types of policies:

- Windows XP wireless policy

- Windows Vista wireless policy

For each type of policy, you can only create a single policy, but each policy can contain settings for multiple wireless networks.

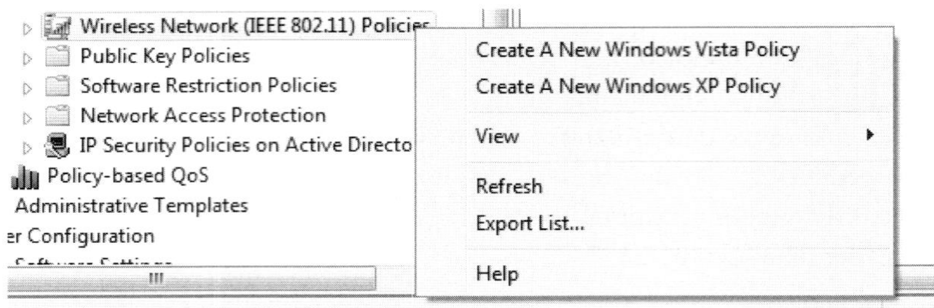

6-5 Configuring a Wireless Network Policy in Group Policy

When only a Windows XP wireless policy is available, Windows Vista will use this policy. When both Windows XP and Windows Vista wireless policies exist, Windows Vista ignores the Windows XP policy and applies only the Windows Vista wireless policy.

The Windows Vista wireless policy allows a number of new wireless configuration settings to be defined. Most significant extra features are:

- Prevention of connection to ad-hoc or infrastructure networks
- Configuration of denied networks
- Configuration of single sign on behavior

6.7.2 Managing Wireless Networks from the Command-Line

Windows Vista provides a new command-line management option for wireless networks with the WLAN interface in NETSH. The command-line interface provides the following options:

- View available wireless networks
- Create a script to copy the current wireless configuration
- Manage wireless network filters
- Import/export wireless profiles
- Connect/disconnect wireless networks
- Show wireless network configuration information

Here are a few common commands for NETSH WLAN.

Use the following command line to enable a filter that suppresses ad-hoc networks in the wireless network networks list:

```
netsh wlan add filter permission=denyall
networktype=adhoc
```

The filter can be deleted using the following command line:

```
netsh wlan del filter permission=denyall
networktype=adhoc
```

Use the following command to show all available information about the current wireless network status:

```
netsh wlan show all
```

Create a script (C:\WirelessConfig.cmd) that creates the current wireless configuration:

```
netsh wlan dump > C:\WirelessConfig.cmd
```

Export the configuration of the SampleWLAN profile to XML:

```
netsh wlan export folder=c:\ name=SampleWLAN
```

Import the configuration of SampleWLAN.xml:

```
netsh wlan add profile filename=c:\SampleWLAN
```

6.8 IPSec

IPSec has been part of Windows since Windows 2000. At first, the technology was just very nice technology, providing security at the IP-level. The introduction of IPSec for domain isolation proved that IPSec can really make a change for network security. IPSec for domain isolation is Microsoft's effort to use IPSec authentication to stop non-managed clients in the network from connecting to specific systems in the network. IPSec domain-isolated systems on the network require authentication from hosts connecting over IP before allowing IP connectivity. When the authentication required is based on Kerberos authentication, IPSec isolation can only allow domain members IP connectivity, virtually excluding any non-domain included clients to connect. More information about IPSec domain isolation can be found at *http://www.microsoft.com/technet/security/topics/architectureanddesign/ipsec*.

6.8.1 New functionality for IPSec

Windows Vista adds a number of new features to IPSec that greatly enhance its flexibility and provide solutions for scenarios that were almost impossible to implement using earlier versions of Windows. The following paragraphs tell a bit more about the most appealing enhancements in IPSec.

Integrated Firewall and IPSec Configuration

IPSec and Windows Firewall have a lot in common when it comes to filtering network traffic. Both provide possibilities for configuring how network traffic is supposed to be handled. The integration of both prevents the creation of contradictory configurations and hard-to-troubleshoot situations.

New negotiation behavior

IPsec in Windows Server 2008 and Windows Vista provides an optional behavior when negotiating IPsec protection. If enabled, when initiating communication with another network node, an IPsec node running Windows Server 2008 or Windows Vista will attempt to communicate in the clear and negotiate protected communication in parallel. If the initiating IPsec peer does not receive a response to the initial negotiation attempt, the communication continues in the clear. If the initiating IPsec peer receives a response to the initial negotiation attempt, the communication in the clear continues until the negotiation can complete, at which point subsequent communications are protected. This optional behavior is recommended for Windows Vista and Windows Server 2008 systems that are configured to require incoming connections and request security for outgoing connections. Those systems will now automatically discover if the system it is communicating with is capable of IPsec, and behaves accordingly. This new behavior greatly simplifies IPsec policy configuration. For example, the initiating node does not need a set of predefined IPsec filters for exemptions for the set of hosts that either should not or cannot protect network traffic with IPsec. The initiating node tries both protected and unprotected traffic in parallel, and if protected communication is not possible, the initiating node uses unprotected communication. This new negotiation behavior also improves the performance of unprotected connections to hosts. An IPsec node running Windows Server 2003 or Windows XP that is configured to request protected communications but allow unprotected communications—a behavior known as fallback to clear—sends the negotiation messages and then waits for a response. The initiating node waits up to 3 seconds before falling back to clear and attempting unprotected communications. With Windows Server 2008 and Windows Vista, there is no longer a 3-second delay when falling back to clear, because communications in the clear is already in progress while the initiating node is waiting for a response.

Client-DC connectivity

Before Windows Vista, a typical chicken and egg situation appeared when trying to protect IP traffic between the client and a DC. Because the DC is supposed to provide the identity to the client, it was impossible to provide identity BEFORE setting up the connection. Windows Vista provides a workaround for this situation when joining a system to a domain. In this situation, IPSec will accept NTLM authentication from the user attempting to join the domain and use that to setup the first IPSec association.

Support for Authenticated IP (AuthIP)

AuthIP is the successor for Internet Key Exchange (IKE) that was used in previous versions of Windows. AuthIP extends IKE with a new possibilities like support for 2-factor authentication. With AuthIP, it is possible to request or require a second method of authentication for IPSec. This enables IPSec to combine computer and user authentication or use new technologies like health certificates for authentication.

6.8.2 IPSec Authentication

IPSec in Windows Vista adds a number of new authentication options:

- New authenticators
- First and Second Authentication

New authenticators

IPSec in previous versions of Windows was always based on computer authentication. Computers with Windows 2000, Windows XP or Windows Server 2003 could use one of the following authentication methods:

- Computer authentication with Kerberos
- Computer authentication with Certificates
- Pre-shared secret key

In Windows Vista, with the introduction of AuthIP, new possibilities are added for IPSec authentication:

- User authentication with Kerberos v5
- User authentication with certificates
- User authentication with NTLMv2
- Computer and User authentication
- Computer health certificate (in combination with NAP)

First and Second Authentication

AuthIP adds the possibility to use multiple forms of authentication for IPSec authorization. When using second authentication, the two forms of authentication can be complimentary or redundant. This creates two scenarios for second authentication:

- 2-factor authentication
  AuthIP has the possibility to require two forms of authentication. For example, a system can be configured to require both computer and user authentication before a connection can be set up.
- Authentication fallback
  With AuthIP, the negotiating nodes can opt to chose the second authentication to try and authenticate when the first authentication method fails. With IKE, there is only one authentication attempt. When that attempt fails, the connection is dropped.

Windows Vista IPSec authentication can consist of two steps:

- First Authentication
  First Authentication takes place during the Main Mode phase of IPSec negotiation and authenticates the computer. The authentication options consist of the same methods that existed in previous versions of Windows. First authentication can be disabled when only user authentication is

required. When choosing a pre-shared secret key, Second Authentication is not available.

- Second Authentication
  Second Authentication takes place during the Extended Mode phase of the Main Mode Phase of IPSec negotiation. During Second Authentication it is possible to use user authentication or computer health certificate authentication. Second Authentication can be disabled when only computer authentication is required.

The default configuration for IPSec authentication in Windows Vista uses Computer authentication with Kerberos v5 and no Second Authentication.

6.8.3 Cryptographic Algorithms for IPSec

Windows Vista introduces a number of new cryptographic algorithms in IPSec for data encryption and key exchange. Most new algorithms were not available in Windows XP and Windows Server 2003. It's a good thing to keep the applied algorithms in mind when creating solutions with those platforms.

Algorithm	Description	OS Supported
AES-256	Strongest security requires more processing power.	Vista or later
AES-192	Less secure than AES-256 and requires less processing power.	Vista or later
AES-128	Less secure than AES-192 and requires less processing power. Default for Vista.	Vista or later
3DES	Less secure than AES-128 but stronger than DES.	XP/Server2003
DES	Not recommended. Only for backward compatibility.	XP/Server 2003
Integrity algorithms		
SHA1	Default for Vista.	XP/Server 2003

MD5	Not recommended. Less secure than SHA1. Provided for backward compatibility.	XP/Server 2003
Key Exchange Algorithms		
Elliptic Curve Diffie Hellman P-384	Strongest security requires more processing power.	Vista or later
Elliptic Curve Diffie Hellman P-256	Less secure than P-256 and requires less processing power.	Vista or later
Diffie Hellman Group 14	More secure than group 2.	XP/Server 2003
Diffie Hellman Group 2	More secure than group 1.	XP/Server 2003
Diffie Hellman Group 1	Provided for backward compatibility.	XP/Server2003

6.9 VPN and Dial-up networks

Just like its predecessors, Windows Vista can handle both incoming and outgoing VPN and dial-up connections. In most corporate environments, incoming connections will not be used for Workstations.

The Windows Vista Virtual Private Network client configuration wizard contains no essential changes compared to the wizard in Windows XP. That does not mean that nothing has changed. Most obvious changes to Windows XP are:

- When using L2TP/IPSec, IPSec can be configured to use a pre-shared key for authentication.
- VPN connections support new encryption algorithms.
- By default, Windows Vista does not support "weak encryption algorithms".
- IPv6 support in VPN connections.

6.9.1 Tunneling Protocols

As the basics of VPN tunneling have not changed, Windows Vista still supports two tunneling protocols for VPN connectivity:

- Point-To-Point Tunneling Protocol (PPTP)
- Level 2 Tunneling Protocol (L2TP)

Both protocols have not changed since Windows XP and can still be used when connecting to existing VPN solutions.

6.9.2 VPN data integrity and encryption algorithms

With the introduction of Windows Vista, Microsoft starts some evangelization regarding the usage of encryption algorithms for VPN connectivity. Vista in fact declares a number of algorithms too weak to safely use over the Internet. Vista does this by disabling the following cryptographic algorithms by default:

- 40- and 50-bit Microsoft Point-To-Point Encryption (MPPE) for PPTP
- DES with MD5 for L2TP/IPSec

The algorithms can be enabled by creating a registry key on the Windows Vista VPN client.

Enabling weak encryption algorithms for a VPN client
Create and set the following registry value: HKLM\System\CurrentControlSet\Services\Rasman\Parameters Name: AllowPPTPWeakCrypto Value: 1 (DWORD)

Windows Vista, on the other side, also introduces a number of new cryptographic algorithms that enable the VPN client to create tunnels based on the latest secure cryptographic algorithms when using L2TP/IPSec. The newly supported algorithms are:

- 128 and 256-bits Advanced Encryption standard (AES)

PPTP with MPPE has only been maintained in Windows Vista for backward compatibility. No new cryptographic support will be introduced for VPN tunnels based on these protocols.

6.9.3 VPN tunnel setup using IPv4 or IPv6

Windows Vista supports L2TP/IPsec-based VPN connections over both IPv4- and IPv6-based networks. PPTP-based VPN connections are supported only over IPv4-based networks, but not over IPv6-based networks.

When establishing a connection with a remote VPN server, Windows Vista will use the following order when all protocols are selected:

1. L2TP/IPSec over IPv6 when IPv6 connectivity exists with the remote server
2. PPTP with MPPE over IPv4
3. L2TP over IPv4

The preference order of IPv4 and IPv6 is configurable by the registry value *DisabledComponents* that is described in the IPv6 section of this chapter.

6.10 Policy-based QoS

QoS policies in Windows Server 2008 and Windows Vista allow IT staff to either label or throttle the sending rate for outbound network traffic.

Using QoS policies, administrators can define outbound traffic policies based on:

- Applications (by executable name or by application folder path)
- Source and destination IPv4 or IPv6 addresses
- Source and destination TCP or UDP ports, or a range of ports

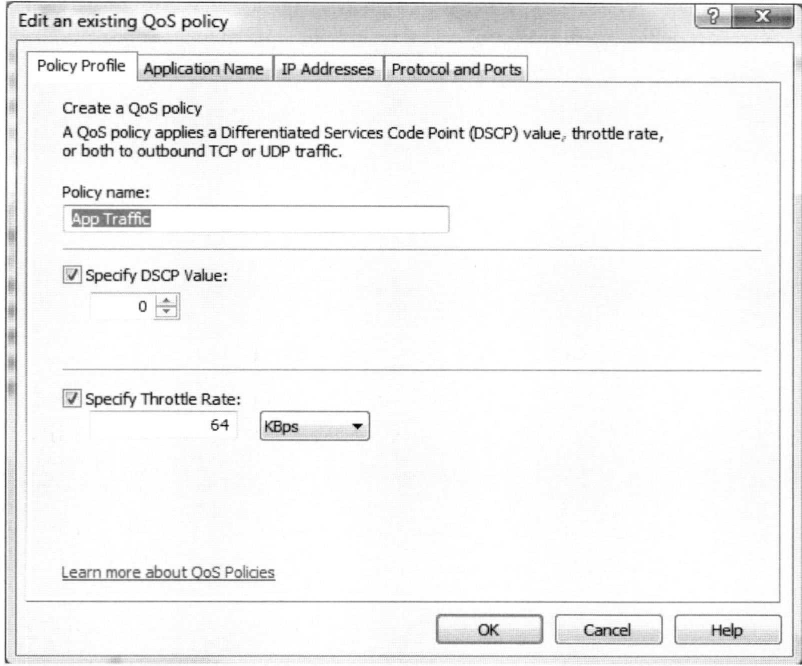

Figure 6-6 Configuring QoS policy

Based on these criteria, network traffic can be labeled using a Differentiated Services Code Point (DSCP) value. Routers in the network infrastructure can place DSCP-marked packets in different queues for differentiated delivery. For Wi-Fi Multimedia (WMM)-enabled wireless networks, DSCP values are mapped to WMM Access Categories. Labeled network traffic can be used to ensure proper working of VOIP and multimedia applications.

QoS can also be used to throttle outbound network traffic. Through throttling, Windows Vista limits the aggregate network traffic to a specified rate. This may keep certain applications from hijacking available outbound network traffic on a system.

Both DSCP marking and throttling can be used together to manage traffic effectively. Because the throttling and priority marking occurs at the network layer, applications do not need to be modified.

6.11 Windows Firewall with advanced security

The first time I looked for Vista's Windows Firewall configuration, I was a bit disappointed. After actually finding the basic version - that is not situated in the NIC properties anymore - I noticed very little difference with what we got used to in Windows XP with SP2 and Windows Server 2003 with SP1. Luckily I was fooled!

For some reason, Microsoft thought it was a good idea to create two Windows Firewall configuration interfaces in Windows Vista. There is the Windows XP lookalike basic version. It is easy to find, on the Control Panel. Then there is the advanced version called "Windows Firewall with Advanced Security". This is an MMC snap-in that contains almost everything you could dream of in the Windows Firewall.

Windows Firewall with Advanced Security uses three profiles to define its configuration:

- Public
- Private
- Domain

At first I thought the three profiles would map to the network location types in the Network Location Wizard described in chapter 6.4.2. When taking a closer look, it appears that Public is indeed the same Public network location as in the wizard, but both Work and Home map to the Private profile in Windows Firewall with Advanced Security. The Domain profile cannot be manually selected, but is selected automatically by Windows when the computer is able to authenticate to a Domain Controller in the network.

6.11.1 What's new in Windows Vista Firewall

Main enhancements in Windows Vista Firewall are:

- Filtering for both incoming and outgoing traffic
  The Vista Firewall filters incoming traffic like its predecessor did. Unlike the firewall in XP and Windows Server 2003, it also filters outgoing traffic. The default configuration looks like the one we got used to in Windows XP and Windows Server 2003:
  - Block all incoming traffic unless it is solicited or it matches a configured rule.
  - Allow all outgoing traffic unless it matches a configured rule.

- Group Policy configuration of Windows Firewall
- Firewall filtering and Internet Protocol security (IPsec) protection settings are integrated
  The new MMC snap-in configures both Windows Firewall and IPSec. This enables much easier configuration of IPSec domain isolation scenarios.
- Rules can be configured for Active Directory accounts and groups
  For rules that specify that incoming or outgoing traffic must be protected with IPsec, you can specify the list of computer accounts and groups or user accounts and groups that are authorized to initiate protected communication. For example, you can specify that traffic to specific servers with sensitive data must be protected, and can only originate from specific users or computers.
- Rules can be configured for source and destination IP addresses
  With the Windows XP/Server 2003 Windows Firewall, you can specify the scope of excepted incoming traffic. The scope defines the portion of the network from which the excepted traffic is allowed to originate, essentially the source IP addresses of incoming traffic. With the Windows Vista Firewall, you can configure both source and destination IP addresses for both incoming and outgoing traffic, allowing you to more closely define the type of traffic that is allowed or blocked. For example, if a computer with a specific IP address is not allowed to originate traffic to a set of servers, you can create a blocking outbound rule specifying the locally assigned address as the source address and the addresses of the servers as the destination addresses.
  For destination addresses, you can also specify the following predefined addresses with the Windows Vista Firewall:
  - Default gateway, WINS servers, DHCP servers, DNS servers
    These predefined addresses are dynamically mapped to the addresses of the host's currently defined default gateway, WINS servers, DHCP server, and DNS servers.
  - Local subnet
    These predefined addresses are dynamically mapped to the set of addresses defined by your IPv4 address and subnet mask, or by your IPv6 local subnet prefix.
- Rules can be configured for IP protocol number
  In the current Windows Firewall, you can create rules based on TCP or UDP traffic, but you cannot specify other types of traffic that don't not use TCP or UDP. The new Windows Firewall allows you to either select the

protocol by name or manually type the value of the IPv4 Protocol or IPv6 Next Header fields for the desired traffic.

- Rules can be configured for source and destination TCP and UDP ports
  With the Windows XP/Server 2003 Windows Firewall, you can specify the destination TCP or UDP port for incoming traffic. With the Windows Vista Firewall, you can configure both source and destination TCP or UDP ports for both incoming and outgoing traffic, allowing you to define more closely the type of TCP or UDP traffic that is allowed or blocked. For example, if you want to block malicious or undesirable traffic that uses a well-known set of TCP ports, you can create blocking outbound and inbound rules specifying the TCP source and destination ports of the traffic.
- Rules can be configured for all or multiple ports
  When configuring a port-based rule with the Windows XP/Server 2003 Windows Firewall, you can only specify a single TCP or UDP port. With the Windows Vista Firewall, you can also specify all TCP or UDP ports (for all TCP or all UDP traffic), or a comma-delimited list of multiple ports. To configure the new Windows Firewall for a range of ports, you must specify all of the ports in the range. For example, if you want to configure a rule for the range of ports 1090-1095, you must configure the following ports: 1090, 1091, 1092, 1093, 1094, 1095.
- Rules can be configured for specific types of interfaces
  With the Windows XP/Server 2003 Windows Firewall, all the enabled rules applied to all the interfaces on which firewalling was enabled. With the Windows Vista Firewall, you can specify that a rule applies to all interfaces or to specific types of interfaces, which include LAN, remote access, or wireless interfaces. For example, if an application is only used over remote access connections and you do not want the rule to be active for LAN and wireless connections, you can configure the rule to apply only to remote access connections.
- Rules can be configured for ICMP and ICMPv6 traffic by Type and Code
  With the Windows XP/Server 2003 Windows Firewall, you can enable rules for a fixed set of ICMP (for IPv4) and ICMPv6 messages. With the Windows Vista Firewall, there is a predefined set of commonly excepted ICMP and ICMPv6 messages, and you can add new ICMP or ICMPv6 messages by specifying the ICMP or ICMPv6 message Type and Code field values. For example, if you want to create a rule for the ICMPv6 Packet Too Big message, you can manually create a rule for ICMPv6 Type 2 and Code 0.

- Rules can be configured for services
  With the Windows XP/Server 2003 Windows Firewall, you must configure a rule for a service by specifying the path to the service program file name. With the Windows Vista Firewall, you can specify that the rule applies to any process, only to services, for a specific service by its service name, or you can type the short name for the service. For example, if you want to configure a rule to apply only to the Computer Browser service, you can select the Computer Browser service in the list of services running on the computer.

6.11.2 Configuring Windows Firewall with Advanced Security

The GUI for Windows Firewall with Advanced Security is a MMC snap-in. A shortcut to the snap-in can be found in the Administrative Tools section of the Control Panel. When started, the GUI shows an overview of the current status of the firewall.

General settings for the firewall can be set up through right-clicking **Windows Firewall with Advanced Security,** and then clicking **Properties**. Firewall behavior can be set per network profile. That provides the possibility to create different firewall rules for a system depending on the connected network.

The tree in the left pane contains four nodes:

- **Inbound Rules**
  This is the set of configured rules for incoming traffic.
- **Outbound Rules**
  This is the set of configured rules for outgoing traffic.
- **Connection Security Rules**
  This is the set of configured rules for IPSec protected traffic.
- **Monitoring** (not available in de Group Policy editor)
  - **Firewall**
    Here you can find information about current firewall rules.
  - **Connection Security Rules**
    Here you can find information about current security rules.
  - **Security Associations**
    Here you can find information about current security associations.

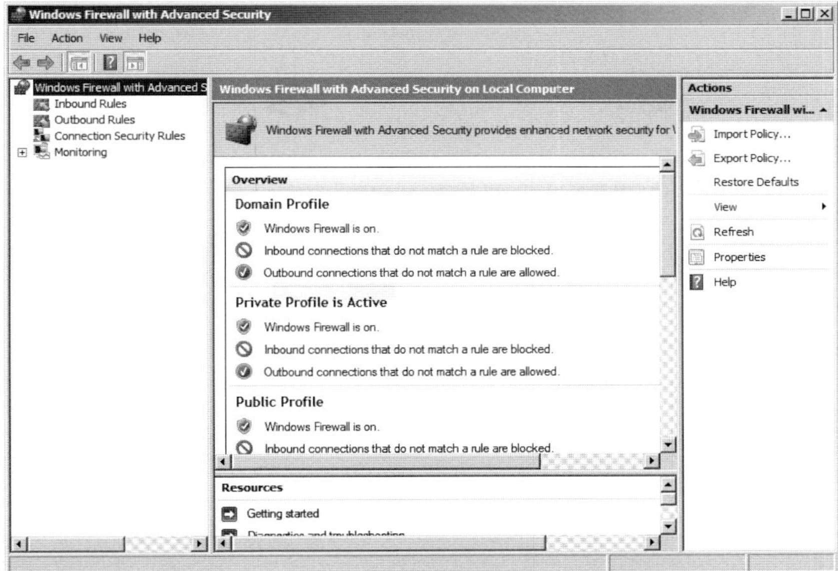

Figure 6-7 Windows Firewall with Advanced Security

Windows Vista by default creates inbound and outbound Firewall rules for all software installed on the system. Rules created for Windows components and those explicitly allowed by the System Administrator are automatically enabled.

Configuring an inbound or outbound rule

To create a new rule, right-click **Inbound Rules** or **Outbound Rules** in the tree, and then click **New Rule**. You can also click on one of the two nodes in the tree, and then click **New Rule** in the Actions pane.

The New Rule wizard will look like this.

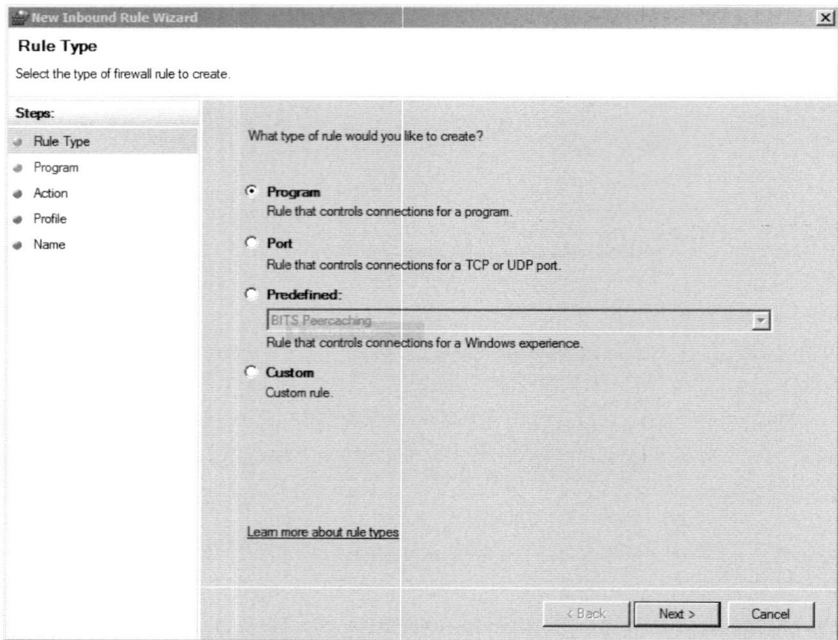

Figure 6-8 New Inbound Rule wizard

In the Rule type page the following options are available:

- **Program**
  To specify a rule for traffic based on a program name (specified by its path and executable name). You must also specify an action (allow, block, or protect), the profile to which the rule applies (standard, domain, or both), and a name for the rule.
- **Port**
  To specify a rule for traffic based on TCP or UDP ports. You must also specify an action (allow, block, or protect), the profile to which the rule applies (domain, public, private), and a name for the rule.
- **Predefined**
  To specify a rule based on one of the predefined services. You must also specify a name for the rule.
- **Custom**
  To create a customized rule. You should select this option when you want to manually configure rule behavior, perhaps based on advanced settings that cannot be configured through the pages of the New Inbound Rule wizard. You must specify a name for the rule.

From the properties dialog box for either an inbound or an outbound rule, you can configure settings on the following tabs:

- **General**
  The rule's name and the rule's action (allow the connections, allow only secure connections, or block).
- **Programs and Services**
  The programs or services to which the rule applies. You can optionally specify both a program or a service. If you specify both, both must match the connection to match the rule.
- **User and Computers** (inbound) or **Computers** (outbound)
  If the rule's action is to allow only secure connections, you can specify the user or computer accounts that are authorized to make protected connections.
- **Protocols and Ports**
  The rule's IP protocol, source and destination TCP or UDP ports, and ICMP or ICMPv6 settings.
- **Scope**
  The rule's source and destination addresses.
- **Advanced**
  The profiles or types of interfaces to which the rule applies and, for inbound rules, whether you want to allow the traffic for this exception to pass through your router that is performing network address translation (edge traversal), using Teredo technology (see paragraph 6.5).

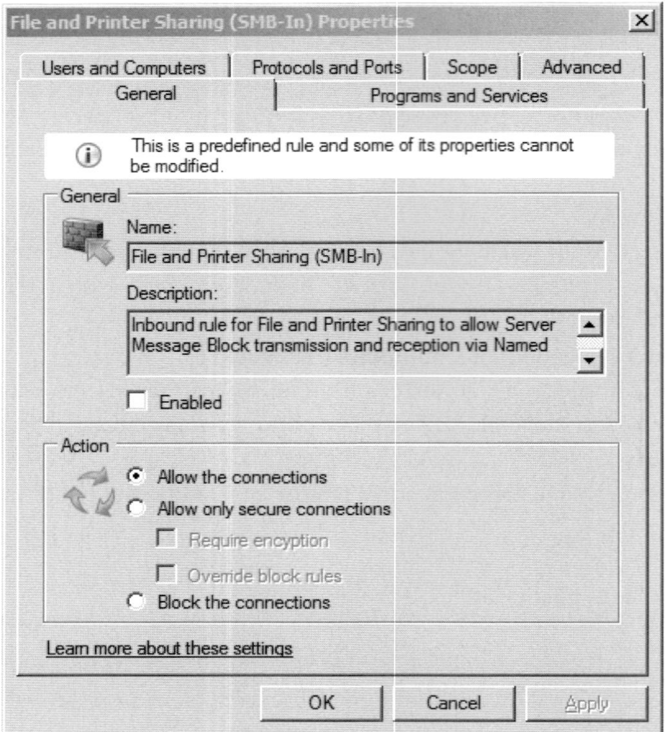

Figure 6-9 Firewall Rule properties UI

Blocking outbound traffic

When you decide to block outbound traffic, be aware this may cause some additional issues. When, for example, you want to block all outbound traffic for the Public profile, this will break the ability for the system to detect if it is on the domain network. Blocking all outbound traffic means there is no DNS, no LDAP, no Kerberos and thus no way to try to authenticate to a domain controller to automatically select the domain network profile. When the connected network is not known as a Private network, Windows Vista will initially select the Public Profile, until the client is authenticated. After successful authentication the client will switch to the Domain Profile.

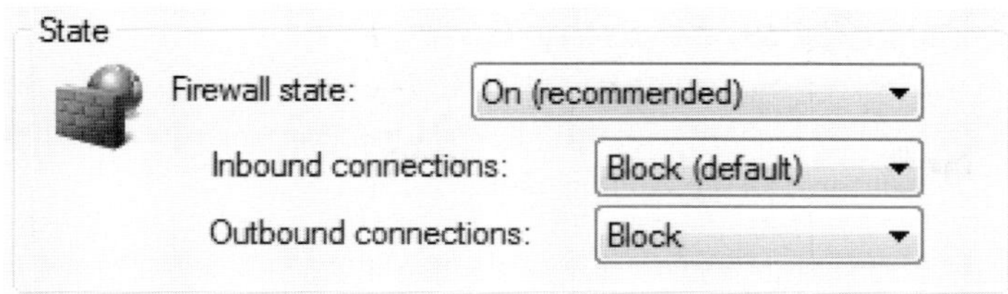

Figure 6-10 Blocking inbound and outbound connections

Here is a list of rules you must at least allow, in order to enable domain authentication for a client to its Domain Controller:

Name	From	Protocol	Local Port	Remote IP	Remote Port
DHCP-Out	svchost.exe	UDP	68	Any	671
DNS (UDP-Out)	svchost.exe	UDP	Any	DNS Servers	53
DNS (TCP-Out)	svchost.exe	TCP	Any	DNS Severs	53
LDAP (TCP-Out)	All Programs	TCP	Any	Any	389
LDAP (UDP-Out)	All Programs	UDP	Any	Any	389
Netlogon Service (UDP-Out)	Netlogon Service	UDP	Any	Any	Any
Netlogon Service (TCP-Out)	Netlogon Service	TCP	Any	Any	Any
Workstation Service (UDP Out)	Workstation Service	UDP	Any	Any	Any
Workstation Service (TCP Out)	Workstation Service	TCP	Any	Any	Any
WINS (UDP-Out)	All Programs	UDP	137	WINS Servers	137
Allow DHCP-In	svchost.exe	UDP	68	Any	67

NB: Windows Vista no longer needs ICMP (ping) to log on to a Domain Controller or apply Group Policies.

Configuring a Connection Security Rule

To create a new connection security rule, right-click Connection Security Rules in the tree, and then click New Rule. You can also click Connection Security Rules in the tree, and then click New Rule in the Actions pane.

The New Connection Security Rule wizard then looks like this.

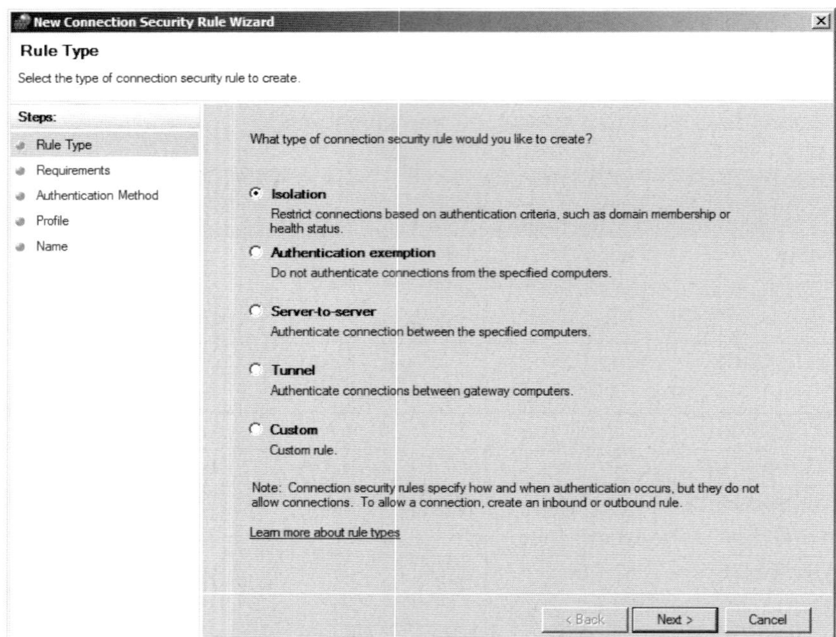

Figure 6-11 Creating an security rule in Windows Firewall

On the Rule Type page, the following options are available:

- **Isolation**

  To specify that computers are isolated from other computers, based on membership in a common Active Directory infrastructure, or because they have an updated and current health status. You must specify when you want authentication to occur (for example, for incoming or outgoing traffic and whether you want to require or only request protection), the authentication method for protected traffic, and a name for the rule. Isolating computers based on their health status uses the new Network Access Protection platform in Windows Vista and Windows Server 2008. For more information, see the Network Access Protection Web site at *http://www.micrsoft.com/nap*.

- **Authentication exemption**
  To specify which computers do not have to authenticate or protect traffic by their IP addresses.
- **Server to server**
  To specify traffic protection between specific computers, typically servers. You must specify the set of endpoints that will exchange protected traffic by IP address, when you want authentication to occur, the authentication method for protected traffic, and a name for the rule.
- **Tunnel**
  To specify traffic protection which is tunneled, typically used when sending packets across the Internet between two security gateway computers. You must specify the tunnel endpoints by IP address, the authentication method, and a name for the rule.
- **Custom**
  To create a rule that does not specify a protection behavior. You should select this option when you want to manually configure a rule, perhaps based on advanced properties that cannot be configured through the pages of the New Connection Security Rule wizard. You must specify a name for the rule.

To configure advanced properties for the rule, right-click the name of the rule and then click **Properties**.

From the properties dialog box for a rule, you can configure settings on the following tabs:

- **General**
  The rule's name and description, and whether the rule is enabled.
- **Computers**
  The set of computers, by IP address, for which traffic is protected.
- **Authentication**
  When you want authentication for traffic protection to occur (for example, for incoming or outgoing traffic, and whether you want to require or only request protection), and the authentication method for protected traffic.
- **Advanced**
  The profiles and types of interfaces to which the rule applies, and IPsec tunneling behavior.

6.11.3 Managing Windows Firewall from the command-line

Here are a few examples of how you can use the command-line to manage Windows Firewall with Advanced Security

Export the current policy to a file:

```
netsh advfirewall export c:\firewallpolicy.wfw
```

Import the policy from a file:

```
netsh advfirewall import c:\firewallpolicy.wfw
```

Restore Windows Firewall with Advanced Security to the default policy:

```
netsh advfirewall reset
```

Restore the default firewall policy and store the current policy:

```
netsh advfirewall reset export
filename=c:\firewallpolicy.wfw
```

Show the properties for the current profile:

```
netsh advfirewall show currentprofile
```

Show the properties for each profile:

```
netsh advfirewall show domainprofile
netsh advfirewall show privateprofile
netsh advfirewall show publicprofile
```

Show the properties for all profiles:

```
netsh advfirewall show allprofiles
```

6.12 Exempt network technology

Besides all new functionality and features, a number of technologies and protocols have been left behind in Vista's new network stack. Here is a list of technologies and protocols which are no longer supported:

- Bandwidth Allocation Protocol (BAP)
- X.25
- Serial Line Interface Protocol (SLIP)
- Asynchronous Transfer Mode (ATM)
- IP over IEEE 1394
- NWLink IPX/SPX/NetBIOS Compatible Transport Protocol
- Services for Macintosh (SFM)
- Open Shortest Path First (OSPF) routing protocol component in Routing and Remote Access
- The following authentication protocols for PPP:
    - Secure Password Authentication Protocol (SPAP)
    - Extensible Authentication Protocol based on MD5 Challenge Handshake Protocol (EAP-MD5-CHAP)
    - Microsoft Challenge Handshake Protocol (MS-CHAP or MS-CHAP v1)

7 Windows Vista Mobility

7.1 Offline Files

Offline Files has been a feature of Windows Clients since Windows 2000. The feature is also known as Client-Side Caching (CSC). CSC provides offline users with local access to files as if they reside on the network. This is especially handy for mobile users who will have access to their network based files that automatically synchronize when they reconnect to the network.

Windows XP however, had some issues with CSC that made the experience a little bit less than seamless for most users:

- Windows XP by default did not synchronize all file types, leading to inconvenient messages when file types like .mdb or .pst were involved in any of the synchronized folders.
- CSC was set on a system basis. The result was that at synchronization time, the system tried to sync all files for all users that ever cached files on the system. When not all files are accessible for the logged on user, this will lead to new annoying messages every time the user tries to sync the system.
- As CSC was a system setting, EFS could only be done by the SYSTEM account. The result was, that every user could access all encrypted files of every user on the system.
- Synchronization only took place at logon/logoff/startup/shutdown. The result was, that you often had to wait very long before all files were synced.
- The contents of the CSC could become corrupted for some reason. The only remedy was to delete the complete contents of the CSC, optionally loosing data.
- CSC was not able to handle open files at sync time. This also caused a lot of annoying messages.

Microsoft certainly sorted out most of these issues and made a good effort to make Offline Files an enjoyable experience in Windows Vista. As a result, Offline Files in Windows Vista has a lot of new and enhanced features.

Delta Sync

Delta Sync or Bitmap Differential Transfer is a new, more efficient way of file synchronization. With Bitmap Differential Transfer, Vista tracks which blocks of a file have changed and only synchronizes the changed blocks to the server. Bitmap Differential Transfer is one of the main reasons why Windows Vista has no issues with large files. In fact, Offline Files in Windows Vista synchronizes any file type. Bitmap Differential Transfer only optimizes file sync when the file has changed on the local disk. Files that have changed on the server side are always completely transferred at sync time.

Bitmap Differential Transfer has no impact on applications that replace files for new ones instead of in-place modifications. Unfortunately, MS Word is one of the programs that work this way.

Periodic Background Sync

Windows Vista Offline Files syncs files continually while you are online (on a fast connection). This means you no longer have to wait for file synchronization to take place when you log off or shutdown the system.

Ghosting

When you make parts of folders available offline, Windows Vista Offline Files creates place holders for files and folders that are only available online. This prevents users from creating files and folders that already exist on the server.

Open files handling

Windows Vista Offline Files transparently handles open files during synchronization. This means that open file handles for files in the local cache will stay offline while the file is in use. The file is than automatically cached when the file is closed. When the file has not changed yet, Windows Vista invisibly recreates a file handle to the online copy of the file when the system transitions to online operation.

Per-User encryption

Windows Vista Offline Files allows EFS encryption on a per user basis. It will automatically encrypt files that are already encrypted on the file server. Other offline files can be manually assigned to encrypt.

Slow Link detection

Windows Vista has a new modus of operation for Offline files. When enabled, it measures the throughput and packet latency of the network every five minutes. When bandwidth is below the set threshold value, Offline Files will start operating in slow-link mode. In slow-link mode, all read and write operations will be satisfied from the local cache. At that moment the system will no longer measure the available bandwidth, and the user must enable online operation manually. While operating in slow-link mode, the user can initiate a manual sync at any time, or return to online operation. When operating online, the system will automatically fall back to slow-link operation when the measured bandwidth gets below the set threshold.

Slow-link mode is not enabled by default. It must be enabled in Group Policy using the "Configure Slow Link" setting under Computer | Administrative Templates | Network | Offline Files.

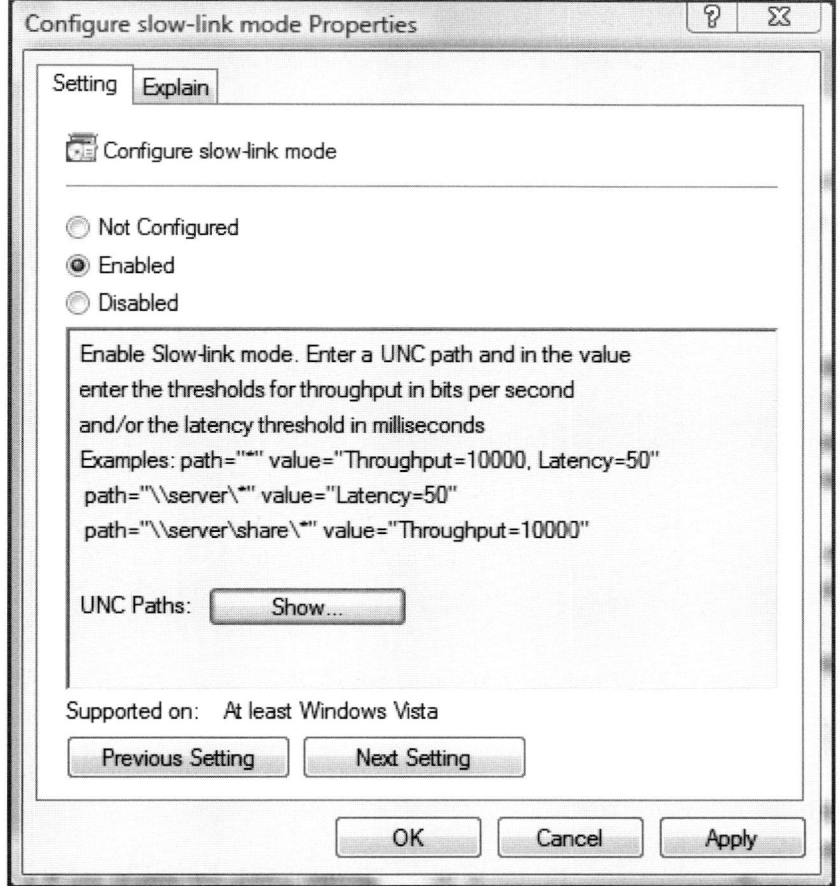

Figure 7-1 Configure slow-link mode for Offline Files

NB: The setting "Configure Slow link speed" is meant for Windows XP only and is ignored by Windows Vista.

The result of all these improvements is a very useful implementation of CSC that actually seems to be workable for about every user, without them having to worry about the way the technology actually works.

7.1.1 Offline Files and server configuration

If and how you can make use of the functionality of Offline Files, is partly defined on the server side. When an administrator creates a file share, there are three caching options available for that folder:

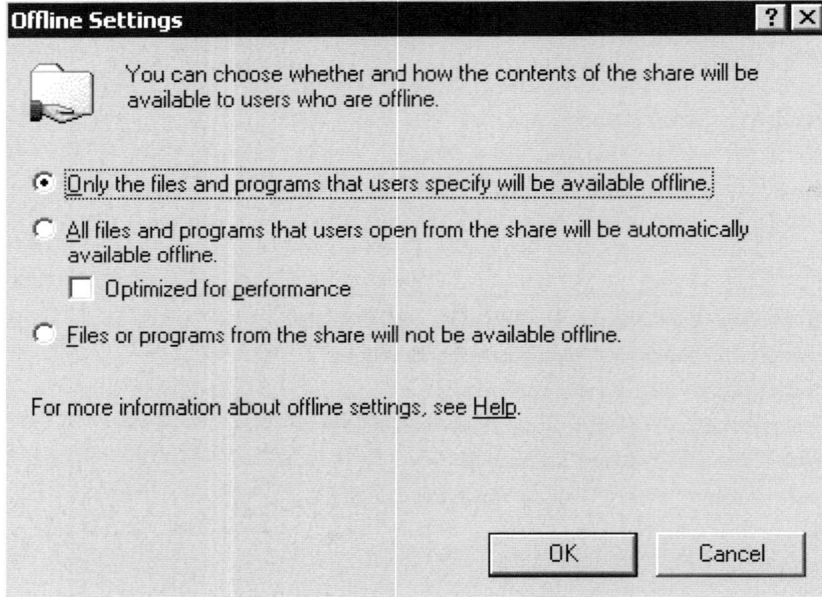

Figure 7-2 Configure Offline caching in Windows Server 2003

- Manual Caching (default)
  A user connected to a share configured for manual caching can pick and choose files and folders to be made available offline.
- Automatic Caching
  A user connected to a share configured for automatic caching automatically caches each opened file for offline use. When the maximum size of the offline file cache is reached, files will be flushed from the

cache based on the last time they have been opened. The user can also manually select each file or folder to be made available offline.

- No Caching
  A user connected to a share configured for no caching, cannot make files available offline from this share.

7.1.2 Managing the offline file cache

Cache Size

Windows XP did not have the option to limit the amount of disk space used for manually assigned offline files. It only contained this option for automatically cached offline files. In Windows Vista, you can configure the maximum size for all files in the offline file cache. Within this size limit you can define how much space is reserved for automatically cached files.

For example, you can specify a 10 GB limit for all offline cached files and a 4 GB limit for automatically cached files. Now the total of automatically cached files can only grow till it reaches the 4 GB limit. When this limit is reached, Windows Vista will automatically remove files from this cache on a least-recently-used basis.

Enter the Offline Files applet from the control panel. The storage limits can be configured by clicking the "Change Limits" button on the Disk Usage tab. Here you can configure the size of the offline cache.

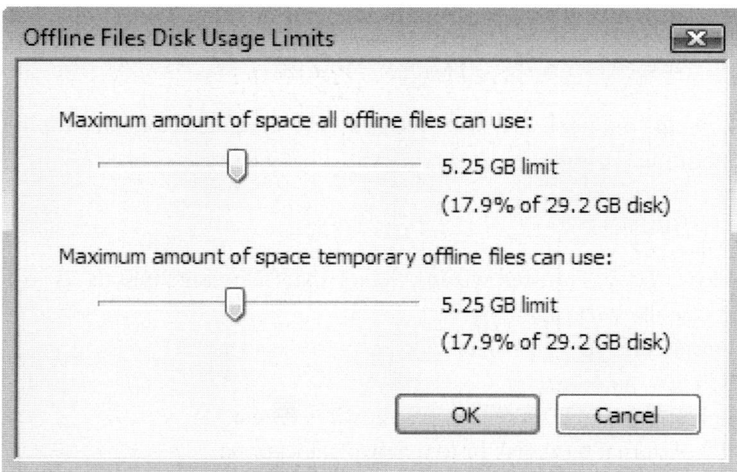

Figure 7-3 Configuring Offline Files disk usage

Reset the Offline File database

Once in a while you may run into a situation where the Offline Files mechanism tries to synchronize files that are no longer accessible. The UI will report this error, but does not supply a method to easily remove the file from the list of items that must be synchronized. The only way to recover from the error situation is by resetting the Offline File database.

Create the following registry value to reset the offline file database:

Key: HKLM\System\CurrentControlSet\Services\CSC\Parameters

Value: FormatDatabase (DWORD): 1

Reboot the system and your offline file cache will be gone. You can now re-assign the files that you want to be cached offline.

Moving the Offline File cache

Windows Vista offers no easy way to move the offline folder cache to a different location. There is a workaround for this omission by using the Windows Easy Transfer Wizard:

Moving the offline file cache in Windows Vista

1. From an elevated command prompt, run the following command:

```
REG ADD
"HKLM\System\CurrentControlSet\Services\CSC\Parameters"
/v MigrationParameters /t REG_DWORD /d 1 /f
```

2. Run the following command as a user who is a local administrator, substituting the drive letter if necessary:

```
c:\windows\system32\migwiz\migwiz.exe
```

3. In the Windows Easy Transfer wizard, select the following options as you progress through the wizard:
   a. Click Start a New Transfer.
   b. Click My old computer.
   c. Click Use a CD, DVD or other removable media.
   d. Click External hard disk or to a network location.
   e. Enter a path where you want to save Savedata.mig, and then click

Next.

f. Click Advanced options.

g. On the Select user accounts, files, and settings to transfer page, do the following:

h. Deselect all check boxes.

i. Under System and program settings (all users), expand Windows Settings, expand Network and Internet, and then select the Offline Files check box.

j. Repeat the previous procedure for each user listed on the page.

k. Click Next to begin the transfer process.

4. In the registry, create a string value called CacheLocation under HKLM\System\CurrentControlSet\Services\CSC\Parameters. To this value, assign the NT format name of the new folder where you want the cache to be located. For example, if you want the cache to be in d:\csc, type \??\d:\csc.
5. Create d:\csc (or whatever path you used in the previous step).
6. Restart the computer.
7. Run c:\windows\system32\migwiz\migwiz.exe and select the following options as you progress through the wizard:
    a. Click Continue a transfer in progress.
    b. Click No, I've copied files and settings to a CD, DVD, or other removable media.
    c. Click On an external hard disk or network location.
    d. Enter the path to the .mig file created in Step 3e.
    e. Map the user account on the old computer to the corresponding one on the new computer.
    f. Click Next, and then click Transfer.
8. Log off, log on, and then make sure you can correctly access your offline files.

Assuming everything got moved correctly, you can delete the old cache by typing the following commands from an elevated command prompt:

```
takeown /r /f c:\windows\csc
rd /s c:\windows\csc
```

7.2 Tablet PC Features

Tablet PC Features is an optional component of Windows Vista that is automatically installed when Vista is installed on a tablet PC style portable PC, or when a pen input device like a Wacom tablet is installed on any Windows Vista based system.

The Tablet PC Features consist of the following components:

- Tablet PC input panel
- Pen flicks for common operations
- Tablet PC calibration tool

7.2.1 Tablet PC Input Panel

The tablet PC Input Panel allows the user to input text using a pen style device in any application. Before logon, it appears as an on-screen keyboard that allows to enter the User password using a pen. After logon, the tool by default sits on the left side of the screen to completely appear when tapped by the mouse or pen. Then the panel allows three input modes:

- Writing Pad
- Character Pad
- On-screen Keyboard

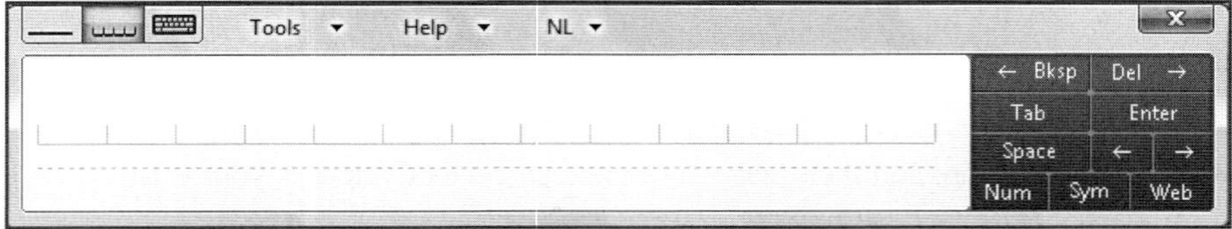

Figure 7-4 Tablet PC Character Pad

When handwriting is used, Windows Vista can learn how to read your personal handwriting when the input language is set to one of the following:

- English
- Japanese
- Chinese
- Korean

In other languages, personalized handwriting recognition is not available.

The options for the Input Panel allow the user to change settings that define when the handwriting in the panel will be copied into the application that is running, and where the panel sits when it is not active.

Compared to Windows XP Tablet PC edition, Windows Vista uses a number of new gestures for scratching out text. Windows XP only allowed the Z-type gesture to scratch-out written text. Windows Vista also allows M- or W-type gestures for scratch-out.

7.2.2 Pen Flicks

Pen Flicks can be used without activating the Tablet PC input Panel, to perform common operations in applications like Internet Explorer to go back and forward to other pages, and to scroll up and down a page without using the scroll bars. Optionally, flicks can also be used for common editing operations like drag and drop, copy/paste, and delete.

Pen Flicks can be configured from the Pen and Input devices tool in the Control Panel.

7.2.3 Calibration Tool

The Calibration tool in the Control Panel is used to recalibrate the pen on the screen when the pen cursor on the screen does not exactly appear where the pen is. When the calibration starts, a cross-type picture is placed in each corner of the screen. When the user then taps the middle of the cross in each corner, the device will be properly calibrated.

7.3 Mobile Device Center

The Mobile Device center is used to connect Windows Mobile devices to Windows Vista, and to allow those devices to sync with, for instance, Outlook, or use the network to connect to Exchange Server. In fact, the Mobile Device Center is the successor of ActiveSync. ActiveSync no longer operates on Windows Vista. Besides synchronizing with Outlook, Mobile Device Center also allows synchronization of Internet Explorer favorites and files, and eventually enables other applications to use their methods to communicate with the Windows Mobile device.

Windows Mobile Device Center is available as a separate download from the Microsoft site at *http://www.microsoft.com/windowsmobile/devicecenter.mspx*.

Figure 7-5 Windows Mobile Device Center

8 Migrating to Windows Vista

8.1 (Roaming) Profiles

Over the decades, Windows has used a predetermined folder structure to store the user environment. This folder structure, which is dubbed the User Profile, contains the following information:

- User data
- Application-specific data
- Registry settings

Windows stores the user profile on the local hard drive. When used locally, the registry part of the profile is loaded when the user logs on and unloaded when the user logs off.

In corporate environments where users must be able to switch between computers when necessary, profiles are copied to a file server at logoff. This makes the profile available when the user logs on to a different system next time. The profile that follows the user is called a roaming profile.

Roaming profiles have never been the ideal solution. As the content of the profiles grows, loading and unloading profiles can take a lot of time. This creates a less than pleasant experience for users, who sometimes have to wait several minutes after logging on before they can start working. Microsoft had a hard time fighting the growing profiles, whose troubles even increased with the introduction of Windows Terminal Server.

8.1.1 What's new in Windows Vista User Profiles

Folder Names

Windows Vista creates a new version of the user profile that is in no way compatible with the profile created by earlier versions of Windows. In order to prevent conflicts, Windows Vista will extend the directory name of its profiles on the network with ".v2". When you used to view user profiles on a file server, they always looked like <username>. The Windows Vista user profiles all look like <username>.v2. On the local system, the profile still looks like <username>.

Default User Profile

With Windows Vista it is still possible to create a default profile for users who don't have a profile yet. The default profile can be defined on the network in the Netlogon share of the Domain Controllers, or locally, in the Users folder. The name of the folder containing the default user profile has also changed. From now on the local default profile is in a different folder than the one on the network.

Windows Vista default user profile locations:

Profile location	Default User folder
Local	C:\Users\Default
Network	\\<domain>\netlogon\Default User.v2

If a user does not have a profile yet, Windows will look for a default profile in the following order:

1. Network profile on the Domain Controllers
2. Local Profile

To create a default user profile, use the following procedure:

How to: Create a default network based user profile
1. Log on to a computer running Windows Vista with any domain user account. Do not use a domain administrator account.
2. Configure user settings such as background colors and screen savers to meet your company standard. Log off the computer.
3. Log on to the computer used in step 1 with a domain administrator account.
4. Use the Run command to connect to the Netlogon share of a domain controller. For example, the path used in the contoso.com domain looks like \\HQ-CON-SRV-01\NETLOGON
5. Create a new folder in the Netlogon share and name it **Default User.v2**.
6. Click **Start**, right-click **Computer**, and then click **Properties**.
7. Click **Advanced System Settings**. Under **User Profiles**, click **Settings**.

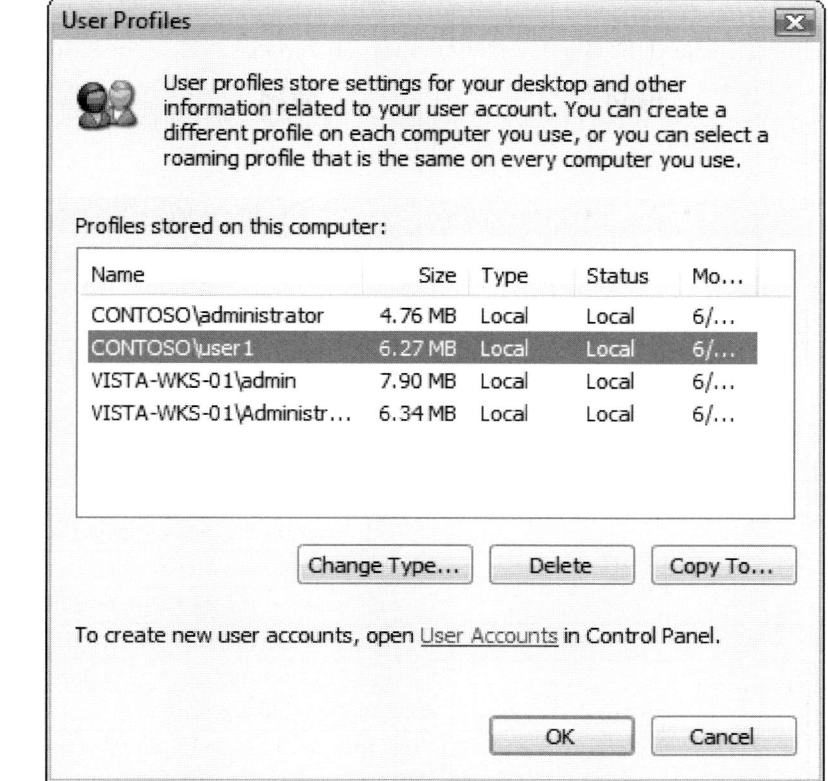

Figure 8-1 User Profile Dialog in Windows Vista

8. The **User Profiles** dialog box shows a list of profiles stored on the computer. Click the name of the user you used in step 1. Click **Copy To**.
9. In the **Copy To** dialog box, type the network path to the Windows Vista default user folder you created in step 5 in the **Copy profile to** text box. For example, the network path in the contoso.com domain is \\HQ-CON-SRV-01\NETLOGON \Default User.v2.
10. In **Permitted to use**, click **Change**. Type the name **Everyone**, and then click **OK**.
11. Click **OK** to start copying the profile. Close all remaining windows and log off the computer when the copying process is complete.

User Profile Contents

Microsoft has changed the Windows Vista user profile to make it look more logical and easier to use. The result is, that there are far more folders on the first level of the user profile. Here is the new list of folders in the Windows Vista profile, with their purpose:

Windows Vista Folder Name	Description
Contacts	Default Location for User's Contacts
Desktop	Desktop items, including files and shortcuts
Documents	Default location for all user created documents
Downloads	Default location to save all downloaded content
Favorites	Internet Explorer Favorites
Music	Default location for user's music files
Videos	Default location for user's video files
Pictures	Default location for user's picture files
Searches	Default location for saved searches
AppData	Default location for user application data and binaries (hidden folder)
Links	Contains Windows Explorer Favorite Links
Saved Games	Used for Saved Games

Not all of these folders used to have an equivalent in Windows XP. The following table gives an overview of profile folders in Windows XP and tells you where that information can be found in the Windows Vista folder structure:

Windows XP Profile Location Documents and Settings*username*\\...	Windows Vista Profile Location Users*username*\\...
Application Data	...\AppData\Roaming
Cookies	...\AppData\Roaming\Microsoft \Windows\Cookies
Desktop	...\Desktop
Favorites	...\Favorites

Local Settings	N/A
Local Settings\Application Data	...\AppData\Local
Local Settings\History	...\AppData\Local\Microsoft\Windows\History
Local Settings\Temp	...\AppData\Local\Temp
Local Settings\Temporary Internet Files	...\AppData\Local\Microsoft\Windows\Temporary Internet Files
My Documents	...\Documents
My Music	...\Music
My Pictures	...\Pictures
My Videos	...\Videos
Nethood	...\AppData\Roaming\Microsoft\Windows\Network Shortcuts
PrintHood	...\AppData\Roaming\Microsoft\Windows\Printer Shortcuts
Recent	...\AppData\Roaming\Microsoft\Windows\Recent
SendTo	...\AppData\Roaming\Microsoft\Windows\Send To
Start Menu	...\AppData\Roaming\Microsoft\Windows\Start Menu
Templates	...\AppData\Roaming\Microsoft\Windows\Templates

All Users Profile

Previous version of Windows provided the "all users" profile. This profile provided a way to add common user data to user profiles, without editing each user profile separately. Windows merges the contents of the Desktop and Start Menu folder under the All Users profile with the user profile when the user logs on. Adding a shortcut to the desktop of the all users profile would result in every user receiving the shortcut on their desktop, when they logon.

In Windows Vista the name of the All Users profile folder has changed to Public. The folder structure is the same as for every other user profile in Windows Vista. Windows Vista will still merge specific folders, such as Desktop and Start Menu, in the Public folder with regular user profiles at logon.

The Public folder does not contain the NTUSER.DAT file because there are no registry settings being merged from the Public folder. When this is a requirement, those settings have to be defined in the HKEY_LOCAL_MACHINE registry hive.

Recycle Bin

Windows Vista has a Recycle Bin for each well known folder in the user profile. This results in separate Recycle Bins for the following folders:

- Each Local Hard disk volume
- Documents
- Desktop
- Download
- Favorites
- Music
- Pictures
- Videos

The Recycle Bins are stored as a hidden file in the root of each volume or special folder. This creates roaming Recycle Bins for each redirected folder in the profile. The size of the Recycle Bin can be defined in Group Policy. Be aware that this definition is a percentage of the volume where the specified folder is located. In cases where this is a very large volume on a centralized file server, a custom solution must be supplied. For example, 1% of a 1TB volume still is 10 GB, which may be much more than you actually wanted to assign to a user.

8.1.2 Profile types in Windows Vista

Windows Vista profile types provide the possibility to adjust the behavior of profiles to the needs of specific situations.

Windows Vista offers four profile types:

- Local Profile
- Roaming Profile
- Mandatory Profile
- Super Mandatory Profile

Local Profile

The local profile in Windows Vista does not differ in behavior from what we have got used to in previous versions of Windows. It just stores the user specific settings in a user specific folder in C:\Users. The user loads the registry information at logon, and stores it at logoff. All other information like application specific data files are edited on the fly in the user profile folder.

Roaming Profile

The roaming profile in Windows Vista does about the same thing as roaming profiles do in earlier versions of Windows. When a user logs off, the local profile is copied to the server location specified in the user object in the domain. This centrally stored version of the user profile will then be used whenever the local copy of the profile is older than the one on the network location, or when there is no local profile. In those cases, the network based profile will be copied to the local profile folder.

Not all information in the local profile folder is copied at logon. In Windows Vista there actually is quite a clear distinction between roaming and non-roaming folders in the user profile. This distinction is especially visible in the AppData folder. This folder contains three subfolders:

- Local
  The local folder contains data that will never be copied to the network-based copy of the profile.
- LocalLow
  This is the folder for processes running in low mandatory process level (i.e. in protected mode). The content of this folder, likewise, will never be copied to the network.
- Roaming
  The roaming folder contains data that will be copied to the network-based copy of the user profile.

Only the roaming folder is copied to the roaming copy of the profile.

Mandatory Profile

The mandatory profile also has not changed in functionality, in respect to earlier versions of Windows. The mandatory profile operates in the same way as the roaming profile, with one exception: changes in the profile are not saved. The result is, that users with a mandatory profile will always get the same settings, no matter what they have changed in a previous session.

In order to create a mandatory profile, the file NTUSER.DAT in the centrally stored profile must be renamed to NTUSER.MAN. Also, make sure the content of the directory is properly protected against changes from unauthorized sources.

Super Mandatory Profile

The super mandatory profile is a mandatory profile with an extra layer of security. When a user logs on with a "normal" mandatory profile, and that profile for some reason does not load, the user will get a temporary profile based on the default user profile. The temporary profile is not saved, and whenever the user logs on again when the mandatory profile is available, the mandatory profile will be applied. When assigned a Super Mandatory Profile, the user will always get the mandatory profile, or will not logon at all. This prevents the user from getting a temporary profile in case the mandatory profile does not load.

In order to create a Super Mandatory Profile for Windows Vista, use the following procedure:

1. Create a mandatory profile.
2. Rename the folder of the mandatory profile to <foldername>.man.v2.
3. In the user properties change the "Profile Path" object property to: <foldername>.man.

8.1.3 User profile compatibility

Windows Vista will store the users' roaming profile on a network share in a folder named: <username>.v2. Due to this naming format, the folder will be different from the folder used for earlier versions of Windows. This also means that the Windows Vista profile will always be different from the profile created in earlier versions of Windows. When migrating to Windows Vista, the following must be kept in mind, in regard to user profiles:

- User-specific registry settings cannot be shared between Windows Vista and earlier versions of Windows.
- In order to share user profile folders between Windows Vista and previous versions of Windows, Folder Redirection is your only option.

8.2 Application Compatibility

As always with the introduction of a new operating system, not all applications that used to work with the previous version will immediately work with the new OS. In an enterprise environment, different approaches can be chosen to overcome these issues. Some companies may choose to avoid compatibility issues using Terminal Services or Application Virtualization (formerly known as SoftGrid), to keep applications away from Vista's way of handling applications.

When you choose to actually run the applications on Windows Vista, the operating system contains a number of options with which to test application compatibility and create fixes when trouble occurs.

Some of the most common issues are:

- UAC issues
  Most issues arise when applications need to write in privileged locations, like HKLM in the registry, or the Program Files or Windows folder on the file system. Some applications are just happy when they are run with administrative privileges at first execution only. Others require those privileges each time they are executed.
- OS not recognized as valid
  Another category of older applications will only feel like running when the application thinks it is running on Windows XP or Windows 95, for example. Just like Windows XP, Windows Vista provides options to make such an application feel good and run just fine on Windows Vista.
- Screen resolution issues
  These issues only occur to me with games, but I'm sure there are other applications that do not like running with any resolution different from 640 x 480. If you happen to run such an application, there are options to make the application run in this resolution, or with fewer colors. Some applications will cause Windows Vista to turn off Aero Glass without the need to configure anything special for that application.
- 16-bit applications on x64
  16- bit applications run just fine on x86 Windows Vista, but not on x64. Sometimes the 16-bit installer for a 32-bit application will keep you from installing the application on x64 systems. Repackaging is your only option here.

Windows Vista offers the following options to fix compatibility issues:

- Using a Manifest
- Using the Compatibility tab for the program or shortcut
- Using the Windows Vista Compatibility Database

Manifests will mostly be used by developers, to define required execution levels, and if Virtualization is allowed for a certain program. More information about Manifests can be found at msdn.microsoft.com.

NB: This process is also called marking the application for compatibility.

8.2.1 Marking application compatibility in the UI

Windows Explorer provides the option to define Application Compatibility settings on a per user or per system basis from the user interface. The compatibility tab allows the user to specify the following options to fix eminent compatibility issues. On the Compatibility tab, the following options are available:

- Compatibility Mode
  A compatibility mode provides a way to make an application think it is running on a previous version of Windows. Some applications accept this trick and just do their job when the correct compatibility mode is selected.

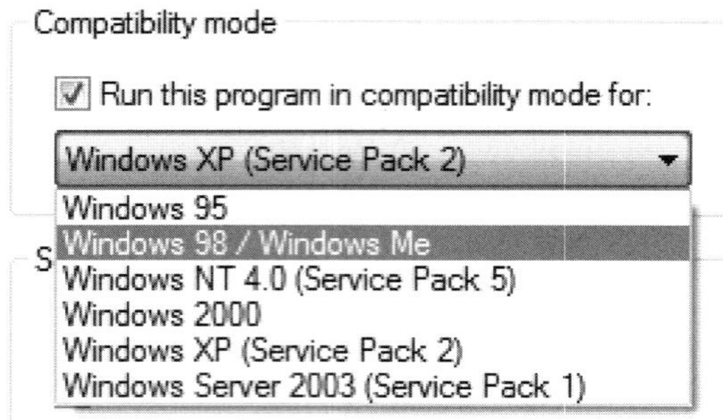

Figure 8-2 OS compatibility modes in Vista

- Screen resolution, colors and effects
  Some (mostly older) applications only run when the screen resolution, the number of colors, or special effects are disabled. The Settings section on the Compatibility Tab provides the options to selectively change these settings for a specific application.

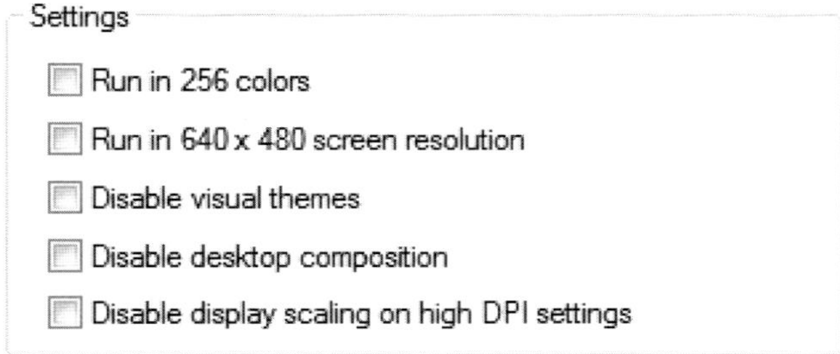

Figure 8-3 Screen resolution and graphics settings

- Run as Administrator
  Even some non-administrative applications only run when started with full administrative privileges. The option Run as Administrator ensures that UAC provides the option to run the application with full administrative privileges.

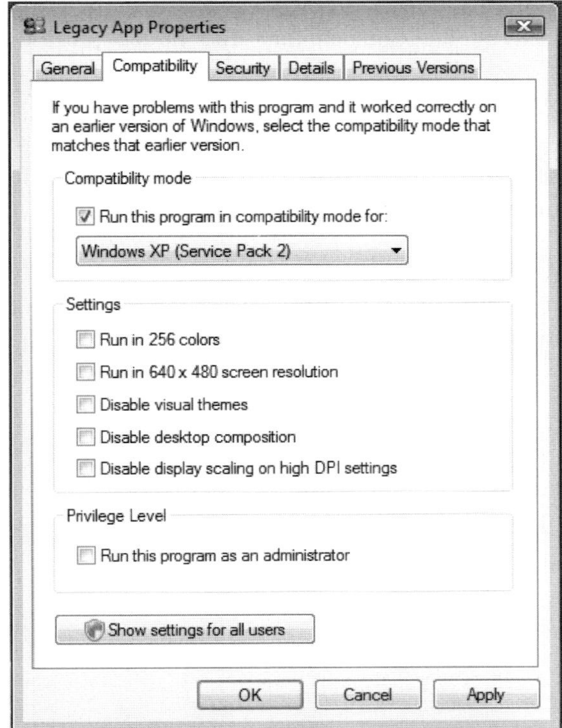

Figure 8-4 Marking application compatibility

8.2.2 The Application Compatibility Database

The Application Compatibility Toolkit 5.0 or ACT 5 is a suite of applications from Microsoft, which will help you find and resolve application compatibility issues. The solutions can then be put in an Application Compatibility Database that can be used to distribute compatibility fixes to other computers. The following three tools provide the functionalities needed to solve most compatibility issues:

1. Standard user Analyzer
   Standard User Analyzer helps to identify compatibility issues for specific programs. Use the tool to start the application with administrative privileges and perform the standard tasks in the application. Then close the application and examine the output of the Standard User Analyzer to identify the compatibility issues the program might have.
2. Compatibility Administrator
   Use the Compatibility Administrator to create an application compatibility fix database. A compatibility fix database contains compatibility fixes for one or more applications for Windows Vista. It contains compatibility fix information as mentioned on the Compatibility Tab in the previous chapter.
3. Sdbinst.exe
   Sdbinst.exe is used to install the compatibility database that you have created with the Compatibility Administrator on a different system, to provide the required compatibility fixes.

Besides the tools mentioned, ACT5 also contains agents to collect compatibility information from systems running Windows XP in your network. On the basis of the collected information you can check for known compatibility issues on the Internet. Microsoft has created a centralized database that allows easy checking for known compatibility issues.

When using the Compatibility Administrator to create compatibility entries, the following options can be defined:

- Requested Execution Level
  In order to fix UAC issues, changing the execution level may cause a program to always run with full privileges. The following execution levels are available:

- RunAsAdmin
  Always run the program as Administrator with full privileges. If the user is not a member of the Administrators group, it is not possible to start the application.
- RunAsHighest
  Run the program with the highest possible privileges for the user that starts the program. If the user is a member of the Administrators group, this program will start with full privileges. If the user is a Standard User, the user token is used to start the program.
- RunAsInvoker
  Run the program with the same execution level as the invoking process.

- Virtualization marking
  Virtualization marking defines if File and Registry Virtualization is used for the program. By default, all 32-bit programs that are not part of Windows Vista will be virtualized. There is one option available to disable virtualization for the specific program:
  - NoVirtualization
- Compatibility Mode
  This is the same Compatibility Mode as mentioned in paragraph 8.2.1, where an application is led into an environment that will make the program feel it is running on a different version of Windows. The following Compatibility Modes are available:
  - Windows Server 2003 (Service Pack 1)
  - Windows XP (Service Pack 2)
  - Windows 2000
  - Windows NT 4.0 (Service Pack 5)
  - Windows 98/Windows ME
  - Windows 95

8.3 User State Migration

Most enterprise networks that I know of don't let users store data and settings on their workstations, but automatically store settings and data on the network. That doesn't mean that in some situations network administrators are forced to store data and settings on the client computer. When you find yourself in such a situation and you need to upgrade your systems to Windows Vista, there are two options available to ensure your data and settings are still available after the upgrade:

- Easy Transfer Wizard
- User State Migration Tool (USMT) 3.0

8.3.1 Windows Easy Transfer

Windows Easy Transfer is a tool in Windows Vista that can be used to transfer files and settings from a computer running one of the following operating systems to a system running Windows Vista:

- Windows 2000 with Service Pack 4
- Windows XP with Service Pack 2
- Windows Vista

Windows Easy transfer does not transfer any system files like fonts and drivers. You can use Windows Easy Transfer to move the following files and settings to a system running Windows Vista:

- Files and folders
- E-mail settings
- Contacts and Messages
- Program Settings
- User accounts and settings
- Internet settings and favorites
- Music
- Pictures and videos

Use one of the following methods to transfer files using Windows Easy Transfer:

- A USB cable connecting the source computer to the system running Windows Vista.
- A network connection between the source computer and the system running Windows Vista.

- Removable media such as a USB flash drive or an external hard disk.
- Recordable CD[9] or DVD[10].

When using removable media, the wizard supports storing the information on multiple media until all data being migrated has been stored.

Use the procedure described in the knowledge base article "How to use Windows Easy Transfer to migrate file and settings from one Windows-based computer to another Windows Vista-based computer" in KB article 928634 at *http://support.microsoft.com/kb/928634* to transfer files using Windows Easy Transfer.

8.3.2 User State Migration Tool (USMT) 3.0

USMT 3.0 is the enterprise equivalent of Windows Easy Transfer. USMT also provides ways to transfer files and settings from one system running Windows to another system running Windows Vista. USMT 3.0 is available as a separate download on the Microsoft site and provides more options to automate user state migration.

USMT contains the following main components:

- Scanstate.exe
  Scanstate scans the source computer to collect files and settings to migrate. By default, scanstate stores the settings in a compressed image file named USMT3.MIG. The contents of the file can optionally be encrypted. Scanstate does not make any changes on the source computer when collecting the data.
- Loadstate.exe
  Loadstate is used to implement the results stored in the migration file on the destination computer running Windows Vista. Loadstate copies each file located in the store one-by-one to a temporary location. During this process it decompresses and if necessary decrypts the file. Then loadstate moves the file to its final destination and destroys the temporary copy, to start implementing the next file.

---

[9] CD burning is not supported on systems Running Windows 2000

[10] DVD burning is only supported on systems running Windows Vista.

- Migration XML files
  Migration XML files contain migration rules that define what and how files and settings must be migrated. Loadstate and scanstate must use the same set of migration XML files for a complete migration. Migration XML files consist of the following XML files:
  - MigSys.xml
  - MigApp.xml
  - MigUser.xml
  - Any custom .xml files
  - Config.xml
    Config.xml contains a list of components that you want to exclude from the migration. It is created using the /genconfig switch on the scanstate command-line.

More information about USMT 3.0 can be found on the Microsoft site at *http://go.microsoft.com/fwlink/?LinkId=56486.*

Index

D

E

F

G

H

I

K

L

M

N

O

P

Q

R

S

T

U